# THE AFRICAN EXPERIENCE
# WITH HIGHER EDUCATION

# THE AFRICAN EXPERIENCE WITH HIGHER EDUCATION

J.F. Ade Ajayi
Lameck K.H. Goma
G. Ampah Johnson
with a contribution by
Wanjiku Mwotia

The Association
of African Universities
ACCRA

in association with

JAMES CURREY
LONDON

OHIO UNIVERSITY PRESS
ATHENS

The Association of African Universities
African Universities House
P.O. Box 5744
Accra-North
Ghana

in association with

James Currey Ltd
54b Thornhill Square
Islington, London N1 1BE
England

Ohio University Press
Scott Quadrangle
Athens, Ohio 45701
USA

The views expressed in this publication are those of the authors and do not
necessarily represent the views of The Association of African Universities

First published 1996
1   2   3   4   5   00   99   98   97   96

**British Library Cataloguing in Publication Data**
Ajayi, J. F. Ade (Jacob Festus Ade), 1929-
The African experience with higher education
1. Education, Higher – Africa, Sub-Saharan   2. Universities
and colleges - Africa, Sub-Saharan
I. Title   II. Goma, Lameck K. H.   III. Johnson, Ampah, G.
378.6'67

ISBN 0-85255-733-7  Paper (James Currey)
ISBN 0-85255-734-5  Cloth  (James Currey)

**A CIP catalog record for this book
is available from the Library of Congress**

ISBN 0-8214-1160-8  Cloth (Ohio)
ISBN 0-8214-1161-6  Paper (Ohio)

Typeset by Jadeas Trust, 1 Ojobadan Avenue, Bodija, Ibadan
Printed in Great Britain by Villiers Publications, London N3

# CONTENTS

## Contents

# List of Abbreviations

| | |
|---|---|
| A-Level | General Certificate of Education at the Advanced level |
| AAI | African-American Institute |
| AAU | Association of African Universities |
| ABU | Ahmadu Bello University, Zaria, Nigeria |
| ACU | Association of Commonwealth Universities |
| AESAU | Association of Eastern and Southern African Universities |
| AFGRAD | African Graduate Scholarship Programme |
| ANC | African National Congress |
| ANU | Agostinho Neto University |
| APPER | African Priority Programme of Economic Recovery |
| ARPPIS | African Regional Postgraduate Programme in Insect Science |
| ASPAU | African Scholarship Programme of American Universities |
| ATTC | Advanced Teacher Training College |
| AUPELF | Association of Partially or Wholly French-speaking Universities |
| BREDA | *Bureau des Recherches Educatifs et Développement Africain* (of UNESCO, Dakar). |
| CHE | Commission for Higher Education (Ethiopia) |
| CIDA | Canadian International Development Agency |
| CMS | Church Missionary Society |
| CURD | *Centre Universitaire de Recherches de Dévelopment* (University Centre for Research and Development, Abidjan) |
| CUSS/UCHS | Centre Universitaire des Sciences de la Sante/University Centre for Health Sciences, (Yaounde). |
| DAAD | German Academic Exchange Service |
| ECOWAS | Economic Community of West African States |
| EMU | Eduardo Mondlane University |
| ENS | *Ecole Nationale Supérieure* (National Schools) |
| ESAURP | East and South African Universities' Research Programme |
| EUS | Ethiopian University Service |
| FBC | Fourah Bay College |
| FIDES | *Fonds d'Investissement pour le Developpement Economique et Social* |

viii

| FRELIMO | Front for the Liberation of Mozambique |
| IAU | International Association of Universities |
| ICIPE | International Centre of Insect Physiology and Ecology |
| IDRC | International Development Research Centre (Canada) |
| IFAN | *Institut Française d'Afrique Noire* |
| IITA | International Institute of Tropical Agriculture, Ibadan |
| ILCA | International Livestock Centre for Africa, Addis Ababa |
| INTERAF | Inter-African Scholarship Programme |
| IUC | Inter-University Council for Higher Education in the Colonies (later, Overseas) |
| MPLA | Popular Movement for the Liberation of Angola |
| MPR | Popular Movement for Revolution (Zaire) |
| MSU | Michigan State University, East Lansing, USA |
| NCAST | Nigerian College of Arts, Science and Technology |
| NCHE | National Council for Higher Education (Sudan) |
| NUC | National Universities Commission (Nigeria). |
| O-Level | General Certificate of Education at the Ordinary level |
| OAU | Organization of African Unity |
| PAC | Pan-African Congress (of South Africa) |
| R & D | Research and Development |
| RTC | Royal Technical College, Nairobi |
| RUA | Rhodesia University Association |
| SANC | South African Native College (Fort Hare) |
| SAREC | Swedish Agency for Research Cooperation with Developing Countries |
| SWAPO | South West African People's Organization |
| TRC (QRC) | Triennial (or Quinquennial) Review Committee |
| UBBS | University of Basutoland, Bechuanaland and Swaziland |
| UBLS | University of Botswana, Lesotho and Swaziland |
| UCAA | University College of Addis Ababa |
| UGC | University Grants Committee |
| U.K. | United Kingdom (England, Wales, Scotland and N. Ireland). |
| UNAZA | National University of Zaire |
| UNDP | United Nations Development Programme |
| (UN) ECA | UN Economic Commission for Africa |
| UNESCO | United Nations Educational Scientific and Cultural Organization |

| | |
|---|---|
| UNICEF | United Nations Children's Fund |
| UNISA | University of South Africa |
| UNN | University of Nigeria, Nsukka |
| UPS | University Productive Sector |
| USA (US) | United States of America |
| USAID | United States Agency for International Development |
| USSR | Union of Socialist Soviet Republics |
| WHO | World Health Organisation |
| YMCA | Young Men Christian Association |

# PREFACE

This study was commissioned by the Association of African Universities as part of the twenty-fifth anniversary celebrations of the Association, and in pursuit of its objective of promoting understanding of the problems of African Universities and seeking solutions to them. The study is, in many ways, a follow-up of the Workshop which the Association held in Accra in 1972 on the theme of *Creating the African University: Emerging issues of the 1970s*. Like that Workshop, this study focuses attention on the Universities of Tropical Africa which share a similar experience, somewhat different from those of North Africa and the 'white' universities of South Africa. It examines their historical background and the issues facing them in the 1990s. Perhaps, rather more than the Workshop, the focus of this study has been on the universities as institutions - issues of governance, finance, autonomy, responsibility - rather than the content of courses or scholarly development, though even these have not been left out. Unlike the Workshop where various scholars were asked to explore various issues and case studies, three former Vice-Chancellors who share a wide experience of African universities were asked to work together and produce a joint study. They are:

J.F. Ade.Ajayi, Emeritus Professor of History, University of Ibadan, former Vice-Chancellor of the University of Lagos, former Vice-President of the AAU, who gave the keynote address at the 1972 Accra Workshop.

Lameck K.H. Goma, a zoologist, graduate of Fort Hare, Cambridge and London, taught at Makerere and Legon; former Vice-Chancellor, University of Zambia, a member of the Executive Board of the AAU at the time of the Accra Workshop; he was also successively Minister of Education, Foreign Affairs, and Higher Education, Science and Technology in Zambia.

G. Ampah Johnson, a biologist with wide teaching experience in France, a pioneer teacher at the University of Abidjan, founding Rector of the Université du Benin, Lome; former President of the AAU and member of the Board of the IAU and AUPELF.

They were assisted by Wanjiku Mwotia, a former teacher of Modern European Languages at the University of Nairobi and, at the time, Programme Officer in the AAU.

The authors visited a number of universities where they held discussions on the subject of the study with a cross section of the university community in each institution. Several of the universities which they were unable to visit sent discussion papers on the issues concerned. The study was funded from special grants made to the AAU by the British Council, the Carnegie Corporation of New York, and the Rockefeller Foundation; from contributions to the core programme budget of the Association from the Netherlands Government, the Swedish Agency for Research Cooperation with Developing Countries (SAREC), and from the International Development Research Centre (IDRC) Regional Office for West and Central Africa; as well as membership subscriptions of the Association's member universities, general grants from the Government of the Federal Republic of Nigeria and the Organisation of African Unity (OAU), and support in kind from the Government of Ghana.

The views expressed in the study are those of the authors and do not necessarily represent the views of the AAU, its member universities, or any of the donors that contributed to the funding of the project.

Donald Ekong,
Secretary General,
Association of African Universities,
African Universities House
Accra, Ghana.

# PART I: HISTORICAL BACKGROUND

Chapter 1

## ANTECEDENTS (before 1900)

### Introduction

We in Zambia are immensely proud of our University. This pride is not simply that this is our first and only University. It is also because the university of Zambia is our own University in a very real sense. The story of how the people of this country responded so enthusiastically to my appeal for support is a very thrilling one. Humble folk in every corner of our nation - illiterate villagers, barefooted school children, prison inmates and even lepers - gave freely and willingly everything they could, often in the form of fish, or maize or chickens. The reason for this extraordinary response was that our people see in the University the hope of a better and fuller life for their children and grand children. (President Kenneth Kaunda , at the Chancellor's Installation Banquet, July 12, 1966, in *Addresses at the Installation* ..., University of Zambia,1966, p.28).

President Kaunda's after-dinner address captured the sense of communal pride and identity which everywhere initially greeted the coming of the University to Africa. In responding so enthusiastically to the University, and pinning so much hope on it for "a better and fuller life for their children and grand children", what picture of the University did the "humble folk", "the illiterate villagers", have in their minds? In what "real sense" was the University their very own? Again and again, the people dance to welcome the University and bring their fishes and best wishes on the day of inauguration but, if they ventured to show up at the gates on the day after inauguration, they find that no one there knows their name or understands their language.

The debate about what constitutes the African University, and how to make the University in Africa the "very own" University of African peoples, is central to the African experience with higher education. This debate is one of a species of intellectual arguments which rage or ebb from time to time about what constitutes African

Christianity, African Islam, African philosophy, African Science or African University; or whether such concepts are in fact contradictions and convey little meaning in practical reality. For example, Islam is universal in its doctrine and centered on Mecca in its practice. Its core message as revealed in the Koran is not even allowed to be translated into languages other than Arabic. Nevertheless, in the practice of the religion, in the rise of different schools of Islamic Law, and the operation of different brotherhoods in the daily life of Muslims, cultural differences are clearly observable. However, is African identity something that Islam in non-Arab Africa should acquire or try hard to get away from? Is Islam in Timbuktu after nine or ten centuries African?

Similarly, the central doctrine of Christianity is in the Bible and is universal. The interaction of English culture and Christianity was such, especially since the Reformation, that the "Church of England" which missionaries brought to Africa in the 19th century, was not just the Church in England. Yet missionaries from that Church could still argue that organizing the Church in Africa into an African Church does not imply the possibility of African Christianity as a concept. Is it, then, possible to adapt African culture to Christianity and still remain African, or adapt Christianity to African culture and still remain Christian?

If it is not easy to separate practice from doctrine in religion, should it not be easier to separate methodology or form from content in branches of knowledge? Though musicology as a universal "science" may be controversial, African music provokes little controversy; it is distinguished from European music not only in content, but also in structure and form. Why, then, has there been so much debate about African philosophy? Many African philosophers insist that it is methodology, not the content, that defines philosophy as a branch of knowledge; that it is the thought of individuals when it conforms to certain methodological criteria that constitutes philosophy and, as such, anthropological summation of the thinking within a community about God or governance or social relations does not constitute philosophy.

The concept of African philosophy has been so controversial partly because of the close link between philosophy and religion, and the fear that African philosophy promotes the idea of African Christianity. Sometimes, the objection is to the lack of precision or definition in the concept of "African". Is it a geographical or a cultural concept? Does it cover the whole continent or just the land of Black people South of the Sahara, or even of Africans in the diaspora? Is it a summation of all the cultures or an analysis of the presumed "African" factor common to all? Thus, many people who have no problem with the concept of Western thought or Western education argue that while you could have Luo or Ewe philosophy or culture, African culture or philosophy is too much of an abstraction. Advocates of the concept of African philosophy have therefore responded by studies of African sagacity, the thoughts of individual African sages or wise men, analyzed within the framework and the methodology acceptable to Western philosophy.

With specific reference to higher education, some people argue that, even though it is possible to distinguish indigenous and Islamic traditions of higher education from the Western tradition, the modern University is exclusively within the Western tradition. This was the view initially taken by Ashby in the 1960s: that indigenous systems of education were "inward looking, conducted by members of the extended family, directed to ensuring conformity with social custom and acquiescence in the hierarchy of the community"; that Islamic traditions of education relied on "the technique of learning by rote" and transmitting truths which "rested on authority and not on observation or enquiry"; and therefore, while it could be adapted to be more responsive to African needs and environment, the University is "essentially a mechanism for the inheritance of the Western style of civilization". (Ashby, 1966 pp.147-8; 1974 p. 2). Even after further research has shown that indigenous education did more than socialize and that Islamic education, especially secular disciplines in Islamic education, promoted observation and enquiry, Philip Altbach warned in 1982 that it is not easy to create "indigenous" academic models: the "institutional patterns, pedagogical techniques and, perhaps most important, the basic structure of knowledge" in our Universities are Western in origin. (Chideya, 1982, Altbach on p.47, Mazrui *cit*. on p.24). As Ali Mazrui put it, in opposition to other scholars like Robin Horton, the very rationality that we employ in our universities is of Western origin. How, then, are the Universities to be made African: how do we adapt the University to African culture so it can provide African development, not westernization? To what extent can a review of attitudes to knowledge in traditional societies or a survey of pre-colonial models of higher education provide useful insights into the intricacies of the problem?

**Indigenous Education**

Studies of sagacity have drawn attention to the role of the sage in traditional African societies. (Oruka, 1991). The sage is recognized as a philosopher, an original thinker whose words of wisdom and advice are widely sought both by private individuals and public officials. He is reputed as a person very knowledgeable about traditional history, laws, customs and folklore, whose testimony is needed in resolving disputes and litigation over issues such as succession to office or property, land, inter- and intra-kinship relationships. He may also be knowledgeable about the properties of different plants and animals, and become a healer or a rain-maker. He may practise as a diviner, arbitrator or consultant. His wisdom may have come as a result of unusual personal experience interpreted as revelation, or from special anointing or possession by a deity associated with wisdom. He is treated with respect and awe because profundity of knowledge was generally viewed as signifying access to supernatural powers. Because of the high status of the man of knowledge in society, there may be an element of individual craving for knowledge and wisdom, and, therefore, self-education. More often, the sage as a leader of thought is a product of the formal or informal processes of indigenous higher education.

It is now clear that indigenous education involved far more than an inward-looking process of socialization. There were no clear-cut gradations, but it is possible to speak of an elementary level where, besides basic moral education and socialization into the kinship group and the larger community, the child learnt from the mother and other adults within the household to talk, to count, and appreciate subtleties of the language. The method is largely informal, between mother and child, but also communal for children of the same age grade within the household, through riddles and conundrums, games, fables and story-telling. At the second level, the child is educated partly through an informal system of apprenticeship to one or more adults to acquire skills in an occupation and the knowledge relevant for the pursuit of that occupation. There was also more formal training in educational establishments organized usually at puberty rites or within age grade associations, sometimes by the state, sometimes by secret societies such as the Poro or Bundo in the Upper Guinea area, about the traditions and values of the community, necessary to get the teenager acceptable as an adult member of society.

Forms of higher education existed primarily for training rulers and priests. Selection of candidates was rather complex, including membership of particular families and some evidence of special vocation or calling by the divinities concerned. Essentially, the training was through attachment and apprenticeship. Favoured children accompanied parents or grandparents to meetings where they learnt the art of public speaking and observed customary ways of dealing with issues. Acolytes were initiated into orders of priesthood and trained to progress from one degree to another. They learnt sacred chants and other esoteric knowledge, varieties of ritual dance and other aspects of religion and folklore. The system of education remained predominantly oral, eclectic and even esoteric. There was keen observation, collation and analysis of the properties of things. But its epistemology placed emphasis not so much on rationality as on the deeper meaning and the power of words, particularly the names of things. Sometimes, the knowledge of sacred chants and traditions acquired by an acolyte was tested at public ceremonies. There were opportunities for retreat and reflection and various exercises during which the divinities were expected to "possess" and teach the acolytes. Although indigenous education was, thus, permeated by traditional religion, and was therefore specific to each culture and language community, occasionally the sage practising as a diviner or healer, acquired such reputation as transcended the local community and could, thus, attract students from a wide region. In this and other ways, knowledge spread from one community to another. Thus indigenous higher education produced and transmitted new knowledge necessary for understanding the world, the nature of man, society, God and various divinities, the promotion of agriculture and health, literature and philosophy.

The man of knowledge or sage often had to earn his living within the household from the occupation prevalent in the community such as farming, hunting or fishing. As he became better known, he may begin to concentrate on specialist occupations as healer, diviner, court historian, judicial advocate or assessor, or several combinations of these. He thus needed recognition and patronage from the community. Those knowledgeable in history, literature and philosophy often made their reputation from "performing" during festivals, sometimes on a competitive basis. Thus, the community in general, and rulers in particular, through their patronage promoted the search for knowledge and skills, for example in healing particular diseases. They conferred titles and various privileges including gifts of land and farming estates on noted men of knowledge, or heads of the guild of court drummers, *griots,* diviners or healers. Yet such groups in their literary compositions and public performances also acted as social critics and conscience of the people. This sometimes bred tension, if not open conflict, with the authorities. Rulers have been known to show their annoyance when diviners failed to divine what the rulers wanted to hear, or if the *griots* became uncomfortably critical.

### The Legacy of Alexandria

The roots of the University as a community of scholars, with an international outlook but also with responsibilities within particular cultures, can be traced back to two institutions that developed in Egypt in the last two or three centuries B.C. and A.D. One is the Alexandria Museum and Library, and the other is the monastic system.

The Ptolemies in the 3rd Century B.C. decided to build their capital in Alexandria with its excellent harbour and nodal point of routes connecting the Mediterranean with the Red Sea and the Indian Ocean. They also built there the

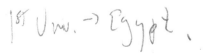

famous Museum and Library with the aim of assembling in one centre, through purchase or systematic copying of manuscripts, the whole of contemporary knowledge. Soon, more than 200,000 volumes were collected. The Library became known as the greatest cultural repository of its time. It attracted all the leading scholars from the Egyptian, North African, Greek, Roman, and Jewish worlds. Illustrious specialists were appointed on fellowships to manage the collection of books and guide the younger scholars within a collegiate system:

> Scientists and men of letters lived in this institution. They were housed and fed and were able to give themselves up entirely to their research and studies, with no menial duties to perform. Its organization was similar to that of modern universities, except that the resident scholars were not required to give lectures. (Riad, 1981, p.192).

Some of the most advanced intellectual work of the period was done in Alexandria. For example, Eratosthenes, the father of scientific geography who measured the circumference of the earth, an African from Cyrenaica, was Librarian there; Strabo, the Greek geographer, the last of whose 17-volume treatise is on Egypt, our best source on the Museum; and there were other famous scholars in cosmography and astronomy; Euclid, Archimedes and others in mathematics, especially geometry; Manetho, the Egyptian scholar-priest, one of the most important sources on ancient Egypt, even though his *Aegyptica* survives only in fragments; poets, historians and other literary men to whom we owe the survival of the tragedies of Aeschylus, the comedies of Aristophanes, the odes of Pindar and Bacchylides, and the histories of Herodotus and Thucydides; Theophratus, the founder of scientific botany; Herophilus, Erasistratus and other pioneers of human anatomy and physiology. The Library suffered damage when Julius Caesar set fire to ships in the harbour of Alexandria. Gradual decline set in during the instability of the period of Roman rule: instability in Rome and the consequent inability to defend the outlying province from attacks from Asia Minor. The scholars scattered and many of the books found their way to Rome, but the legacy of Alexandria remained:

> ...the fascination of the ancient Alexandria lies in the fact that it was at the root of a remarkable scientific movement which remained unrivalled until modern times. For well over a millennium, the scholarly achievements of ancient Alexandria served as guiding lights for the great humanists of the European Renaissance. It is perhaps legitimate to say that before the Alexandrian era, knowledge had been to a great

extent regional, but with the creation of the Alexandrina as the first universal library in the history of mankind, knowledge too, became at once universal. (El-Abbadi, 1990, pp. 15-16).

It was because of the strength of the intellectual foundations laid by the Library and Museum that Alexandria played such a notable role in the doctrinal controversies of the Early Christian Church. It was the unique contribution of Alexandria, through the work of St. Clement, "a man of prodigious erudition" and his pupil Origen, "under whom philosophical speculation and philological interest reached their summit", and other scholars to situate the message of Christianity within classical tradition and attempt to reconcile them. Secondly, the Patriarchs of Alexandria, notably St. Athanasius and St. Cyril, played a prominent role in the Arian controversy of the 4th and 5th centuries. This was a theological debate on which the unity of the Latin and the Greek Orthodox or Byzantine Church foundered. The Council of Chalcedon eventually ruled that Christ was one person with two intimately united natures, whereas the Patriarchs of Alexandria held fast to the belief that Christ had but one nature, a divine nature, and that the apparent human nature was but an outward show. This is the doctrine of Monophysitism which has remained central in the theology of the Egyptian and Ethiopian Coptic Church. (Donadoni, 1981).

The spirit of resistance and local patriotism thus symbolized by Alexandria bred the monastic system. Monophysite Christianity together with the spirit of resistance spread fast among the peasants of Egypt on whom Roman taxes fell so heavily. It is said that the practice developed of many peasants abandoning their farms and fleeing into the desert to make a new life as hermits away from tax gatherers. Soon, this developed a religious dimension, of people leaving as a group not only to escape tax gatherers but in fact to escape from the world, to seek contemplation, and mystic union with God. They were called anchorites (tax evaders) in derision. They often pooled their resources, lived communally and frugally, cultivated farms and traded their produce jointly. In their search for contemplation, they attracted teachers and religious guides. Thus arose the monasteries, with leaders emerging later to found different monastic orders to regulate the monastic way of life. Monasteries developed not only within Christianity but also Islam and became models for communal living favouring the search for knowledge as a joint enterprise.

## Islamic Education

By contrast with indigenous education, Islamic education operated within a unified structure, based on the written word of the Koran which had to be comprehended in Arabic. Teachers could therefore migrate from one place to another, and the pattern remained the same. There were teachers who made their living from teaching children rudiments of Arabic and the Koran usually in the open verandahs of their own homes. They received alms and gifts from the children's parents, while the children also helped with various occupations on the side, such as farming, leather work and various crafts, including even buying and selling. The informality of the system ensured that the children were brought up within particular cultures. The local particularities, however, diminished the higher the student climbed towards the sophistication of universal Islamic culture. A few of the teachers were qualified to take on more advanced pupils at the secondary level in introductory courses to Arabic philosophy, exposition of the Koran, and the life of the Prophet. Alternatively, some mosques organised *madrasas* or colleges along monastic lines for such advanced students, and supplemented the teaching by public colloquia, especially during the month of Ramadan. Some of the madrasas attracted enough reputable teachers and the courses of instruction were organised more formally like universities, with princely endowment, adequate libraries, and curricula built around one or more of the schools of Islamic law, advanced philology, Hadith, History, and Geography. More usually, the most reputable teachers were engaged in a variety of other activities as judges, diplomats, etc. and attracted students to study at their feet in a range of authorities and move on to other reputable teachers. The itinerant scholar, therefore, remained an important feature of Islamic higher education.

Thus, Islamic education, like the indigenous pattern of education, was rooted in religion. Particularly in the case of Islam, learning was an aspect of religious life. As Islam spread in Africa, - in Egypt and the Nile Valley, North Africa, the Maghreb and Western Sahara, from those centres to the Western and Central Sudan, and from Arabia to the Coast and islands of East Africa, - Islamic education spread with it. Islam spread initially through conquest and colonization, and the warring leaders patronized Islamic education as a weapon of state building. Later, Islam spread more through commercial and missionary activities followed by periodic reforms through jihads, with Muslim teachers and scholars rather than rulers taking the initiative. There were, thus, two major factors in the expansion of learning and scholarship within Islam. The first was the need of rulers to use scholars in their administration, especially in building up Islamic arts and culture in urban centres. The rulers employed learned men as diplomats, imams of mosques, judges, jurists, advisers on governance, law and taxation. The more prosperous the regime became, the more the rulers built not only palaces but also mosques and madrasas, and the more they attracted scholars from far and near. Thus a community of scholars ('ulama) grew up, often international, but also usually with a core of local scholars who had themselves travelled and studied at the major international centres of Islamic higher education. The second factor was the need of pious Muslims seeking contemplation. There were holy men who sought retreat in desert oases or fortified centres (ribat). More often the seat of the holy man develops into a monastery where mysticism is combined with advanced study in theology or jurisprudence. The monasteries became centres of learning which may or may not have developed formally into madrasas or organised colleges or universities.

The oldest Islamic University in Africa is Karawiyyin founded in 859 in the Old City of Fez around the Mosque by the Idrisids, a Sharifin dynasty, one of the many struggling to conquer the Maghrib, and hold it, if possible, as part of the wider Muslim empire. The Idrisids brought in Arab merchants and scholars from Kayrawan in Tunisia and Cordoba in Spain to establish an urban centre, propagating Sunni Islam in the midst of the Kharijite heresy of the Berbers, and upholding the supremacy of Arab and Berber Muslims in the midst of non-Muslim Berber groups resisting such domination. Fez thus became a centre for propagating Arab orthodox Islamic culture. The assemblage of scholars around the Karawiyyin Mosque became a powerful tool in that endeavour. The Idrisids endowed the University well. But as empires rose and fell - the Almoravids, the Almohads, the Marinids, etc. - the community of influential scholars acquired a certain independence of their own and became an important prize that awaited whoever controlled the capital city of central Morocco, but whose favour and loyalty also had to be specially courted. Karawiyyin University thus became a major force in the history of Islamic scholarship not only in the Maghrib, but also in the Sahara, and the Western Sudan. It played a notable role in the spread of the Maliki Code, the blending of the cultures of the Maghreb and Andalusia, and the rise of a distinctive Moroccan impact on Islam, especially Sufism and religious Brotherhoods, with their Shaykhs and marabouts. (Talbi, 1988).

The Fatimids founded the city of Cairo in 969 and decided to make it the capital of a Caliphate in succession to the Abbasids of Bagdad. They at once built barracks for their army, a palace and a mosque named Al-Azhar. Religious ideology played a prominent role in the contest to build a stable Caliphate: between Sunni and Shiite, between dynasties originating in the Hejaz, and those originating from Ifriqiya, or even further West in Berber country. The Fatimids were soon replaced by competing Ayyubid princes and they in turn soon lost power to the Mamluk garrison - white Turkish slaves, recruited early into the army, trained and exercised in the wars of the Crusades. They were stationed in Egypt to protect important trade routes and the Holy Land. With the divisions among the Ayyubids, they began to select the Sultan from among their own leaders and they maintained stability and prosperity in Egypt from 1250 - 1517 when they lost power to the Ottoman Sultan in Istanbul. Much of the trade and financial administration was in the hands of Christians and Jews. Thus with Mamluk nobles controlling the administration both in the capital and the provinces, they welcomed the community of scholars at Al-Azhar who concentrated on training students, promoted Sunni orthodoxy, and attracted an international staff from Andalusia, the Maghreb, Syria, the Hejaz, etc., that made Al-Azhar so famous and influential throughout the Islamic world, especially in Africa. Among the most famous teachers was Ibn Khaldun, the historian and sociologist, who arrived in Cairo in 1382 and lived there till his death in 1421. It was in Cairo that he did most of the work on his *Universal History*, and he was appointed again and again the grand Kadi of Maliki law. At the same time, while preserving their international character, the 'ulama of Al-Azhar fulfilled the important function of creating a specifically Egyptian stamp on Sunni orthodoxy, and they began to make themselves spokesmen of the Egyptian people, protesting against the luxury and exploitative practices of the Mamluk nobility. (Garcin, 1984).

Because of its location on the southern edge of the desert and at a strategic point on the routes linking the trading cities of the Niger Bend to the trade routes southwards to the gold producing areas, Timbuktu rose in the 12th and 13th centuries as a cosmopolitan urban centre which the different hegemonic powers - Mali, Mossi, Songhai, Bambara and even Morocco - tried to control. In fact, the foreign merchants there came to enjoy a high degree of autonomy. Partly for this reason, it also attracted scholars and students from far and near. Timbuktu became famous as a holy city of many Muslims distinguished by their piety and their quest for learning. The scholars became the greatest defenders of Timbuktu's claim to be a "little state within a state". (Hunwick, 1966, p.313). In the 14th and 15th centuries, the trend was for rulers of Mali or Songhai going on pilgrimage to import scholars from Al-Azhar, or for Sudanese students to go to Fez or Al-Azhar and surprise their teachers with their great ability. By the 16th century, the bulk of the teachers and holders of such offices as imams, kadis and khutabs, not only in Timbuktu but also in the other major centres like Walata, Jenne and Gao were Sudanese. Accounts of visitors to the Sudan suggest that the population of Timbuktu was about 80,000; that in the 16th century, there were about 180 koranic schools, and thousands of students from all parts of the Sudan and the Sahel who lived with their teachers or as lodgers.

The University of Timbuktu was not as centralized as al-Karawiyyin of Fez or Al-Azhar of Cairo, but consisted of a number of independent schools ("of transmission") of which those around the Mosque of Sankore (Sankara) were the best known. The scholars did not receive regular stipends, but some of them lived in communities or monasteries where their material needs were taken care of by the Mosque and they could devote their attention to their teaching. The best known "schools" were loose associations of outstanding scholars and their circle of friends, relations and students, differentiated from others in their curricula depending on the preferences of their masters. This tendency to differentiate curricula was counterbalanced by the integrative role of the Mosques, especially Sankore, where the courses of study offered were essentially open to all students who could qualify.

It has been said that in the 16th and 17th centuries, the intellectual life of Timbuktu was in fact dominated by three families of which the best known was the Aqit family. The school financed itself from patronage, and from official positions of the master and other prominent members of the school. The student attached himself to a particular scholar of repute, and not only attended the lectures and tutorials of the master, but also acted as his assistant and secretary, and was present at his audiences at all times. (Saad, 1983, chapter 3). The courses of instruction covered the usual ones of theology, exegesis, traditions, Malikite jurisprudence, as well as grammar, rhetoric, logic, astrology, astronomy, history and geography. Science and mathematics was very little developed. Malikite jurisprudence was a particular speciality. The method of instruction was essentially exposition and commentaries on texts and authorities in the scholastic fashion.

In spite of the constraints of this methodology, it is unlikely that the initially international staff could have been transformed to a predominantly Sudanese one without leaving a distinctly Sudanese imprint on their scholarship. Moreover, the 'ulama were actively involved in the expansion of Islam to the Central Sudan and other parts of West Africa. They contributed to the development of other notable centres of learning, especially in Kano, Katsina and Ngazargamo. Yet, Cisoko's verdict that through the University of Timbuktu "Sudanese humanism became a fundamental part of world-wide Islam" (1984, p. 208) has to be balanced with the views of Dramani-Issifou that "Islamo-centrism made the universities of Timbuktu seem less brilliant than black Africans today would wish, as they can discern in those universities, as far as our present knowledge goes, hardly a trace of their cultural past". This, he added, was because the Muslim scholars belonged to a fairly closed world and were a small minority group facing a mass of adherents of African traditional religion whom they thought themselves duty bound to convert. (1988, p.112). The issue then is whether their passion for Islam and their operating within a closed system of universal Islam meant that they had lost all traces of Sudanese culture.

Unfortunately, little of the writings of the scholars at the University of Timbuktu survived the vandalism of the Moroccan invaders in 1591. The two outstanding works that we have - Al-Sadi's *Tarikh al-Sudan* (History of the Sudan, 1655) and the *Tarikh al-Fattash*, (Chronicles of the Researcher, 1664) compiled by Mahmud Ka'ti from various notes recorded by different members of his family - show clearly that the Sudanese scholars might have written completely within the traditions of Islamic scholarship and historiography, but they were certainly not remote from local oral traditions of the peoples and cultures of the Sudan.

## Afro-Christian and Western Education

In Ethiopia, education was the exclusive preserve of the Orthodox Church which organised and supported a wide range of educational establishments which dominated the cultural, religious, literary, artistic and even scientific life of Ethiopians. However, while Koranic schools tended to become universal in Muslim communities, especially in the urban areas, because of the necessity for every mature Muslim to comprehend the message of Islam in Arabic, only the children of the ruling class and others aspiring to be monks or priests went to school in Ethiopia. Traditionally, there were three levels of schools: the *Nebab Bet* (School of Reading) at the elementary level; at the secondary level were the *Quedasse Bet* (School of Holy Mass) and the *Quine Bet* (School of Poetry); and a variety of institutions of higher education referred to collectively as the *Metshafit Bet* (School of the Holy Books or Scriptures).

This pattern went back to the Zagwe period (c.1100-1270), but it became more widespread and established during the expansion and consolidation of the Solomonid dynasty from the late 13th to the early 16th centuries. The emperors preferred to retain the arrangement by which the Bishop at the head of the Ethiopian Church was chosen from the Coptic Church in Egypt, which required the cooperation of the Mamluk Sultans. Sometimes the cooperation was not easy to obtain - there was no Bishop between 1458 and 1480 and therefore no ordinations, with the consequent shortage of priests. The emperors put up with the situation because of the strong links with the traditions of Alexandria, and the Egyptian connection was the main guarantee of contact with the outside Christian world, through Alexandria to the Byzantine Church, the Holy Land and even the Latin Church. With such an arrangement, the educational system of the Church was a vital factor in the development of an indigenous culture and outlook.

The pillar of the system was the monastic school that Iyesus-Mo'a established on Lake Hayk, and others patterned after it, including Debre Libanos. Later, two monastic orders rose to establish and regulate life in the monasteries. The monasteries were generally located in remote areas, initially for people seeking contemplation and personal salvation, and this tended to encourage the autonomy of each institution. But the more successful ones also began to attract scholars and train students for the priesthood and administrative and other state functions. The monastic schools thus became an essential "preparatory ground for national leadership. Apart from being born into a rich and powerful family, gaining meritorious distinction as a religious scholar was the most reliable way of joining the Christian elite". (Tadese Tamrat, 1984, p.441). There was the special monastery on the inaccessible Mount Geshen where all eligible princes were confined so as to simplify the process of succession. The princes were kept fully engaged there on the study and practice of Ge'ez poetry, Sacred Music, Church History, and Exegesis of Holy Scriptures, away from any possible intrigue. If a vacancy occurred, the selected prince was sent for to ascend the throne.

The emperors gave generous grants of land to the monasteries, but could not always effectively control them. In return, the monasteries produced candidates for ordination as priests who were to preside over different congregations, manage elementary schools and lead the Church into newly conquered areas. The aim of the highly elaborate system of education in the Orthodox Church was, thus, to conserve and to extend an existing culture, rather than to change it. Nevertheless, as an Ethiopian educationist reminds us:

> the notion of prescribed school curricula varying from one level of schooling to another, administration of examinations to test the completion of prescribed curricula, ceremonial manifestations marking graduation ceremonies, the awarding of a diploma with a seal affixed to it, and other aspects of present day formal education had existed for many centuries, especially in the northern provinces of Ethiopia.(Habte, 1976, p.116).

The expansion of Islam and Arabic influence succeeded in choking up the Latin Church in North Africa, reduce the Coptic Church in Egypt to a minority sect and the Church in Ethiopia into a beleaguered one. The Latin Church eventually made contact with West, Central and Southern Africa from the 15th Century onwards in the era of the slave trade. The Portuguese voyages of exploration and trade were sent out under royal charter, and monastic orders, notably the Benedictines and later the Jesuits, were invited to send missionaries and establish schools. Other European countries soon joined in the trade, - the British, Dutch, Danes, French - usually through chartered companies. As a result, small colonies of Europeans, mulattos and

Africans developed at the main trading stations, notably in St. Louis and Goree in Senegal; Cape Coast, Elmina and Accra on the Gold Coast, Benin and the Kingdom of the Kongo. For the needs of these colonies some form of elementary schools began to be established to teach reading, writing and accounting in the different European languages. To provide teachers for such schools, boys were sent abroad for further education. Some of them became famous scholars abroad like Anton Amo from the Gold Coast who became a philosopher at the Martin Luther University in Halle, Germany, or Jacobis Capitein and Philip Quaque who returned as teachers, pioneers of an increasing number of Africans who went abroad for higher education.

The overall effect of the slave trade, especially the trans-Atlantic slave trade in the period 1600-1850, was profoundly disruptive of African social and intellectual life. The competition among European powers to control the trade, and the increasingly dehumanized capitalist mode adopted, promoted depopulation of youths, able-bodied men and women of child-bearing age on a scale that no society could contain without severe damaging effects. It strengthened some communities along the coast who, in self-defence, preyed on their neighbours until they themselves became victims of the internecine conflict. It encouraged the growth of slavery as the preferred mode of production. It disrupted intellectual life, the arts, crafts, manufacturing, agricultural production, peaceful trade and all notions of communal solidarity. The focus of the trade, and periods of worst disruption, shifted from place to place - Senegambia, Upper Guinea, Volta Region, Niger Delta, the Congo Basin. In the 19th century, the trans-Atlantic trade merged with the Arab trans-Indian Ocean trade with devastating effect in Central and East Africa. The movement for the abolition of the trade thus involved the need for rehabilitation of the peoples and reconstruction of a badly battered continent, and the renaissance of African civilization.

In the circumstances, the demand for Western education was certainly growing in Africa by the nineteenth century. The French mission to Egypt under Napoleon Bonaparte demonstrated some of the advances that scientific and industrial revolution were making in Europe. Several rulers in Africa, like Muhammad 'Ali in Egypt and Tewodros in Ethiopia, wanted Western schools as precursors of such changes, especially in military technology. Muhammad 'Ali certainly achieved considerable success in setting up a network of secular Western elementary and secondary schools and research institutes, side by side with the traditional koranic schools, madrasas and al-Alzhar. He also sent several students to France, Italy, Britain, Austria and other places in Europe to train as teachers, return to replace the initial international staff, and train the next generation of teachers within the new system of Western education.

However, most of the initiative for stimulating this demand came from Christian missionaries who saw in the campaign for the abolition of the slave trade and the promotion of Western education their most effective weapons for the propagation of Christianity. They did their best to attract children to school for religious instruction and to learn to read and write, usually in European languages. At the same time, they organised Sunday schools and Bible classes for adult converts and candidates for baptism to learn to read the Bible, if possible in African languages. Many of the missionary societies also realized that, if they wished to promote rapid evangelization, they could not ignore some form of training for African teachers and pastors either locally for larger numbers, or abroad at greater expense for a limited few. The missionaries had a fair measure of success in parts of West and South Africa. Their most spectacular success, however, was in Madagascar. There, because of competition between the Protestant London Missionary Society and the Roman Catholics, involving rivalry between Britain and France, and the Malagasy response of trying to play Britain against France, and shifting policy from active encouragement to outright proscription of missionary activities, Christianity took firm root on the central plateau of Imerina. When the Hova oligarchy seized power, a major plan in their reforms of 1869-70 was to organize a universal and compulsory system of state-run elementary schools, a little ahead of similar reforms in Britain. The success in Sierra Leone was also notable, if not so spectacular.

Both Sierra Leone and Liberia originated from the philanthropic venture of catering for the welfare of freed slaves who were viewed as constituting a social problem in Europe and America and were, therefore, repatriated to the West Coast of Africa. The British government took over Sierra Leone as a Crown Colony in 1808 so that it could be used as a base for the activities of the Royal Navy in its determination to enforce the abolition of the trans-Atlantic slave trade. That campaign became the motive force for British activities in West Africa leading eventually to the establishment of colonial rule towards the end of the nineteenth century. In the task of rehabilitating the freed slaves brought from Europe and North America, or freed in the course of the abolitionist campaign, the British depended very much on the cooperation of various missionary bodies, notably the Church Missionary Society and the Methodists.

Apart from a few who sought for commercial opportunities in Freetown, most of the recaptives were settled in various agricultural villages around Freetown under magistrates who were usually missionaries. Evangelization among the adults, and western education for the young, were the basic weapons of acculturation in creating the Creole society. This produced a network of elementary schools that compared with, and sometimes surpassed, what was available in most parts of rural

England.  The high mortality rate among European missionaries and officials encouraged the CMS to go further in the 1840s to develop two secondary schools, one for boys and another for girls.  Both the CMS and Methodists also took steps to improve the training of teachers and pastors locally and to encourage the brighter candidates to study abroad.  They encouraged as many of the affluent parents as could afford it to send their children to Britain for professional courses, especially in law and medicine.  In one such project, the CMS encouraged the Royal Navy to sponsor four graduates of the Freetown Grammar School to go abroad and study medicine.  Two of them, Africanus Horton and Broughton Davies,  qualified and were employed as medical officers in the Navy.  It was then that the issue of higher education in Sierra Leone became a matter of public debate: local training versus overseas training; the relevance of African culture in African higher education; and what kind of higher education was most relevant to African development.

## The Freetown Debate, 1872-73

Fourah Bay College, founded in 1826, was the main Church Missionary Society (CMS) institution for training its African auxiliaries.  It began as a trade school inculcating the virtues of hard work.  Gradually its literary content began to be improved.  As the grammar schools began to function, the level of Fourah Bay was also raised to the level of an institution of further education for the products of the boys' Grammar School interested in becoming teachers or candidates for ordination as pastors.  In 1859, the CMS authorities in London observed that in all the previous ten years, the College had trained only 10 students at a cost of nearly 800 pounds sterling and decided to close it down "as a collegiate establishment" until the demand for it improved.  This raised controversy in Freetown as many people saw the closure as a retrograde and hostile action, arguing that the demand was low because the quality was poor and the range of subjects covered was too narrow.

Various African leaders, like Africanus Horton in 1861 and again 1862, put forward suggestions as to how the College could be made to broaden its appeal, but the suggestions were ignored.  The College was reopened in 1863, but by March 1871, the newly appointed Principal, the Revd. Metcalfe Sunter, complained that there were only a handful of students, the buildings had fallen into disrepair, and the grounds were overgrown.  To facilitate revival of the College, Sunter and Bishop Cheetham conceived the idea of throwing the College open to fee-paying children of wealthy parents who could at least benefit from a few years there on preliminary studies prior to going abroad for professional courses.  There was little enthusiasm at the CMS Headquarters in London even for such limited reforms. Henry Venn who usually favoured progressive pro-African projects was cool: he did not like the idea of mixing lay fee-paying students with the Society's theological students.

That was how the leaders of the educated elite in Freetown turned the discussion about the future of Fourah Bay College into a public debate in which the case for a secular African-controlled university was made. Africanus Horton, himself a product of Fourah Bay College who, as mentioned above, had been sponsored under CMS auspices to study medicine in Edinburgh, was then practising with the British Navy as Assistant Surgeon at Cape Coast. There, he lived in close contact with the Fante and later became a champion of Fante nationalism and self-government for the Fante Confederation. A prolific writer and entrepreneur, he had suggested in 1862 that the British government should take over Fourah Bay and endow various chairs, especially in the sciences - Botany, Chemistry, Mathematics, Mineralogy, Engineering, Architecture. He repeated this in 1868, but in 1873, he added his voice to those demanding a government or public financed university located in Africa, emphasizing Science and Technology to develop the resources of Africa. It was by promoting such development that the university would become an instrument for restoring to Africa its lost place of glory in the world:

> Africa, in ages past, was the nursery of science and literature; from thence they were taught in Greece and Rome, so that it was said that the ancient Greeks represented their favourite goddess of Wisdom - Minerva - as an African princess ... Origen, Tertullian, Augustin, Clemens Alexandrinus, and Cyril, who were fathers and writers of the Primitive [i.e. Early Christian] Church, were tawny African bishops of Apostolic renown ... Herodotus describes them as 'wooly-haired blacks, with projecting lips' ... And why should not the same race who governed Egypt ... who had her churches, her universities and her repositories of learning and science once more stand on their legs and endeavour to raise their characters in the scale of the civilized world? (cit Thompson, 1930, pp.54-6).**

One of the most vocal in the debate was James Johnson, a product of both the Grammar School and Fourah Bay College, at the time without any overseas experience. By 1870, he was emerging as an introverted, puritanical, passionate and dedicated Anglican pastor. He knew and appreciated the extent to which African development depended on the missionary enterprise, but he was a radical critic of missionary education which he said laid "a fetter on our minds". In a letter to the

Acting Governor of Sierra Leone in December 1872, published in *The Negro* in January 1873, he said that the missionaries had ignored the history, culture and "peculiarities" of the African people, and proceeded in every way to give them a foreign model to copy. The result, he said, was that "we as a people ... have lost our self-respect and our love for our own race, are become a sort of nondescript people...and are in many things inferior to our brethren in the interior countries." (cit Blyden, 1896).

The coordinator of the debate and most widely recognised spokesman of the radical group was Edward Blyden. Born in the Dutch West Indies, and singled out as unusually gifted in languages, he was sent to be educated in the United States. Refused admission into Rutgers University, he migrated to Liberia where, at Alexander High School in Monrovia, he received a good basic education in the classics. After a period as a journalist, teacher and Presbyterian Minister, he was appointed professor of classical languages at the foundation of Liberia College in 1862 by the Board of Trustees for Donations for Higher Education in Liberia, a philanthropic group based in Boston. Besides Latin, Greek and Hebrew, he took particular interest in Arabic and, as Secretary of State for Liberia, he was able to visit Beirut in 1866. He left Monrovia in 1871 in the tumult that led to the death of President Roye. He went to London where the CMS offered him the job of professor of Arabic at Fourah Bay and evangelist to the interior Muslim communities in Futa Jallon. He was discharged when the CMS learnt of the scandal in Monrovia involving him and the wife of President Roye, but with a recommendation to the government in Sierra Leone to profit from his undoubted skills, especially in making contact with the Muslim communities in the interior. James Johnson, who was very particular about such things, said he had

---------------------------------

** Compare the Speech of the Public Orator, C.J. Potter, at the Inauguration of the University College, Ibadan in November 1948:

> The continent of Africa has a great and long tradition of learning. The valley of the River Nile was the very nurse and cradle of scientific research. The Library of Alexandria was among the wonders of the ancient world. At the time when the imperium of Rome extended to this continent, its northern shores were the home of many learned men. When the glory that was Greece and the grandeur that was Rome had become but memories in Europe, the tradition of learning     was still alive on the banks of the Niger ... So, the Secretary of State has come to inaugurate not the first, but the latest of the houses of learning in these regions. As his aeroplane crossed the coastline of Africa, it must have passed close to the place where one of the greatest African scholars of all time spent many years of his life - Saint Augustine, Bishop of Hippo, whose writings have profoundly influenced the thoughts of Europe. He loved to quote a phrase from an earlier inhabitant of Alexandria which might be borne in mind today - *Multitudo sapientum sanitas est urbis terrarum*. (*University Herald*, Ibadan, March 1949).

investigated the allegations and found no fault with Blyden.

This situation allowed Blyden, for a while, to practise as a free-lance journalist, editing a newspaper which he christened *The Negro*. The proposed University of West Africa was the most important of the causes he took up. In December 1872, he exchanged a series of remarkable letters with John Pope Hennessy, the Irishman who was Acting Governor and who, to the embarrassment of the Bishop and the resident missionaries, responded sympathetically to the radical criticism of missionary education. Blyden, with Hennessy's agreement, published the letters. Because of the support which *The Negro* gave to the state subsidy to the work of the Anglican Church, the Methodist authorities championed a rival newspaper, *The Independent*, which attacked Blyden's views, thus widening the area of debate.

Edward Blyden's criticisms of missionary education were similar to James Johnson's, namely, that it was narrow, sectarian and stifling. Liberal education, Blyden said, "has, with very few exceptions, been substituted by the narrow and dwarfing influence of ecclesiastical dogmatism." What was needed, he added, was education that would first unfetter the African mind and then enlighten it. To do this, it was necessary to promote race consciousness in the African. He did not separate the ill effects of missionary education from the cumulative effects of the slave trade. However, by praising the moral character of interior peoples who had suffered from the slave trade but not from missionary education, in contrast to that of the coastal people who had suffered from both, Blyden gave the impression that missionary education - slavery of the mind - was worse than slavery of the body. About the slave trade, he said:

> Europeans owe us a great debt, not only for the unrequited physical labours we have performed in all parts of the world, but for the unnumbered miseries and untold demoralization they have brought upon Africa by the prosecution for centuries of the horrible traffic to promote their own selfish ends... (cit. Ashby, 1966, p.455).

Therefore, as a form of restitution, he urged the Acting Governor to take the initiative in seeking approval and funds for a secular, government-financed, well-established African University,

> in keeping with the advancing spirit of the age and adapted to the inherent necessities of the race...an Institution with able African teachers brought, if necessary, from different parts of the world - even a Negro Arabic Professor from Egypt, Timbuctoo or Futah - would have great influence in exposing

and correcting the fallacies upon which our foreign teachers have proceeded in their utter misapprehension and, perhaps, contempt of African character. (ibid. pp 453, 52).

In his exchange of letters with Hennessy, perhaps for reasons of strategy, Blyden did not specify details of curriculum reform that would achieve the general objectives. He tackled this in an inaugural lecture he gave in 1881 to the Liberia College, entitled *The Aims and Methods of a Liberal Education for Africans*. His basic approach was to avoid the study of modern European civilization, the period when "the trans-Atlantic slave trade arose and those theories - theological, social and political - were invented for the degradation and proscription of the Negro." Rather, he would concentrate on the Classics which he said were capable of providing intellectual "nourishment ... without ... race poison". To the Classics, he would add Mathematics as well as Arabic and major African languages. The great value of Arabic and African languages that he emphasized was that they would open up communication with the peoples of the interior from whom a fount of African culture and traditions would come with which to reinvigorate the creativity of the coastal peoples. We must listen, he said,

> to the songs of our unsophisticated brethren as they sing of their history, as they tell of their traditions, of the wonderful and mysterious events of their tribal or national life, of the achievements of what we call their superstitions; we must lend an ear to the ditties of the Kroomen who pull our boats, or the Pesseh and Golah men who till our farms; we must read the compositions, rude as we may think them, of the Mandingoes and the Veys. (Blyden, 1882).

This echoed James Johnson's reference to "our languages enriched with traditions of centuries; our parables, many of them the quintessence of family and national histories; our modes of thought, influenced more or less by local circumstances, our poetry and manufactures which, though rude, had their own tales to tell ..." However, how the University was to utilize this treasure of African culture to foster regeneration and creativity, neither Blyden nor Johnson could tell, since neither of them spoke any indigenous African language nor, up to that time, had any close contact with indigenous African people. It was not until 1876 when James Johnson, who was born in Freetown, was transferred to Lagos where he was able to make contact with his father's Ijesha and mother's Ijebu people, that he could speak more authoritatively about African culture.

## Fourah Bay College, 1876

John Pope Hennessy forwarded the exchange of letters to London with a covering letter addressed to the Earl of Kimberley, supporting the demand for a Government-financed University which was responsive to the cultural needs of Africans. He added that he had a long conference in Freetown with the Hon. William Grant, African member of the Legislative Council and thirteen African pastors of the Church of England on the subject, and he had discussed it with others in Lagos and Elmina. He predicated his views on the Report of the Parliamentary Committee of 1865 that the aim of the British Government should be to train the peoples of the West African Coast to be self-governing. It was therefore necessary to have a University so as to reduce the necessity for sending people to Europe at a tender age, at the risk of their health, their morals, and continuity with their historical traditions. It is painful, he said,

> to notice the contrast between such young men, who ought to be the natural leaders of public opinion in their own country, and the Chiefs and people from the Interior who have been untouched by Europeans. The latter have a manly bearing, a natural courtesy, a very keen intelligence and a frank and honest disposition. The negroes who have been educated in Europe, or who have been forced here into a sort of Semi-European mould, are the very reverse of all this ...

> I think a West African University founded on a very humble basis ought to be established, where not only the sons of rich Africans could be educated but where, like in the early Irish Universities and some of the Continental Universities of our own times, even the poorest youths who had talents and a real taste for knowledge might by sizarships or fellowships have an opportunity of cultivating learning. (cit. Ashby, 1966, p.457).

The response in the Colonial Office was sympathetic but cautious. If education in Europe was the cause of the degeneration, what of the large numbers educated locally who were reported to be degenerate? And if they were degenerate, why should their views be accepted? The main worry voiced out, however, was whether there was enough demand. Lord Kimberley decided to remit the matter to the substantive governor to give his "careful attention" to the matter and conduct a feasibility survey.

The reaction of the CMS authorities both in Freetown and in London was very hostile to what they called the Hennessy-Johnson-Blyden fever. They were not impressed by the arguments about the need for race consciousness or for regarding "African culture and traditions" as a treasure house, a source of intellectual invigoration and creativity. The official reply of the CMS to the Freetown debate appeared in the *CMS Intelligencer* of 1873: Concerning the charge that missionary education Europeanized the African, "the answer might be, what else could ever be done? We have already shown that Africa has no past ... How, then, were race instincts [i.e. culture] to be respected which either had no existence or which [if it existed at all] were fatal and soul-destroying to the Negro?" They regarded the views of Blyden and others as impractical, due to mere fancy, and arising from sheer ingratitude for all that the missionaries had done or were doing. On the specific issue of "race sentiment", Bishop Cheetham said, using the controversial term "Negro" that Blyden had adopted to refer to all Africans:

> national feeling & so forth is not finding expression in the *Negro* but the Negro is spreading it on thick before the people are ready ... patriotism & national feeling etc. are plants that grow with a nation's growth & here there is not a nation yet, only a collection of persons of different tribes who heartily hate & distrust one another: & in the present condition of Soc$^y$. to write about race sentiment is understood to mean by the commonfolk - be good haters - hate well - everybody else but yourself. (cit Ashby, 1966, p.464).

The Methodist establishment who were bitter rivals of the Anglicans because of the controversy over the state subsidy, were similarly incensed at the disparagement of missionary work and played their part separately in frustrating Government support for the proposed University.

The CMS further saw Pope Hennessey's influence as that of a dogmatic Catholic out to destabilise Protestants. They objected to the idea of a secular, Negro-controlled University where, at best, "Mohammedanism" would be placed on an equal pedestal with Christianity or, at worst, would be a "Godless University". Bishop Cheetham advised the new Governor that the Hennessey-Johnson-Blyden scheme would be too expensive; that it was better for government not to take the initiative, but to help the Africans only to the extent that they were able to help themselves. Then, in a confidential letter, he urged the CMS to move quickly to frustrate the scheme...

I would so open Fourah Bay & announce it open, as to cut to the ground the plea of necessity for another college: I would for a long time to come keep in my own hands, if I were you, the Higher Education of the Coast using Governors' names & all the rest of it for ornament and patronage but you being at the base. (*ibid.* pp.463-4).

Up to June 1873, Sunter was still of the opinion that "the time has not yet arrived ... for the establishment of a University, unless 'White Man's money' should not only establish it but also maintain it: the time has not yet arrived for the establishment of a College in affiliation with an European University: but the time has arrived, I think, when we may fairly begin to look forward in the direction of the latter and prepare for it ..." However, the Parent Committee appreciated the need to move fast. They invited James Johnson to visit London to advise on the University project and other matters. Thus they heightened his loyalty to the CMS and diverted his attention away from a secular University towards a reform of Fourah Bay College. Soon after, they transferred him away from Freetown to face fresh challenges in Lagos.

The Parent Committee decided in November 1873 to proceed with the idea of opening up Fourah Bay to fee-paying students desirous of education "in advance of what has been hitherto given in our Grammar School." The religious and missionary character must be preserved and observed by all students. A Theological department for training youths for missionary work must be maintained. "For some time yet", Europeans should remain in charge. These proposals were endorsed by the missionary Conference in Freetown in June 1874. The initial intention was to approach London for affiliation, but when it was known that Durham had just granted affiliation to Codrington College in Barbados, an approach was made to Durham and affiliation became effective in May 1876. The curriculum was drawn up in Durham. Durham teachers were to set the papers and mark the scripts. For both the B.A. (pass) degree and the Licentiate of Theology, the needs of candidates for the Ministry of the Church of England dictated the contents of the course - Biblical Studies, the Classics, English History up to the Conquest, and Mathematics. The only adaptation that was possible was to supplement it with a non-examining course in Arabic and Islamic Studies. Proposals for Law, Medicine, Science, Agriculture, Economics, Engineering and Architecture, not to mention African Studies, were washed off.

Thus, the University institution at Fourah Bay, affiliated to Durham University, was a pale shadow of the Blyden-Johnson-Hennessy proposed West African University. The Revd Metcalfe Sunter, who was not a university graduate, remained Principal till 1882. He shouldered the bulk of the teaching. A converted Jewish Rabbi, Alexander

Schapira, taught Hebrew and Arabic, while a German missionary and linguist, C.A.L. Reichart was in charge of Classics. Of the two African Assistants, N. S. Davis was himself a candidate and the first person to obtain the B.A. under the Scheme of affiliation in 1878.

Perhaps James Johnson became reconciled to the idea of Fourah Bay College, or his new pastoral and evangelistic duties in Lagos were enough to divert his attention from the problems of higher education. Africanus Horton turned to the idea of private sponsorship of higher education. When he died suddenly in 1883 at the age of 48, he left his house, Horton Hall as a bequest in his will for a Horton Collegiate High School for the advanced study of science to the level where it would be accepted in affiliation to an English University. It was the failure of his business ventures in mining and banking that left no funds to support his many bequests that killed the proposal. Edward Blyden continued to explore official channels to take the initiative and attract private funds. Eventually, he secured employment as Director of Muslim education throughout British West Africa and as such remained an influential adviser on education generally. In 1896, he suggested to the Governor of Lagos a plan for the Lagos Training College and Industrial Institute, based on joint sponsorship by government and the business community, the College being a centre of higher education "with an emphasis on the Classics, Mathematics, Mental and Moral Philosophy and Natural Science." The Governor and the Colonial office were attracted because of the emphasis on the vocational training Institute, but the plan was dropped because of the "apathy" of Lagos businessmen for whom colonial rule meant declining opportunities, revenues, prospects, and capacity to sponsor such projects. His 1899 proposal for a university level "Central Training Institution for Muslims", anticipating the Gordon Memorial College of Khartoum as a centre to give Muslim/Arabic teachers good grounding in English and Western education so as to make them useful agents of British imperial rule in the Western Sudan, did not receive adequate official support.

Fourah Bay College remained the only University institution in West Africa until 1948. Its one attraction was the opportunity to obtain a university degree without leaving West Africa. Its fortunes continued to fluctuate as before the time of affiliation, partly because of its unexciting quality, partly because of shortage of funds from the CMS to subsidize its work, and partly because of discrimination against educated Africans in the Sierra Leone public service. Its most distinguished alumni tended to be students from Nigeria who became well known as Principals of schools or made their mark in the Church ministry. In 1908, the College announced that it might have to close down its Collegiate section, but it managed to carry on until 1918 when negotiations for Methodist cooperation in the running and funding of the College eventually yielded some fruit. The degree course was lengthened to three years. The B.A. pass degree in Theology was instituted to replace the L.Th. In particular cases, with the support of part-time teachers, it was sometimes possible to arrange for the B.A. in Law, but down to the Second World War, very little had changed at Fourah Bay.

## Towards African Renaissance

The 19th century was a period of rapid and multiple changes in the Western world. The history of Fourah Bay College reflects two of these changes which were of particular importance to Africa. The first was the growth of imperialism, the European desire for overseas empire, particularly in Africa and South-east Asia. This began as part of the social reforms consequent upon the growth of industrialism - improved education, increase of parliamentary democracy, rise of an urban industrial working class, Evangelical revival, the missionary enterprise and abolitionist movement. The settlement in Freetown was an offshoot of the abolitionist movement. When FBC was founded in 1827, it was to train evangelists not only in theology but also in habits of labour as part of the effort to develop export crops as alternatives to the slave trade. By the time Blyden and others were demanding an African University, and the CMS decided to use the affiliation of FBC to Durham to frustrate it, the desire to stop the export of unpaid African labour across the seas was already being transformed into a desire to acquire territories in Africa where the land, the human and mineral resources could be exploited with African labour for the benefit of Europe. Some educated Africans co-operated with this European desire in the belief that colonial rule might prove a necessary step to African development. Colonial rule proved to be both an opportunity and an obstacle to African development.

The second change reflected in the history of FBC was the transformation of higher education in Europe and America. The Medieval university which grew out of the monastic traditions of Alexandria shared various aspects of indigenous African higher education described earlier - the oral, eclectic and sometimes esoteric character, not to mention the affinity of some kinds of knowledge in African epistemology to magic. Since the 17th century, the scientific revolution had been reducing these areas of congruence. There were also similarities with Afro-Christian and Islamic universities in the religious basis of higher education, the reliance on a number of set texts, the pursuit of vocational and professional training, - beyond law, medicine and theology, - in institutions other than the universities. It was the industrial revolution that brought scientific research, and vocational and professional training, more and more into the universities. Much of the reform of the universities in the mid-19th century - to have regular lectures, systematize research, promote national languages etc. - was taking place under the auspices of the state which showed increasing interest in relating the universities to the economic, military and managerial effectiveness of the nation. The clamour of Blyden and others for an African university was, in fact, partly a reflection of similar clamour in Europe and America for reform of education as a factor in national invigoration. Durham University, the third University in England following after the medieval Colleges of Oxford and Cambridge, was founded in 1832 four years before University College, London. In 1861, there were only 41 students in the University of Durham. It was a royal commission that initiated reforms which improved its quality in the 1870s and made it possible for the C.M.S. to consider affiliating Fourah Bay College to it. Thereafter, new universities and university colleges were established in London, Manchester, Bristol, etc. and, therefore, development was rapid.

In the early 20th century, the clamour for universities in Africa was muted as people learnt to cope with colonial rule. By the 1920s, the debate was resumed, and the usual theme was the regenerative power of universities, provided they were modern universities which reflected the reforms of the 19th century. Thus, Nnamdi Azikiwe of Nigeria, on his return from studying in the US, published a book in 1937, entitled *Renascent Africa* in which he took up the issue of the nature and function of the African University. Universities, he said,

> have been responsible for shaping the destinies of races and nations and individuals .. The universities of Europe and America have been responsible for the great movements in the national history of these continents ... Give the Renascent African a university, ... With twelve million pounds there is no reason why the best libraries, laboratories, professors cannot be produced right here, and this continent can become overnight "A Continent of Light".

Universities, he added, are mirrors "which reflect (the) particular sociological idiosyncrasies". An African graduate of European or American universities, "unless he has developed his individuality, is nothing short of a megaphone, yea a carbon copy of these societies". Yet, in his description of the African University, his emphasis was not on the factor of cultural heritage but of ownership and commitment: "an indigenous university sustained through African initiative ... maintained at (African) expense". If such universities had existed in Africa, he said, they could have had their curricula filled with important divisions of knowledge which would have hastened their intellectual emancipation, and would have enabled them to make scientific researches into some of the quackeries which some of them are wont to elevate into an unmerited apogee by calling them a phase of `Super-Science'. (cit Fafunwa, 1971, p 179-80).

In other words, the African University is to be defined not merely by its historical continuity with the African past, but even more by its commitment to the renaissance of Africa. Renaissance could not be achieved by merely reflecting the "quackeries" of the past. Rather, there must be intellectual emancipation from both the limitations of the past and the shackles that colonialism placed not only on the mind, but also on the freedom of choice.

Chapter 2


## COLONIALISM AND HIGHER EDUCATION

### Education and Social Change

During the colonial period, education was probably the most critical issue in the relationship between European rulers and African subjects. A few Europeans learnt African languages and were thus able to communicate directly with the people. The vast majority of Europeans had to depend upon interpreters and mediators. Western education provided the means of recruiting Africans into this role of mediators through whom traditional African societies and institutions were adapted into the colonial mould. Adaptation was going on in three different sectors: (i) colonial administration and services, including tax collection, law courts, public works, agriculture, and health; (ii) mining, finance, commercial enterprises, including farming establishments, production of raw materials, produce collection, distributive trade, importation and exportation; and (iii) missionary activities, including evangelization and the provision of western education itself. The provision of Western education thus became the most important factor of social change within the different colonial territories.

For that reason, education policies were also the most effective instrument for the colonial administrations to try to control the pace and direction of social change. For most of the colonial period until the Second World War, the priority of the different colonial administrations was the maintenance of law and order, not the fostering of social change. Even where the official policy was one of "assimilation" and racial equality, the colonial administrators tended to regard educated Africans with any pretensions to claim racial equality as dangerous radicals who were no longer suitable for the role of "interpreters". Some Europeans preferred to dispense with African "interpreters" altogether and rely on missionaries or other European residents, who learnt African languages, to act as intermediaries. At all events the prevalent attitude of the colonial regimes was to neglect education or seek to limit its provision. Neglect or restriction was evident at the elementary level, more severe at the secondary level, and virtually total at the level of higher education.

## Stimulating the Demand

Once conquered, the traditional authorities were obliged to give up resistance, learn to cooperate with the colonial rulers, and accept the status of dependence. One condition of this was to renounce warfare and interest in military technology and industrialization which, in the nineteenth century, had been behind much of the interest of traditional rulers in Western education. In return, the colonial rulers re-organized the traditional institutions, appointed their own candidates and tried to make some provision of secular elementary education to train "sons of chiefs" and other functionaries to run modernized traditional institutions.

The different missionary societies were obviously interested in continuing to stimulate and to try to satisfy the demand for Western education. It was good for their purpose of evangelization, and the subsidy they received from the colonial administrations, often a substantial part of their revenue, was an added advantage. However, they had to abide within laid down policies and observe regulations. Although they often disagreed over details, such as policies restricting their access into Muslim areas or extending Muslim rule over non-Muslim and potentially Christian populations, the missionaries were usually allies of the colonial rulers in trying to see the pace and direction of change controlled.

Thus, the most important group stimulating the demand for Western education were the Africans who had benefited from, or had witnessed the benefits of, Western education from the activities of missionaries in the 19th century. The educated elite created by the mission schools and their offsprings, especially in West and South Africa were anxious to sustain and, if possible, to increase the momentum in the expansion of Western education. They had come to realize that the acquisition of Western education was the necessary condition for obtaining jobs in the different modernizing sectors of the economy, and, thus, to join the influential modern elite. Many Africans, some barely literate, became evangelists both for Christianity and Western education as the essential ingredients for social change and development in the different communities. Sometimes it became a matter of community rivalry to secure the services of some evangelist or missionary body to establish schools. In this way, once introduced, the expansion of a network of elementary schools could be sustained by the community itself exerting pressure on the missionary society concerned, so as to remain competitive in the race for development.

Some of the missionaries and several of the break-away Ethiopian Churches and sects were not interested in education beyond bare literacy to facilitate studying the Scriptures. For the development of education, the critical sector was at the post-primary level and here the pressure for expansion was exerted by the educated elite who were themselves largely the product of a specific policy of missionary societies in the middle of the 19th century to create an African elite who could work side by side, and not merely under, Europeans for the development of Africa. This mid-19th century liberalism was part of the movement that led to the establishment of the University of London with a view to extending university education to working class people and others kept out of Oxford and Cambridge, by awarding degrees to candidates prepared in various Academies or Colleges, or even by private study. This same liberalism was evident in the development of universities in India - and the self-governing overseas colonies. (Ashby, 1966, chapter 3).

More than anything else, that policy was implemented in the establishment of the two secondary schools by the CMS in Freetown - the Grammar School for boys in 1845 and the Female Institution (later Annie Walsh Memorial School) in 1849. It had its counterpart in the Four Communes of Senegal declared in 1848 to be part of overseas France, and the establishment in St. Louis of General Faidherbe's école des otages ("School for the sons of chiefs"), basically a comprehensive secondary school, providing courses also in commerce, elementary law and administration, and teacher training. These schools set off a chain reaction that later changes of policy could not easily undo. Some of the products of the schools were sent to Europe for further training. In Freetown, they were partly responsible for upgrading Fourah Bay College as a Training Institution to a University College affiliated to Durham University in 1876. The advantages that these conferred on the CMS as a missionary body ensured that similar schools were established by the CMS in Lagos - a Grammar School for boys in 1859, and a Female Seminary for girls in 1876; by the Methodists - Wesleyan Boys High Schools in Freetown 1874, Cape Coast 1876, and Lagos 1878, followed by a Methodist Girls High School, a Baptist Academy and a Roman Catholic St. Gregory's College in Lagos in quick succession, as well as the CMS Training Institutions in Bonny and Onitsha and the Presbyterian Hope Waddell Institute in Calabar. (Ajayi, 1963).

The demand for an African University, raised in the public debate in Freetown in the 1870s, did not easily die down. With all its constraints, Fourah Bay College received students from Nigeria and Ghana (Gold Coast), though less so from Ghana because of the predominant influence there of Methodists and Presbyterians rather than Anglicans. The products of Fourah Bay played a notable role in seeking to establish more secondary schools in Nigeria, usually by acting as Founding Principals, persuading a congregation as a patriotic duty to put up buildings and initial capital, and requesting the CMS to adopt the school, secure government recognition, and assist with recruitment of staff, additional graduates if possible, or the ablest products from the Training Institutions. In that way, secondary schools were established between 1900 and 1920 in the 6 most prominent Yoruba towns. In Ghana where this partnership between Fourah Bay graduates and the CMS in the founding of secondary schools was not feasible, the educated elite, tried to raise funds for National Institutes or Collegiate establishments from the chiefs or businessmen. Such efforts led eventually to Mfantispim and Adisadel Colleges in Cape Coast and the Grammar School in Accra. (Kimble, 1963, pp.84-87). Both in Ghana and Nigeria, the dearth of graduate teachers became the main factor limiting the spread of secondary schools and that ensured that the thirst for higher education was kept alive. It was also an important factor in ensuring that the mission Teacher Training Colleges, - the CMS at Oyo, Methodists at Ibadan, and CMS at Awka - maintained an increasingly high standard, such that the St. Andrew's College at Oyo seriously considered seeking affiliation to Durham as a University College in the 1920s.

The demand for post-primary education in general, and specifically for higher education, became an essential platform in the rising tide of nationalism in West Africa, which was linked up with the Pan-African movement both of Marcus Garvey and of William DuBois. At the same time, changes of emphasis can be detected in the mission assigned to the University. J.E. Casely-Hayford a graduate of Fourah Bay College and leader of the National Congress of British West Africa had published a book in 1911 entitled *Ethiopia Unbound*. In it, he had imagined a Fante University teaching in Fante and making the development of African languages and cultures its major area of concern. By the 1920s, the emphasis of the National Congress was on a university whose degrees would have world-wide recognition, and provide access for its holders into responsible, decision-making posts in the Civil Service, hitherto reserved for Europeans. Such graduates would of course also provide teachers for secondary schools and teacher training colleges and help to speed up the spread of education.

The developments in South Africa were similar, though the outcome was rather different. In the 1840s and 1850s, the missionary societies in South Africa, especially the London Missionary Society in the Eastern Cape, the Methodists in Natal, and the Paris Evangelical Mission in Lesotho (Basutoland), placed emphasis on the need for post-primary education, industrial and agricultural schools, as well as Training Institutions for African teachers and pastors. The most famous was the Lovedale Institution established by William Govan of the Scottish Presbyterian Mission in 1841. With a grant from the liberal Sir George Grey, provided for in the Act granting self-government to the Cape in 1854, "to train Bantu youth in industrial occupations and to fit them to act as interpreters, evangelists and school masters amongst their own people", Govan added an industrial section with masonry, carpentry, wagon-making, smithing and, later, printing and book binding. (Groves, 1954, vol.ii, p.136).

Lovedale became a model, similar to the Hampton Institute and Booker T. Washington's Tuskegee Institute of the Southern US, but with undoubted thoroughness in its academic work as well. It was meant to educate both Africans and whites together but from the 1870s, with the retreat from the liberalism of mid-19th century, it was decided to concentrate on the specific needs of Africans. Lovedale influenced the development of secondary education for blacks throughout Southern, Central and East Africa, being replicated at Blysthwood and Livingstonia in Malawi, and copied at Adams College in Natal and several other places. Swiss missionaries working with the Paris Evangelicals at Morija in Lesotho established a comprehensive secondary school along the same lines in 1868, and a Training College in 1880. Anglican and Methodist mission schools tended to imitate the English public schools. Quite notable were the Methodist Clarkebury Institute founded in 1825 and Healdtown College, near Fort Beaufort, which by the 1930s was reputed to be "the largest African School below the equator, with more than a thousand students, both male and female". (Mandela, 1994, p.31-2). As in Freetown, the spread of secondary schools and Training Institutions further stimulated the demand for higher education.

## UNISA and Fort Hare College

The British administrations of the Cape Province in South Africa were content to leave education largely to private initiative, mostly missionaries and Churches serving different racial and even ethnic communities, supplemented by Government grants through which the Government tried to influence policy. As a result of private initiative, a few of the better colleges tried to push beyond secondary education, the best known being the South African College at Cape Town, established in 1829 for the English-speaking community and the Victoria College at Stellenbosch for the Afrikaans-speaking community. The first major Government initiative in higher education came in 1858 with the establishment of a Board of Public Examinations in Literature and Science to examine candidates from the various Colleges, particularly those seeking civil service employment. The Board was replaced in 1873 by the University of the Cape of Good Hope, an examining body with no teaching facilities, with power to grant degrees like the University of London as then constituted. It obtained a royal charter in 1877.

After the Boer War, and the Federation of the independent Orange Free State and Transvaal with Natal and the Cape in 1910, the Union Government reorganised the University of the Cape of Good Hope into the University of South Africa (UNISA) in 1916. It was still an examining body, but now incorporated six university colleges as constituent colleges, with agreed syllabuses, and taking the degrees of the University. The colleges were: Rhodes University College at Grahamstown; Huguenot University College, Wellington; Grey University College, Bloemfontein; Natal University College, Pietermaritzburg; Transvaal University College, Pretoria; and the Kimberley School of Mines and Technology which became the Witwatersrand University College, in Johannesburg. Other Acts of the Union Parliament recognized the South African College as the University of Cape Town, and the Victoria College as the University of Stellenbosch. They were meant specifically for the white communities, Bloemfontein, Pretoria and Stellenbosch being Afrikaans-speaking, while the others were English-speaking. In 1921, the Dutch Reformed Church Christian College at Potchefstroom was incorporated into UNISA as a University College, thus strengthening the Afrikaans element in UNISA and greatly reducing the English dominance of the earlier University of the Cape of Good Hope.

The Afrikaans-speaking University and University Colleges specifically barred the admission of non-Europeans. Without saying so, the English-speaking ones rarely admitted non-Europeans. There was little enthusiasm for university education for the Africans. The prevalent racism was compounded by the fear that education would enable the majority Africans to "swamp" the white communities who began to see themselves as defenders of an island of European civilisation in a sea of African barbarism. Many of the missionaries, even those who counted as liberals, shared the racist prejudices of the white communities, but at least they believed that with the inspiration of the Bible, the Africans could be helped to make some advance, though never to the level of Europeans. Thus, some of the whites supported the establishment of limited facilities for African higher education, if not out of Christian charity, then on the principles of the old Greek principle that "if you don't destroy your enemy then you must make him your friend". (Hofmeyr in the "Introduction" to Shepherd, 1941, p. vi).

It was reported that by 1878 Dr. James Stewart, who had taken over from Govan as Principal of Lovedale, saw the need for a College to cater specifically for the needs of Africans for higher education. He declared in a public lecture in Edinburgh in 1902 that higher education for Africans

is not altogether discouraged, but assisted to a small extent on the ground that education spreads among a people from above downwards rather than the reverse. The desire for it is kindled among the mass by their seeing its effects and advantages to the few who have really gone beyond the most elementary stage". (Shepherd, 1941, p. 173).

It was not till 1904, after the Boer War when the British began to transfer power to the white communities, that he made definite proposals on the matter to the Inter-Colonial Native Affairs Commission. The Commission responded positively in January 1905 with a recommendation "that a Central Native College or similar institution" be established, with contributions from the various Provinces, "for training Native teachers and in order to afford opportunity for higher education to Native students". In December 1905, representatives of different groups of Africans met in a Convention at Lovedale and endorsed the idea of a Central College. By October 1907, a Committee under the Rev. James Henderson who had succeeded Dr. Stewart in 1905, was established to raise funds. The Presbyterian mission pledged £5,000 (five thousand pounds) and offered a site near Fort Hare as part payment. The Transkeian Territories General Council (African Local Council) voted £10,000 (ten thousand pounds).

However, little progress could be made until the Act of 1910 when the Union Government could provide the necessary assistance on behalf of the different Provinces. But it was not until November 1914, after the onset of World War I, and the demand for African support in the war effort, that the Government of the Union finally endorsed the idea, agreed to the constitution, voted an annual subvention of £600 and appointed its representatives on the Governing Council of the proposed College. The College, hitherto referred to as the Inter-State Native College, now christened the South African Native College, was declared open by General Botha, the Prime Minister, in February 1916. It started with 18 African male and 2 African female students but also included two Europeans.

To begin with, the College offered courses at secondary school level for students making up for deficiencies in post-primary education and preparing for university matriculation. The bulk of the students studied for the 2-year College Diploma in Education, Commerce or Agriculture. There were at the time only 2 academic staff: the Principal (1915-48), Mr. Alexander Kerr, an experienced teacher and graduate of Edinburgh University, specifically recruited for the post; and D.D.T. Jabavu, a graduate of English from the University of London, the son of J. Tengo Jabavu, a Methodist preacher and one of the prime movers in the foundation of the College. At the inauguration of the College, Alexander Kerr echoed the sentiments of James Stewart, emphasizing the importance of higher education for social change:

More is accomplished for the civilization and education of the masses by supplying every part of a country with good professional men than by teaching everybody the ABC. The educated professional few carry with them a standard of life wherever they go while serving their fellowmen in all that concerns their daily needs and highest interests. (Shepherd, 1941, p. 288).

As at Lovedale, the Tuskegee Institute exerted a powerful influence on the College. D.D.T. Jabavu had visited Tuskegee after his degree in London and Alexander Kerr also visited it in 1923. Jabavu promoted African languages and agriculture, and built up a famous choir. It was only gradually that a sprinkling of the students began to sit for the degrees of UNISA.

In 1923, the College was incorporated specifically as an institution of higher education recognized as preparing students externally for degrees of UNISA. Gradually, it won some of the privileges of the internal University Colleges of UNISA: it was able to nominate some staff as supernumerary members of the Faculties and Senate of the University, and the professors and lecturers began to be recognized as internal examiners. However, this was not extended to the few African staff who were not allowed to sit down with European colleagues to discuss syllabuses, even for African languages and literatures. This further discouraged the appointment of African staff, and no arrangements were made for African staff training and development. A major development took place in 1937 with a substantial grant of £75,000 from the Chamber of Mines for developing the sciences and embarking on medical education. That, among other factors, made it possible from 1937 for the College to begin to concentrate on post-secondary work, even though the onset of World War II delayed the full effects of the new changes. In 1937, the enrolment stood at 150 students.

The Provincial Governments and the High Commission territories, especially Lesotho, sponsored African students to the College. The College also sought for donations from the private sector. But it was the different missionary groups that built up day to day support. The Methodists, Anglicans and Presbyterians each erected a hostel, managed by a Warden who looked after the accommodation of the majority of the students. They transferred to the College or began to offer there courses in Theology for the training of their non-European ministers. In addition, the YMCA of the US and Canada raised funds for a Christian Students Union Building. The Union Government agreed to cooperate with the missionary bodies, and the constitution laid it down that "The College shall be a Christian College and, while no special religious tests may be applied, all members of the staff shall be professing Christians and of missionary sympathies".

This missionary background of the College did not preclude the government from playing a significant role in the running of the College from the start. The Higher Education Act of 1923 empowered the Government of the Union of South Africa to nominate four representatives to the Council of the College. Government involvement was essential to raise funds to enable the College to go beyond Theology, Old Testament Greek and Latin, Church History and English, to offer courses in Science, Agriculture, Commerce and Medicine. The price was that the missionaries could not retain, even if they had wished to, the liberal policies of the mid-19th century so evident in West Africa. (SANC, Calendar for 1940). In 1951, the running of the College was taken out of the hands of the missionaries as the College was affiliated with Rhodes University in Grahamstown, about 100 km away, and renamed the University College of Fort Hare. The arrangement with Rhodes University was, however, shortlived. The Nationalist Party that won the 1948 election soon embarked on extending apartheid policies fully to education. In 1960, in applying "Bantu Education" to higher education, Fort Hare was placed under the direct management of the Minister of Bantu Education, operating largely through the predominantly Afrikaans-speaking UNISA. Admission was restricted to the Xhosa from Transkei and Ciskei, Xhosa-speakers from the rest of the country and the Sotho from Transkei. It was under those circumstances that the College was granted University status in 1969 and was transferred to the control of the Ciskei homeland government with effect from 1986.

In spite of these severe limitations, Fort Hare has played a role in pioneering higher education for Africans in Southern, Central and East Africa comparable with that of Fourah Bay in West Africa. With its programmes covering Education, Commerce, Agriculture, Science, Para-medical sciences and later Medicine, it offered a much broader curriculum than Fourah Bay College. With the active support of Alexander Kerr, and with Jabavu taking charge of the Department, Fort Hare gave early attention to African Studies, particularly in the study of the languages, literatures and traditional societies of the Xhosa, Sotho, Tswana and Zulu, before African Studies became politicized and distorted under the apartheid system. The Principal remarked that the African students were "obsessed with topics like the franchise, the colour bar and social segregation in public amenities and conveyances... They had a passionate faith in the efficacy of education to make good these and similar deficiencies". But the reality was the grosser forms of discourtesy by some Europeans, such as being called "Kaffirs" or "Natives" or "Indian coolies". They were thus likely to have been cool to speeches such as were given at the first graduation ceremony in 1924, - with Z.K. Mathews and E. McWanna as the two graduates - by Professor Dingemans of Rhodes University who wished that the College would develop "a rich but marked individuality ... a *Native* college in no way inferior to white colleges ... specifically adapted to the needs of Native students and to the circumstances in which they were to exercise their particular calling". Or Senator Roberts, a former missionary, speaking with his tongue in his cheek:

> Let there be among your people a select body of cultured educated men and no posts for which they are fitted by education and by ability will be closed to them. No doors will be shut against their entrance into a larger room if they are fitted to enter. Slowly, as the level of education rises among your people, this barrier and that barrier will be broken down: this way and that way opened up. But the men must be there: men fitted and equipped for this wider field. (Kerr, 1968, pp.115-6).

The staff remained predominantly white, mostly from the Eastern Cape, at best paternalistic to the African student, at worst downright racist and little tempered by the Christian environment. But the thirst for higher education was such that students learnt to adjust and cope with the attitudes of their teachers. The degrees of UNISA were widely recognized and, until the College began to enforce the restriction to Xhosa- and Sotho-speaking students, Fort Hare attracted students from as far away as Zimbabwe, Malawi, Zambia, Kenya, Tanzania and Uganda. In that way, it has a record of distinguished alumni including frontline leaders like President Robert Mugabe of Zimbabwe, the former Botswana President Sir Seretse Khama, and Prime Minister Ntsu Mokhehle of Lesotho. Nearer home, it produced black leaders like Oliver Tambo, Mongosuthu Buthelezi, P.A.C. founder Robert Sobukwe, and the legendary Nelson Mandela, President of the ANC and of South Africa.

**Colonial Policies**

In French West and Equatorial Africa, there was not the same policy of cooperation between the local administrations and missionaries. This arose partly because of the streak of anti-clericalism in the French Third Republic, and partly from the attempt at the centralization of policy in the hands of officials in Paris. Without abolishing the Four Communes, there had been a retreat from mid-19th century liberalism before a critical mass of educated elite had been created, able to influence policy as in Freetown, Cape Coast/Accra or Lagos. From 1903 onwards, a series of directives from Paris tried to consolidate policy and regulate practice in education. The insistence that the purpose of western education was the spread of French secular culture, not evangelization, undermined the spread of even elementary education in mission schools. It meant that in their evangelization the missionaries placed little emphasis on education, and did little to encourage either government or the people to contribute towards the cost of education. Being predominantly Catholic, they did not encourage Adult literacy or Bible reading. African languages were used orally in church, but all instruction in schools was in French. In some mission stations, some 2-year courses of elementary education were available to teach spoken French and trades necessary to boost production for the French market.

The French administrations began after 1920 to build up a network of secular schools in the main urban areas, providing 3-year senior primary education including written French language, literature and history. This was under the energetic Albert Sarraut, Minister for the colonies, who said in his book in 1923 that "To educate the natives is assuredly our duty ... But this fundamental duty in addition coincides with our obvious economic, administrative, military and political interest." (Crowder 1968, p.379). The virtues that the schools were expected to teach can be seen in the advice which a European gave to two young boys, Moussa and Gli-Gla, in a textbook for village schools:

> It is always necessary to love those who deserve it and merit it. Difference in race makes little difference. Goodness has nothing to do with colour. It is, on the one hand, an advantage for the native to work for the white man, because the whites are better educated, more advanced in civilization than the natives, and because, thanks to them, the natives will make more rapid progress, learn better and more quickly, know more things, and become one day really useful men. On the other hand, the blacks will render service to the whites by bringing them the help of his arms, by cultivating the land which will permit them to grow crops for Europeans, and also by fighting for France in the ranks of native troops. Thus, the two races will associate and work together in common prosperity and happiness of all ... (cit. Crowder, 1968, pp.378-9).

Within such a programme for "association", the French obviously had no thought for establishing institutions of higher education locally. The two young boys, on the other hand, were not likely to agitate for one either. Their hope would be to manage to escape from their local predicament to join the rank of the *evolues* in France.

One aspect of the French policy of anti-clericalism was that the administrators favoured the consolidation and expansion of Islamic education as an autonomous system, independent of western education. However, this was only at the elementary level, and Islam as a local, not an international or universal, religion. The French cooperated with local sufi orders and marabouts, but discouraged Islamic secondary and higher education, and contacts with the major intellectual centres of Islam in the Middle-East, for fear of radical anti-colonial influences. Rather, research into Islamic and other African societies were encouraged by French experts of the Arab bureaux, and this eventually led to the establishment of the *Institut Français d'Afrique Noire* (IFAN) in Dakar in 1938, with branches later at the territorial headquarters.

Thus, until the Second World War, the only Teacher's College for the whole of French West Africa was the Ecole Normale William Ponty, the teacher training section moved from St. Louis to Gorée. There were only two secondary schools: the rest of Faidherbe's institution in Saint Louis, now called *Lycée Faidherbe*, and the recently established *Lycée van Vollenhoven* in Dakar, not only for Africans but, in fact, predominantly for children of European officials and settlers taking the *brevet de capacité colonial* which was comparable with the baccalaureate. With the introduction of the baccalaureate in 1924, the possibility of making any substantial adaptation in the curricula of the lycee dwindled as every candidate hoped to obtain a certificate fully recognized in France. Thus, for the Africans, the French policy aimed to leave the mass uneducated, and to groom a select few as *evolue*, co-opted as loyal upholders of French culture and colonial rule, encouraged to complete their education in France and to feel more at home in Paris than in Africa. This enabled the French citizens to monopolize all employment in the administration, commercial enterprises and schools, including even lowly clerical jobs. The Medical Institute established at the secondary level in Dakar in 1918 produced African assistant doctors, dispensers, midwives and district nurses who were to look after the health of Europeans as much as that of the Africans. Also in Gorée there was a school for Marine engineering, and the *Ecole William Ponty* for training teachers and preparing cadets for the medical profession. It became the most important centre for the formation of the African educated elite in all of Francophone West Africa. Later, there was established also a school of Veterinary medicine in Bamako. It was not until 1939 that a Polytechnic was opened in Bamako to produce technical personnel required in public works - draughtsmen, land surveyors and estate managers and engineers.

In the coastal parts of Togo, Benin (Dahomey) and, to some extent Cameroun, some modification of this general picture is necessary. The effects of 19th century missionary activities on the coast of Benin, proximity to Nigeria and Ghana, as well as the record of German support for elementary education in African languages between 1900 and 1915 could not be easily ignored. As a result, a disproportionate number of students from Benin and Togo acquired secondary and higher education abroad, joined others from the Caribbean, and cooperated with the Pan-African movement or other radical groups in France. They engaged in various anti-colonial activities, such as the so-called Porto Novo riots of 1923, followed ten years later in 1933 by a similar riot in Togo.

In Madagascar, the French policy of controlling the pace of educational development was reinforced by the people's reaction against Westernization. The French conquest, in spite of the tremendous effort of the Malagasy rulers to pursue modernization in the 19th century, and the ferocity of the French conquest and repression, provoked a reaction against Christianity and Western education in favour of reviving traditional religion and cultural values. The French felt called upon to insist even more rigidly on their policy of cultural imperialism. The emergent middle class were therefore rather ambivalent in their attitude to Western education. Nevertheless, they could see that the French policy was not in their best interest, and they too began to demand a more liberal approach to education, including more respect for Malagasy language, culture and values. Thus, while the network of elementary schools survived, the development of secondary and higher education was severely limited. A number of technical and trade schools emerged, like the Tananarive Medical Institute established in 1896 but, like in the rest of French Africa, the policy of control and restriction was not reversed until after the Second World War.

French and Belgian Catholic missionaries as well as Protestants, mostly American and British, were already established in the Congo before the Belgian government took over control, after the scandal of the misrule of King Leopold which provoked international outcry. The policy of the government was to cooperate fully with the missionaries provided they were prepared to operate strictly within the rules and regulations laid down by the government. The Catholics were willing to cooperate, but the Protestants cavilled at government control of education, and thus of their principal activities. This meant in effect that the Protestants financed the building of their own schools, the maintenance and staffing to the best of their ability while the state fully financed Catholic schools. Both sets of missionaries were nevertheless bound by the rule that instruction in elementary schools had to be in African languages, and only the few selected to be pastors and other mission agents were to receive any secondary education in French, the official language. The result was the emergence of an impressive network of elementary schools, in Zaire (the Belgian Congo) as well as Burundi and Rwanda, managed by mostly Roman Catholic Fathers in a very paternalistic manner.

Even elementary schools were run like convents. The brightest and most obedient boys were selected to serve at mass. The graduates were sent to training colleges which were run like seminaries. The content of education was classical and clerical, with strong emphasis on vocational, trades and technical education for those not considered suitable for the priesthood. Self-help, community involvement or, anything that might encourage a liberal secondary or higher education was frowned at. The result was that all the senior administrative and technical posts were monopolized by Belgian officials while the Congolese with basic education filled the minor cadres, and the bulk of the people were made to produce as much as possible for the Belgian economy.

The Portuguese pursued a cheaper version of the Belgian policy of cooperation with the missionaries. The Portuguese Government had less to invest on African education. The willingness to rely on the missionaries, therefore, represented a greater degree of laissez-faire. There was also a larger community of Portuguese settlers and stronger tradition of concessionaire companies and settlers controlling policy locally. The result was that even elementary education was limited; whatever secondary, teacher training, technical or higher education that existed were intended more to cater for the needs of the children of Portuguese settlers, officials, and a handful of the *assimilado* than for the needs of the African population.

The Italians were relatively late comers to colonialism, and they found it difficult to evolve or sustain any particular policy while meeting perpetual resistance, sometimes with professions of peace and conciliation, sometimes with intimidation and brutal war. In Somalia, they were willing to cooperate with missionaries, but the Somali rejected missionary education. The rulers of Ethiopia had embarked on a policy of modernization involving the development of a state-sponsored secular system of education parallel with the traditional educational system of the Orthodox Church. Ras Tafari Makonnen, as Regent and later as Emperor Haile Sellaise, had followed Emperor Menelik's example by establishing a network of elementary schools and a few post-primary institutions in Addis Ababa and the Provincial capitals. His policy was to invite different nationalities to take charge - Egyptian Copts, French, Swiss, Swedish, and British. By 1935, there were some 14 such government schools in Addis Ababa, employing 30 foreign teachers, and several hundred Ethiopian students sent abroad to study. The Italian invasion disrupted the development as the invaders were out to punish not only the ruling class but also the emergent Ethiopian class of officials and professionals. It was not till after World War II that the Emperor was able to pick up the pieces. (Moumouni, 1985, 88-91).

British colonial policy on education went back to 1882 when the policy of government subvention to missionary schools was established in West Africa. An Inspector of Education, the Revd. Metcalfe Sunter, former Principal of Fourah Bay College, was appointed to determine which schools met the criteria for approval, and to report on the performance of as many of the approved schools as possible. The formula for cooperation worked very well. The missionaries were interested in elementary and vocational education and the occasional teacher/evangelist training institution. However, the demand for secondary schools was already so strong that, as noted before, whichever mission refused to establish one risked losing ground to its rivals. The educated elite, therefore, took the initiative to get congregations and communities to build secondary schools and the missionary societies to adopt them, help with recruiting staff and getting government approval. The duty of the Government Inspectorate was to encourage improvements in quality, less learning by rote, more relevance to local conditions. The administrations later established a few government elementary and secondary schools to act as models and thus help to raise standards. These developments were ad-hoc. It was not until 1923 that the missionaries prevailed on the Colonial Office to set up an Advisory Committee on Education in Tropical Africa, with terms of reference later extended to other colonial territories.

**The British Advisory Committee**

The British Advisory Committee on Education in the Colonies deserves to be singled out of all agencies for the formulation and implementation of colonial policies on education. It was established in 1923 largely to ensure that adequate attention was paid to the views of the Phelps-Stokes Commission to Africa in their Report of 1922. The charitable Foundation based in the US had funds to promote appropriate policies for the education of blacks in America and in Africa, and had taken the initiative to send a Commission to examine education policies and practice in West, Central and South Africa. The Commission included J.K. Aggrey, a Fante who had gone to the US and taken a degree, and had been teaching and providing leadership at the Livingstone College, North Carolina for almost 20 years. The Commission was led by the Executive Secretary of the Foundation and President of Hampton Institute, Dr. Jesse Jones, a Welsh-born American who joined missionaries in pressurizing the Colonial Office to set up the Advisory Committee to achieve continuity and consolidation of colonial office policies on education. The Committee was so impressed by the philosophy of the Commission's Report that they co-sponsored a return visit to South, Central and East Africa which yielded a second Report published in 1925. This American connection ensured that the Advisory Committee took a broad and long term view of its responsibilities. In the period between the two World Wars, the two Reports of the Commission and the pronouncements of the Advisory Committee were regarded as the most authoritative statements and guiding philosophy for educational reform in Africa as a whole, and not just in the British controlled parts of Tropical Africa alone. The focus of the Committee was, of course, on elementary, secondary, vocational and technical education, as well as teacher training institutions. However, while other colonial agencies ignored or rejected the demand for higher education out of hand, the Advisory Committee could not; it was obliged to keep the demand under constant review and propose alternatives.

The emphasis of the Commission's Reports was on adapting education to suit the condition of Africans, to develop crafts, and occupations existing in society, to conserve and limit the pace of change. It was the philosophy already at work in Lovedale especially since the 1870s, and the philosophy of Fort Hare which was later taken to an extreme in the philosophy of Bantu Education. It is to be noted that Dr. C.T. Loram, a member of the Commission, was also a member of the Native Affairs Commission in South Africa and his work, *The Education of the South African Native*, laid the basis of the apartheid philosophy of separate development in education. The Advisory Committee endorsed the views of the Commission, but were themselves not so united in viewing the function of education as conservative rather than as a facilitator of change. This ambiguity could be detected even in the first major policy statement of the Committee:

> Education should be adapted to the mentality, aptitudes, occupations and traditions of the various peoples, conserving as far as possible all sound and healthy elements in the fabric of their social life; adapting them where necessary to changed circumstances and progressive ideas as an agent of natural growth and evolution. (cit. Brown, 1964, 370).

The more progressive members of the Advisory Committee had to compromise and accept "natural growth and evolution" rather than change as the function of education. Its "aim", the Committee said, "should be to render the individual more efficient in his or her condition of life, whatever it may be, and to promote the advancement of agriculture, the development of native industries, the improvement of health, the training of the people in the management of their own affairs, and the inculcation of true ideals of citizenship and service." The emphasis is on service within the black community, but since the black community already exists to serve the white, "the ideals of citizenship and service" could not have been too far from the philosophy of "association" which the European urged the two young Africans, Moussa and Gli-Gla to embrace. But the Committee went further. "The first task of education", they said,

> is to raise the standard alike of character and efficiency of the bulk of the people, but provision must also be made for the training of those who are required to fill posts in the administrative and technical services, as well as of those who as chiefs will occupy positions of exceptional trust and responsibility. As resources permit, the door of advancement, through higher education, in Africa must be increasingly opened for those who by character, ability and temperament show themselves fitted to profit by such education. (*ibid.*)

The Committee was "advisory" to the Colonial Secretary, but it was high powered in its membership and the range of expertise that they covered. Their opinions and advice on controversial policy issues were very influential. In the last resort, the Colonial Secretary could accept their advice and issue it as a directive. Short of that, the colonial Governors enjoyed a large measure of autonomy and they compared notes at regional meetings of Governors. The Advisory Committee preferred to act as a pressure group interacting, through individual members, sub-committees and various Commissions, with the Governors and Directors of Education. They endorsed the policy of cooperation with the missionaries and other Voluntary Agencies, but noted that government "reserves to itself the general direction of education policy and the supervision of all educational institutions".

The Advisory Committee operated in the 1920s on the assumption that Europeans, assisted by traditional rulers would, for the foreseeable future, determine policy in the African colonies; that Africans needed in the administration would function as clerks, messengers, interpreters, craftsmen, tradesmen, agricultural and veterinary assistants, and technicians; and that it was these cadres that the schools needed to produce. The Committee inspired the series of Ordinances in each colony setting up Departments of Education and Inspectorates, and regulating the conditions for operating different levels of education, and attracting government subsidies. These regulations succeeded in raising the standards of the schools, particularly the secondary schools and teacher training Colleges. They encouraged the opening of secular government schools in Muslim areas and other places not adequately served by the missions. But they could do nothing in a place like Zambia (Northern Rhodesia) where European settlers continued to block avenues for development of African populations. The Government established its first Junior Secondary School at Munali in Lusaka in 1939. In 1966, on the occasion of his installation as Chancellor on the inauguration of the University of Zambia, Kenneth Kaunda complained bitterly that

> as far as education is concerned, Britain's colonial record in Zambia is most criminal. This country has been left by her as the most uneducated and most unprepared of Britain's dependencies on the African continent. This record is even treasonable to mankind when it is recalled that in the seventy years of British occupation, Zambia has never lacked money, and, except for a year or two, her budget had never been subsidized by the British Treasury. However, financial exploitation was preferred to human development ... (in Addresses, 1966, p.5).

In responding to the demand for higher education, the Advisory Committee selected a number of central government institutions and tried to develop them more or less like Lovedale. These were:

**Gordon Memorial College**, Khartoum, established in 1898 by Lord Kitchener in memory of General Gordon. It was intended to be a major centre of Western education to rival the existing system of Islamic education and to combat the fanatical doctrines of the defeated Mahdi. In practice, the local officials showed little interest until James Currie became its Principal and later Director of Education of the Sudan, and subsequently, member of the Advisory Committee. It was then developed as a full Secondary School with excellent physical facilities. A students' protest in 1925 was used to justify slowing down any further developments.

**Makerere Government College**, Kampala, Uganda, established in 1921 as a trade school to train carpenters and mechanics, more for private employers than for Government. In 1922, a para-medical course was added, and later veterinary, surveying and agricultural courses. Academic classes were introduced in 1926, and clerical and Teacher Training courses established in 1929. Makerere did not offer a full Secondary School course until 1933.

**Yaba Higher College**, Lagos, was preceded by King's College, established in 1909 as a model Secondary School to help raise the standard of the 6 missionary secondary schools in Lagos and a growing number of others in Nigeria. The aim was to produce a better standard of clerks to meet the insatiable demand both in government and the private sector. Soon, the curriculum and performance of the students began to be regulated by the introduction of British examining bodies. The government also tried to use the comparatively generous number of qualified staff and others available in Lagos to run a part-time teacher training programme in the evenings and at weekends. But the Teacher Training Course was short-lived and King's College settled down as a regular Secondary School.

In 1929, two other Government Secondary Schools, with adequate facilities for teaching science, were established in Nigeria. The government then responded to the demand for higher education by establishing the Yaba Higher College. At that time, there were about 30 government assisted Secondary Schools and a great dearth of qualified teachers. The Higher College started classes in 1932 to provide "training of a university or professional character, although as a great deal of attention will be devoted to the practical side ... the course will not be so wide, especially on the theoretical side, as would be necessary to obtain university or professional qualifications in the United Kingdom". It offered 2-year courses in Arts or Science, followed by professional courses of teacher training (additional 2 years + 1 year practical); 2 years engineering, or agriculture or surveying; 5 years medical course, 5 years veterinary. Whereas the medical graduate was employed as assistant medical officer on a salary of 120 pounds sterling rising to 400 pounds in 15 years, the European medical officer earned 400 pounds rising up to 720 pounds for performing similar duties. The College attracted the cream of available students and proceeded to frustrate them. The College was part of the Department of Education. Success in examinations was tied more to vacancies and character evaluation than to performance. Registration for overseas examinations was discouraged and courses essential for such examinations were often eliminated from the curricula, thus ensuring that the College Diploma remained strictly of local significance.

**Prince of Wales School and College, Achimota**, elaborately planned by Governor Guggisberg, a Canadian who saw sound education as the most effective tool of development. He recruited a high powered team - A.G. Fraser, former Principal of Trinity College Kandy, in Sri Lanka (Ceylon), W.E.F. Ward, and J.K. Aggrey, and others. They were to establish a comprehensive model school, running classes in kindergarten, elementary and secondary, as well as a University College affiliated to the University of London. It was to give strong emphasis to local languages and cultural heritage, to conduct research and interact with other schools and associations of teachers. It was to have respected Ghanaian professionals on its Board, though qualified Ghanaian teachers were scarce.

It began with kindergarten and secondary classes, but soon decided to concentrate on the critical area of secondary and give a comprehensive education, sound on the academic, as well as in vocational and practical courses, drama and sports. The Advisory Council considered University courses premature. It was not till the 1930s that courses up to London University Matriculation and Intermediate were allowed. In this, Achimota proved even more liberal than Yaba Higher College as students of Yaba discovered during World War II when many of them were transferred to Achimota because the British Army requisitioned for use of their campus. One issue which the Advisory Committee used to stall development of full University courses at Achimota was the division within the Council itself on the wisdom of affiliation to British Universities. Affiliation meant taking the examinations of the British universities, which undermined the principle of adaptation. But those demanding higher education in Africa had become very suspicious of the principle of adaptation if it meant creating local certificates and diplomas that were not recognized even by the Colonial administrators themselves as equivalent to European degrees for purposes of securing employment, and could therefore be used to tie down the holders to whatever conditions of employment the colonial administrations chose to impose. (Agbodeka, 1977)

Indeed, one relic of mid-19th century liberalism which neither the retreat since the 1870s, nor the discouraging policies of the Advisory Committee, could undo was the extension of British university external examinations service to the colonies. The affiliation of Fourah Bay College to Durham University, and of Fort Hare and Pius XII College in Roma to UNISA, were examples of this liberalism. However by far the largest number of Africans were affected by the School examinations. Besides other examining bodies like the College of Preceptors, the Oxford Delegacy and the Cambridge Local Examinations Syndicate offered examinations at the Preliminary, Junior and School Certificate levels to measure the achievements of students in Secondary Schools in Britain and they offered the same examinations, through arrangements with the Colonial Office, the Crown Agents and approved local Supervisors to the colonies. Eventually, they withdrew the Preliminary and Junior Certificates, and the Oxford Delegacy also withdrew, leaving the Cambridge Local to dominate the field. These foreign examinations made adaptation difficult, but they did much to raise the standard of secondary education and helped to weaken the reluctance to embark on higher education locally. By offering a uniform standard and external yardstick, they provided objective criteria for evaluating performance in the

Secondary Schools in the English-speaking territories. The French did the same with the international baccalaureate. They held out a uniform level to which teaching in the schools could be geared. This stimulated competition among the schools as to the level of achievement of their students.

The University of London Colonial Examinations offered service at the level of higher education: Matriculation, Intermediate and Final Degrees. Some schools preferred the London Matriculation to the Cambridge School Certificate. But the bulk of African candidates other than British settlers in Mauritius, Kenya and Zimbabwe (Southern Rhodesia), were clerks or trained teachers who prepared themselves through correspondence courses - British University Correspondence College, London; Wolsey Hall, Oxford; Rapid Results College, London - and private study. Eventually the Advisory Committee allowed Gordon College, Makerere, Achimota and the Yaba Higher College to enter for the Intermediate examination, and only such approved institutions could enter candidates in science. For candidates attempting the Intermediate and Final Degrees by private study, the favourite subjects were Philosophy, History, Law, English, and Classics. The failure rate, especially at the Matriculation, was high. But at least the scheme provided the opportunity for the odd persevering candidate to get a University degree without travelling abroad. The first such graduate in Nigeria, a tutor at the St. Andrew's College, Oyo, took the Matriculation examination in 1922, the Intermediate in 1925, and the B.A. in Philosophy in 1927 in the Third Class. Another, a tutor at the CMS Training Institution in Awka, took the B.A. in Philosophy in 1929, and passed in the Second Class Lower. Two others, both at St. Andrew's College, Oyo, one in History, another in Philosophy, took their B.A. in 1933. (Namie, 1989; Omolewa, 1993). The first University graduate in Zambia took his B.A degree in History and Native Administration in 1949 by private study. The next three took their degrees, two in Arts Subjects (English and Psychology; Geography and History) and one in Science (Botany and Chemistry) from Fort Hare in 1951.

Of considerable importance, too, were the number of Africans who managed to go overseas for University education. One of the effects of the mid-19th century liberalism in West and South Africa were the number of Africans holding important positions or engaged as entrepreneurs, able to afford to send their sons, and occasionally their daughters, to Europe and America for higher education. They trained as teachers, others as lawyers or medical doctors, professions which did not depend upon employment in the colonial service. This tradition continued until the colonial period, even though fewer people were able unaided to sponsor their children. The missionary bodies sponsored many more to train as teachers, pastors and evangelists. Most missionaries trained their employees in Seminaries and Training Institutions not attached to Universities. The training programmes of others, especially U.S. missionary bodies and Roman Catholics, usually involved university level training in humanities and theology. During the Second World War, a few of the demobilized soldiers stayed back in Europe and tried to work their way through College, as some others encouraged by the Marcus Garvey movement and J.K. Aggrey had been doing in the U.S. At the same time, post war nationalist efforts to stimulate educational development sometimes involved whole communities contributing money to sponsor selected qualified citizens to study in Universities abroad.

## Cracks in the Wall

By the 1930s, perceptive observers began to see that future constitutional development in Africa depended more on the educated elite than on the hitherto favoured traditional rulers. As a result, the demand for higher education began to be listened to with better understanding. A conference of Directors of Education in East Africa, meeting in Zanzibar in 1932, recommended that Makerere College be allowed to enter for the London Matriculation and Intermediate examinations. The Advisory Committee then set up a Sub-Committee under Sir James Currie to review anew the whole issue of higher education in Tropical Africa. Among others, the Committee interviewed some Africans resident or studying in Britain. His Report of December 1933 represented the first major crack in the obstructive wall that the conservative members of the Advisory Committee had erected. He seemed to be trying to persuade such members:... the African thirst for higher education remains unabated; if this is not satisfied at home it can only lead to an increasing efflux of undergraduate African students towards the Universities in Europe and America....

There is reason to think that the absence of any African institutions for adequate higher training already cripples to some extent the recruitment of properly trained natives for higher posts where they are wanted for Government and private service in Native administrations and Judicial systems. It seems indefensible, for example, that the Gordon College should, at all events till very recently, have had to rely substantially upon the American University at Beyrut for the advanced training of natives needed for its own staffing. From another slightly different point of view it appears equally indefensible that intelligent Africans from the Gold Coast should most easily obtain further training of a university type by taking advantage of American bounty and American institutions.

There is a grave danger, as we see it, of the Africans' zeal for education being neglected and ignored by the Government to whom they ought to be able to look for its reasonable satisfaction. There appears no prospect - nor is it in any event a prospect that can in the least be wished or desired - that the present vehement demand for higher education will slacken off. (Ashby, 1966, 477-8).

It appears, therefore, that a major consideration with the Sub-Committee was the political implications of the new interest in studying in America which the return of Aggrey and the doctrines of Marcus Garvey and the Pan-African movement had generated not, as in the past, among would-be African pastors and missionaries, but among young radical nationalists like Nnamdi Azikiwe, Kwame Nkrumah and others, especially in West Africa. It also appears that some members of the Advisory Committee may have begun to question the wisdom of basing British imperial policies so firmly on ideas generated in the United States. At any rate, the Committee seemed to have begun to distance itself from orthodox Phelps-Stokes ideas and to move towards accepting the necessity for an African educated elite. However, unlike the French, they preferred to have such an elite trained in African institutions where they could be better influenced than at British or American universities. The Sub-Committee recommended that Gordon's College, Khartoum and Makerere College be groomed to become University Colleges training students to the level of University Pass Degrees, emphasizing Education, and concentrating attention on producing teachers to meet the needs of the Sudan and East Africa. Achimota and Yaba were to cooperate to meet the needs of West Africa, with a role being assigned to Fourah Bay College in Theology and Education.

The Report was not published but it was referred to the Conference of Governors both in East and West Africa. The Governors referred it to their Directors of Education and were in no hurry to reply. Their comments did not come till 1936, saying, in effect, that they had not encountered any "vehement" demand and would do nothing to instigate one. The feeling generally with officials on the spot was that the time had not come, and dwindling resources during the Great Depression of the 1930s made the recommendations inopportune. Meanwhile, they preferred responding to individual needs for scholarship to study in British universities when necessary and if funds could be found. This was the alternative preferred for training African staff for Achimota. Thus, T.A.M. Dowuona and Akufo Addo were sent to Oxford in

1931 and 1932; A.L. Adu to Cambridge and E. Amu to the Royal College of Music in 1937. (Agbodeka, 1977, p 73-74.).

Yet the pressure did not die down. The next positive move came, strangely enough, from East Africa where secondary education lagged so much behind the development in West Africa. Perhaps for that reason, the officials were personally not as hostile to the African educated elite as were the officials in West Africa. It was the Governor of Uganda who reacted to the Currie Report by asking for a review of the possible role of Makerere in higher education. The result was the high-powered De La Warr Commission which took evidence in London, visited Uganda, and reported in 1937. The Commission included 2 Members of Parliament, Heads of two British universities (Exeter and Leeds), a Member of the British Institution of Civil Engineers, a female teacher in the University of London, Alexander Kerr and Z.K. Mathews of Fort Hare, and F.J. Pedler of the Colonial Office as Secretary. (Kerr, 1968) The Commission recommended the establishment at Makerere of "a University College in the near future and of a University at no very distant date". The Commission realized the risk in too rapid a pace of development considering the "present very flimsy foundations of primary and secondary education ... Nevertheless we are convinced that the material needs of the country and the intellectual needs of its people require that such risks as there may be should be taken". The College, they proposed, should begin by awarding its own Diplomas, then be affiliated to London, granting London external degrees, before it obtains a charter to grant its own degrees. In that way, the College will have "the opportunity to fashion an indigenous culture which would be no less African because it represented a synthesis of both African and European elements ...

> The African background today comprises not the native alone, and not the European alone, but the interaction between the African theory of traditionalism and the European theory of progress (Ashby. 1966, 198).

Then, the Council of Achimota College revived the issue of affiliation with the University of London. A Committee under Pickard Cambridge in 1938 carried out a quinquennial review of the College and was asked to consider what contributions it could make to a West African University. The Committee's Report was negative, saying there were not enough secondary schools to support a University, and the demand in government and industry for university graduates was not large enough yet. However, in considering the Report among others, a conference of West African Governors meeting in Lagos in 1939 at last agreed that there was need for one

University in West Africa. It should be "West African in spirit and reality as well as in name, and not a mere colourless imitation of a British University". They, therefore, "welcomed the proposed Institute of West African Culture at Achimota as a means of achieving this. Secondly, it should be of high quality, its degrees standing comparison with those of a first-class university in Britain, and for this, a period of affiliation with a British University or Universities would be necessary". How affiliation with a British University was to produce a University that was truly West African and no colourless imitation, was not explored. Perhaps they set it as a conundrum to put off their critics. Perhaps it was an admission that they had run out of arguments to defend colonial obstructions to educational development in the colonies.

Chapter 3

# DECOLONIZATION AND HIGHER EDUCATION, 1945-1960

## Decolonization

The years 1945-60 are usually described as the period of decolonization in Africa. Decolonization should mean the rolling back of empire, achievement of national independence, and local autonomy and control over the political and economic destiny of the country. It is now being increasingly recognized that these were not years of *decolonisation* as such, but transition from colonialism to neo-colonialism, increasing dependence and under-development. This is as true in the field of education as in the field of political economy. During the colonial period, Africans were starved of education. They had been offered all kinds of inferior alternatives to higher education. When in the period 1945-60 the colonial powers began to offer colonial universities - identical in structure, curriculum and statutes, granting metropolitan degrees, staffed, financed and monitored by the colonial authorities, - African nationalists grasped at them.

In 1945 which marked the beginning of decolonization in Africa, colonial higher education also entered a new phase. The end of the Second World War, which had been preceded by a long decade of economic depression, and which presaged some economic boom, raised the expectation of major structural changes - constitutional, economic and social reforms, especially in the area of education. A major impetus towards reform was the declaration by the Allied Powers in the Atlantic Charter of 1944 reaffirming the right of peoples to self-determination. Although it soon became obvious that the Allied Powers had in mind the peoples in Europe, the Middle East and the Far East under Nazi and Japanese military domination, other peoples like in India, Indonesia, and Indo-China could not be held back. Similarly, while the British and the French colonial rulers did not consider that the Atlantic Charter could apply to Africa for another 50 years, African nationalists claimed the necessity to move immediately towards self-government. French colonial administrators in Africa gathered in Brazzaville in January 1944 to celebrate the fall of Vichy France and discuss what social, economic and political benefits Free France could offer the African colonies for their war efforts. French colonial authorities argued that such rewards had to be within the framework of a French Community, similar to the British Commonwealth. As de Gaulle said at the Conference, it was in the colonies that Free France "found her refuge and the starting point for her liberation ... as a result of this there is henceforth a permanent bond between the Mother Country and the Empire", a bond which was supposed to rule out any possibility of self-government. (cit. Crowder, 1968, p 499). However, an African elite was to be encouraged to play a role not only in the proposed French Community, but also in new territorial consultative assemblies. Another meeting was convened in Dakar in July 1944 to discuss specifically educational reforms, and it advocated considerable expansion of elementary, secondary, and teacher-training institutions and initiated plans for higher education. In 1946, the *Fonds d'Investissement pour le Développement Economique et Social* (FIDES), to mobilize funds for investment in socio-economic development, comparable to the British Colonial Development and Welfare Fund, was established.

For African leaders, the most critical issue in reforms was the training of Africans capable of taking over the administrative and technical jobs hitherto reserved for Europeans. They renewed the pressure for an accelerated Africanisation of the civil services through carefully planned overseas scholarships and training programmes, and the establishment locally of institutions of higher education, specifically universities. Thus, the priority expectation was that the new universities should produce administrative and technical staff for the civil services, as well as teachers for secondary schools and teacher training colleges. Many African leaders did not expect that new colonial universities would, for some time to come, meet the standards of European universities or cover adequate range of disciplines and they therefore usually accompanied their pleas for institutions of higher education locally with demands also for overseas scholarships.

The British were the first to act. The initiative taken by the Governor of Uganda in 1936 to ensure that, despite the neglect of secondary education or, perhaps, because of it, there was an urgency to develop Makerere as a University College, eventually made an impact on other governors both in East and West Africa. What is more, the Channon Report of May 1943 convinced both the Advisory Committee on Education in the Colonies and the Colonial Secretary of the need, even during the War, to devise a machinery by which all the British Universities would cooperate to sponsor colonial University Colleges, where the syllabuses for the London University external degrees could be suitably adapted, and degrees of London University would be awarded. The Colonial Secretary, at the end of May 1943, called upon the Universities in Britain to consider how they could contribute to university education in the colonies: "The universities of this country have in the past", he said, "made their vast contributions to the successful growth of the overseas dependencies by themselves training and nourishing the administrators and specialists on whom their progress has depended. We are now entering on an era when this contribution may become more indirect [sic] but no less vital by taking the form of assistance in the development of Colonial Universities which will rear the local leaders of the future." He then proposed the appointment of a Commission

> to consider the principles which should guide the promotion of higher education, learning, and research and the development of universities in the Colonies; and to explore means whereby universities and other appropriate bodies in the United Kingdom may be able to cooperate with institutions of higher education in the Colonies in order to give effect to these principles. (Ashby, 1966, p.212).

The Commission under Mr. Justice Cyril Asquith covered East, West and Central Africa, as well as the West Indies. There were no representatives of the colonial territories on the Asquith Commission. There were, however, two other Commissions, the Irvine Commission on the West Indies and the Commission under Sir Walter Elliot on West Africa, on which the colonies were represented. There was no separate Commission on East Africa because the De La Warr Report on Makerere and Gordon's College remained current. The emphasis of the Asquith Report was on the need to ensure high quality education in the colonies so as to produce an elite of good quality leaders. The University Colleges should aim to become centres of learning, promote research, be wholly residential, and emphasize liberal Arts and Science above professional/vocational studies. Beyond that, the Asquith Report laid the basis for the scheme of Special Relations between the University of London and the Colonial University Colleges, under the supervision of the Inter-University Council (IUC) for Higher Education in the Colonies. The IUC was responsible for allocating funds under the Colonial Welfare and Development Act; it was to process advertisements for the University Colleges and recruit staff for them largely, but not exclusively, from the British Universities. To ensure that good quality staff were recruited, such staff received various allowances which created a differential between their salaries and those of the local staff. The staff of the Colonial University Colleges were to approach London with proposals (if any) for adapting the London external degree syllabuses; they were to set the examination papers, have them vetted in London; mark the scripts, which were to be vetted in London, and the results were then to be agreed at joint meetings in London of the London University and Colonial University College examiners.

Neither the French nor the Belgians saw any need for such an elaborate scheme. Their emphasis was not on the possibility of adaptation but on the provision of higher education identical in quality and content with that provided in France or Belgium. There was not the same insistence as in British West Africa for the establishment of universities locally, partly because the development of secondary schools lagged behind. However as elementary and secondary education were expanded and aligned with French practice, provision was made for all Africans who had the equivalent of the baccalaureate to obtain scholarships to study at the Universities of Bordeaux, Montpellier, Toulouse or Paris. There was thus a significant increase in the number of young Africans studying in French Universities in the years 1945-55. The radical politics of the African students in France was a major factor that urged on the French Government the initiative to establish University Centres in Dakar and Tananarive. Like the Belgian Catholic, Protestant and State University Centres in Zaire, these were overseas campuses of metropolitan universities meant to cater not only for the emergent African elite but also for the needs of the considerable numbers of children of the resident European officials and settlers.

## The Asquith Colleges

The Asquith, Elliot and De La Warr Commission Reports provided the framework of the Special Relationship with the University of London and with other British universities through the IUC, on which the Colonial University Colleges in British Africa were based. This provided for the possibility of adaptation of the content, if not also the structure, of the degree programmes, but, in practice, the emphasis was on transplantation, not adaptation. The Elliot Commission which had among its members Arthur Creech Jones, a trade Unionist and future Labour Colonial Secretary, also included I.O. Ransome-Kuti, K.A. Korsah and E.H. Taylor-Cummings from Nigeria, Ghana, and Sierra Leone, respectively. The Commission was thus able to reflect some of the aspirations of Africans, and that might be why it could not reach consensus. A majority of the members, including the Chairman and all the three African members recommended developing Yaba Higher College, Achimota College and Fourah Bay into three University Colleges for Nigeria, Ghana and Sierra-Leone, with a distribution of professional faculties between them, and coordinated by a West African Council on Higher Education. They also recommended that entry to University should be at the School Certificate (0-Level) and not at the Higher School Certificate (A-Level). However, a minority of five members, including Creech Jones, disagreed and opted for a single West African University, located at Ibadan, with the existing Colleges - Yaba, Achimota and Fourah Bay - acting as territorial Colleges, preparing students for admission to the single University.

On the publication of the Colonial Secretary's Despatch on the Elliot Commission Report in July 1946, the immediate concern of the educated elite in West Africa was certainly not the problem of adaptation. They saw the Government's acceptance of the Minority Report as a major setback and decided to struggle to get the decision reversed. The educated elite in Ghana, through various political and nationalist groupings, rejected out of hand the proposal to stunt the development of Achimota College and turn it into a "Preparatory School" for a new University College in Ibadan. Even the colonial administration agreed that it was a retrograde step and it took immediate steps to convey to the Colonial Office the strength of local feelings and to seek for a review of the proposal. Eventually the British Government agreed that any country able to find the initial capital cost could establish its own University College. Ghana was thus allowed to build the University College at Legon with a million pounds sterling from the funds of the Cocoa Marketing Board.

**The University College of Ghana** thus started in October 1948 with 92 students on the western campus of Achimota College while the buildings were going on in Legon. David Balme, a classical scholar, was the first Principal of the College. He announced that his instruction was to build a University that would eventually grow to accommodate 5,000 students but that seeing how few secondary schools there were, and in order to keep standards high, he planned for a first 10-year phase in which he envisaged a maximum of 800 students. He proceeded to build a fine set of buildings on the model of Cambridge - Halls of Residence, self-contained departments, each with its own set of offices and class rooms, central administrative offices and the Great Hall, - enough to cater for the 800 students, but exceedingly difficult to expand in order to cater for many more. No one questioned his judgement at the time. As with other "Asquith Colleges" which aimed to be wholly residential, not only Halls of Residence for students, but also staff quarters, workers villages nearby, and municipal facilities like water, electricity and transportation had to be provided. Later, in place of the territorial College proposed for Achimota, the Government of Ghana decided to establish the Kumasi College of Technology, which was subsequently developed as a second University.

Similarly, the proposal that **Fourah Bay College** which had for so long been the only beacon of higher education in West Africa should now become a territorial college/preparatory school for Ibadan was unacceptable to the educated elite in Sierra Leone and, indeed, to many friends of Fourah Bay College throughout West Africa. The proposal merely indicated the extent to which the Colonial Office was insensitive to African opinion. Eventually, it was agreed with the CMS in 1948 to expand the Council of Fourah Bay College to allow for the representation of more secular interests; and that, for an interim period of five years, Fourah Bay was to continue as a University College affiliated to Durham, offering a degree programme in Arts and Theology, but to be run jointly with a government-financed territorial College offering Intermediate Science, Economics and Commerce. In 1954, Fourah Bay embarked on degree programmes in science and diploma courses in engineering. It was eventually incorporated as a public-financed University College of Sierra Leone under a Royal Charter in 1960.

Kenneth Mellanby, a research scientist, was appointed the first Principal of the **University College, Ibadan**, in 1947. He opened the College on a temporary site in January 1948 in Ibadan with 104 students, including three female students, from the Yaba Higher College and the Survey School, Oyo, to complete the Intermediate Arts and Science of London University. In October 1948, a fresh set of 148 students (113 Science and 35 Arts) were admitted also for the Intermediate. The pattern of development of the College may be regarded as typical of the Asquith Colleges. The Intermediate, not School Certificate, was accepted as entry to the degree programmes. Admission to the Intermediate or Concessional Entry class was by selection through a stiff examination, with about 700 students competing for 150 places. Nevertheless, the failure rate was very high, with many of the students who were refused admission or weeded out gaining admission and doing well in U.K. or US universities. The Classics Department was the first to admit students to the degree programme of the London External before the Special Relationship Scheme had been put fully in place. Until 1954, only General Degree Courses were available and, even after that, entry into Single honours degree courses was restricted. Basic Arts Degrees included Religious Studies, but not Philosophy. Medical students did the Intermediate Science and the pre-clinical courses, but were encouraged to go abroad to complete the clinical programme in various Teaching Hospitals in London. Agriculture was slow in developing. It included some Animal husbandry, but students of Veterinary Science or Forestry were few and were sent abroad. Engineering, or applied science and technology was available in Colleges of Technology or Polytechnics, but not in the University College. In fact a Faculty of Engineering of the University College, Ibadan was established in 1955 and located in Zaria, in the interest of geographical spread of higher education. It was granting degrees of the University of London under the Scheme of Special Relations. But is was absorbed into the Nigerian College of Arts, Science and Technology and made Ibadan appear even less involved in technological education than was in fact the case. Education was not offered till 1958 on the grounds that Education had been allocated to Achimota in the Elliot Report. Similarly, law, commerce, banking and other developmental professional courses were not offered. Even Economics and the Social Sciences were not on the priority list. Economics was introduced in 1957 as a Department of the Faculty of Arts, and the Faculty of Social Studies was introduced in 1961.

Two other Asquith Colleges were the Gordon Memorial College which in 1947 was reconstituted with the Kitchener Medical School into the **Khartoum University College**, and **Makerere** which, also with the Medical School, became a University College in 1949, both under the Special Relationship Scheme. The pattern of development was similar to the West African Colleges, with an emphasis on residential communities, municipal facilities, basic Arts, Science and Medicine, preparing cadres largely for administrative positions rather than for professional careers. The Islamic background, and the influence of Egypt encouraged the study of Law, as well as Agriculture and Veterinary Sciences in Khartoum. Similarly, some of the vocational programmes at Makerere survived as Diploma courses in the University College, for example in Art.

In Kenya, while African leaders were struggling for access to secondary education, European settlers were pressing for technical education and the Asian community for commercial education. By 1949, it was agreed that Makerere as an inter-territorial College was adequate to cater for University education for all of East Africa, and that higher education in Kenya and Tanzania (Tangayika) should aim only to complement it. Thus the **Royal Technical College**, Nairobi, was incorporated by Royal Charter in 1951. The Asian Community believed that Commercial education was inadequately provided for in the plans for the College and established the Gandhi Academy for Arts, Science and Commerce. This was eventually incorporated into the College. The surge of nationalism and the racial tensions generated by the Mau Mau revolt indicated the need for a closer study of the needs for higher education in East Africa. The Carr-Saunders Working Party eventually recommended developing Makerere, Nairobi and Dar-es-Salaam as three co-ordinated University Colleges of East Africa, sharing responsibility for different Faculties - Makerere (Arts, Science and Medicine); Nairobi (Arts, Science and Engineering); Dar-es-Salaam (Arts, Social Studies and Law), all three in Special Relationship with the University of London. Other subjects - such as Art, Architecture and Commerce at Nairobi - featured as Courses for the Diploma of the University College.

### Dakar and Tananarive

Apart from the Befelatanana School of Medicine established in 1896, the University of Tananarive traces its origin to the courses in Law which judges of the Court of Appeal organized for training magistrates in 1941 when communication with France was difficult if not impossible. The Faculty of Law in Aix-Marseille adopted the courses, thus creating an Institute of higher studies in law. The Faculty of Science in Marseille followed up with Institutes for Physics, Chemistry and Biology in 1952 leading up to a Faculty of Science in 1954. Similarly, in 1950, there was established an Institute of Higher Studies in Dakar, under which the Faculties of Science and Medicine of the Universities of Paris and Bordeaux seconded staff to Dakar to pioneer higher education. In 1955 a similar Institute of Higher Studies was established in Tananarive to coordinate the existing institutions of higher education in law and science. In 1959 Pharmacy and Arts were added. Eventually, the Institute in Dakar was constituted into a University in 1957, and the one in Tananarive in 1960.

They were constituted under decrees of the French Ministry of National Education, creating French universities located overseas. The decrees specified that the universities were to be governed by the statutes which governed the other universities of France; that the academic staff of the new universities were part of the cadres of French universities, and eligible for all the rights and privileges of academic staff in France; that the regulations in force for Universities in France, particularly those dealing with admission, examinations and standards of achievement, were applicable equally to the new Universities; and that as in France, each Faculty should enjoy its own administration and financial autonomy. On independence in 1960, these provisions were then embodied in a series of Cooperation Agreements between France and Senegal, beginning with France accepting full financial responsibility, and gradually reducing the extent of its commitments. The first of the Agreements signed August 5, 1961 still included a clause in the Preamble which stated that teaching French, the official language of Senegal, was for the Senegalese people "the historical instrument for promoting modernization as well as the culture, political, economic and social development in accordance with their African traditions" (Ashby, 1966, 369; *Accord de Cooperation*, signed Aug. 5, 1961).

### Colonial Universities of Belgian Congo (Zaire)

The Catholic University of Louvain in Brussels (founded in 1425) established a medical foundation and an agricultural centre in (Leopoldville) Kinshasa. This became known as Lovanium (little Louvain) University Centre in 1949 when it was accorded official recognition as a public institution. There was little effective demand from Africans locally for the expansion of higher education, but pressure came from three other sources: the resident officials and settlers seeking university education for their children; the UN Mandated Territories Commission seeking university education for the mandated territories of Rwanda and Burundi; and thirdly, religious and ethnic rivalries in Belgium. When in 1950, it was decided to develop the Lovanium University Centre into an overseas campus of the Catholic University of Louvain, the Protestants decided to create their own University, and those who believed that it was wrong to encourage religion-based Universities in Africa pressed the Government to establish a State University. Hence Lovanium opened its doors in Kinshasa in 1954, the Free University (Protestant) established a University in Kisangani (Stanleyville) in 1955, and the official or State University of Lubumbashi (Elizabethville) was established in 1956. A block taken from the wall of the oldest building in Louvain, engraved 1425/1954, was buried in the foundation of the Faculty of Science in Lovanium in 1954.

Each University started with a pre-University Course to give more Africans the opportunity to matriculate. Lovanium enrolled 30 Africans mostly in Latin and Humanities. Only 11 matriculated. To these were added 10 others, Africans and Europeans. By 1956, there were 119 African and 50 European students and 32 academic staff, all Europeans. There were courses in basic Arts and Science, as well as Medicine, Engineering, and Commerce, and an Economic and Social Research Institute. In 1957, a Faculty of Technology was established. By 1959, there were 365 students and an academic staff of 68. The State University of Lubumbashi was located to serve Rwanda/Urundi and a sizable resident European population in the Katanga copper mining region. It enrolled 20 Africans in its matriculation course in 1955 and 11 students passed. In its first year degree programme however, out of 104 students, there were only 8 "Congolese" and there may have been 3 or 4 others from Rwanda. In 1959, there were 264 students of whom 32 were Africans.

Lovanium was administered by a Higher Academic Council consisting of the Rector of Louvain, the Rector of Lovanium and one representative of each Faculty of Louvain that operated in Lovanium. The Council was located in Brussels. To supervise the work locally in Lovanium, there was a Governing Board presided over by the Rector, and consisting of his nominees among the staff who had all been seconded from Louvain. It was further provided that:

The Higher Academic Council shall collaborate with the Governing Board in all academic matters. The Council shall be consulted by the Governing Board on all matters concerning teaching and research in the University, and particularly on the establishment of new faculties, schools or institutes. The Council may recommend to the Board any measures which it deems useful for the development of teaching and research in the University.

Similarly, the Administrative Council of the State University of Lubumbashi consisted of representatives of all Belgian universities, and the Council was based in Brussels.

### Pius XII College of Lesotho

The growing influence of the doctrine of apartheid provided the stimulus for the decision of the Catholic Bishops in Southern Africa, including the High Commission Territories of Botswana (Bechuanaland), Lesotho (Basutoland) and Swaziland to come together and work out strategies for the emergence of a local institute of higher education comparable to Fort Hare College of South Africa. The outcome of this initiative was the establishment in April 1945 of what later became known as Pius XII College, located in Roma, 25 miles south of Maseru, the capital of Lesotho. The mandate of the College from the beginning was to prepare the brightest of the African matriculants for the Bachelor of Arts degree of the University of South Africa (UNISA).

It began very humbly in a spare classroom, with four priest-lecturers teaching five students offering such courses as theology, philosophy, psychology and social anthropology. This programme was later expanded to include courses leading also to the degrees of Bachelor of Commerce, Bachelor of Science, and a postgraduate Diploma in Education. Even so the enrolment of candidates remained very small and attempts at reform were not pursued with vigour. By the special agreement of 1955, the College was recognized as a University College of UNISA with full responsibility for the teaching and examining of its students. This new relationship did not last long as UNISA began to place racial restrictions on the admission of students, a dilemma which was compounded by financial problems at the College.

It took the concerted efforts of those individuals and institutions who recognized the needs for higher education and manpower development of the three High Commission territories to transform the Roma College into a full University College. Prominent among these were Dr. C. W. de Kiewiet of the American Council on Education, Sir James Cook, Vice-Chancellor of University of Exeter (UK) and Dr. J.F. Leddy, President of Windsor University (Canada) who worked out the modalities to put the proposed University on a firm academic and financial foundation, and free from the encumbrance of racial discrimination.

This was a crucial period in the history of the institution in the sense that it marked the transition from an essentially clerical background to a secular institution of higher education. When the University of Botswana, Lesotho and Swaziland (UBLS, formerly UBBS) was inaugurated in 1964 it had 31 academic staff and 180 students. Out of these the largest number came from Lesotho with smaller numbers from Botswana and Swaziland and a quite considerable contingent from countries such as Zimbabwe and South Africa.

## Liberia University and Haile Selassie I University

Colonial influences in university development were not restricted only to colonies in the process of "decolonization"; they were important features of university development in Liberia and post-Italian-occupation Ethiopia. These were in fact important precedents for neo-colonial influences in post-independence Africa.

Liberia College which was founded in 1862 with grants from a philanthropic organization in Boston continued as an autonomous institution plagued, like Fourah Bay College, by various crises. In the late 1940s, it was razed down completely in a fire disaster. This roused the Liberian public to pressurize the Legislature to seek foreign assistance largely from America to revive the institution. The College was reconstituted as the University of Liberia by an Act of the Legislature on February 15, 1951. The first two presidents were Americans; so were the majority of the staff who were thereby subject to rapid turnover, while the University suffered from frequent breaks in programmes. The expatriate staff insisted on autonomy of the University and the cost was that the University failed to be integrated into the development process of the State. The level of support from the Liberian government for research or general maintenance was very low. Up to 1970, it was shown that the Liberian government spent more money on sending students on scholarships abroad than in subventions to the University.

In 1949, also in Liberia, the Protestant Episcopal Church re-opened the Cuttington College and Divinity School which had been closed since 1929. The roots of the College went back to the Hoffman Institute established near Cape Palmas in 1889 to provide vocational education. To this was added the Divinity School in 1897. The School was re-opened in 1949 as Cuttington University College. The staff was predominantly American and the Bishop of the Episcopal Church, also American, was the President of the Board of Trustees. The College continues to be administered and financially supported by the Protestant Episcopal Church, and receives a grant from the Government of Liberia. The College offers instruction only at the undergraduate level in Education, Humanities, Science, Social Sciences, Nursing, Theology and Agriculture.

In Ethiopia, in 1949, the Ministry of Education established a new institute of higher education called Trinity College, and appointed as its head a young Canadian Jesuit, then the Director of what is today the Entotto Comprehensive School. Trinity College began with an initial intake of 71 students and 9 academic staff. Under the name of the University College of Addis Ababa (UCAA), it was granted a charter in July 1950 as an autonomous state institution wholly financed by the government. Largely because of the strong American influence and the heterogeneity of the academic staff, the University College did not seek Special Relationship with any one overseas institution. Each Department or Faculty was linked with a different institution for purposes of staff recruitment, visiting professors and external examiners, usually offered on the basis of technical assistance.

Between 1954-61, a number of small colleges and post-secondary institutions were opened by the Ethiopian Government, often with the assistance of external agencies. A College of Agriculture was launched in Jimma around 1952-3, with substantial assistance from the American Government, through Oklahoma State University, a land-grant university. It was soon moved to its new campus at Alemaya with modern facilities and up-to-date equipment. This was closely followed by the establishment of a College of Building Technology largely through Swedish assistance. A public Health College followed, built at Gondar with the help of grants from WHO, UNICEF and the United States. The Theological School, first established in 1942 as a secondary-level institution, was given the status of College of Higher Education in 1960. It was to coordinate the various Colleges under one unified university system that Haile Sellassie I University emerged in December 1961, through an imperial charter. The emperor also bequeathed to the University the Genete-Leul Palace which had been the scene of the bloody revolt of the Imperial Guard during the attempted coup d'etat of 1960. The students had demonstrated in favour of the coup attempt and the former palace now houses the University main administrative offices, the Institute of Ethiopian Studies, Research Library, Museum etc.

From the beginning, every effort was made to ensure that the courses of study at UCAA were relevant to the needs of the country. With the restoration of the country's independence under Emperor Haile Sellassie I there was acute shortage of trained man-power to run the various arms of the bureaucracy and other technical services. It was in recognition of this need that a two year programme in Port

Administration was started in the academic year 1951-52. In the same year a School of Law started offering courses in the evenings and on a part-time basis. New facilities for students to major in Education and Public Administration were opened in 1952-53, and, in 1953-54 an Extension Department began offering Diploma courses to public servants in the evenings.

In August 1954 degrees were conferred upon 13 successful graduates of UCAA. 10 received Bachelor of Arts degrees in General Studies and the remaining 3 in Education. Science education did not make rapid progress either in terms of student numbers or of curriculum development. The Faculty of Science continued to offer Certificate and Diploma programmes until 1959 when, for the first time, 6 students graduated with the Bachelor of Science degrees in Biology. The diversification and development of academic programmes continued at a relatively rapid rate. A major programme in education developed into a four-year degree programme for secondary school teachers in 1955-56, and a Faculty of Education was established in 1958-59. The curriculum of the School of Law was expanded to include both Advanced Courses in Law and pre-Law options for non-specialists. A commerce section offering courses in advanced accounting and business administration was opened in 1957-58. A two-year diploma programme in social work started in 1959-60. Two important research centres, the Geophysical Observatory and the Forestry Institute, started work in 1957-58 and in 1960-61, respectively.

A major reorganization in 1960-61 rationalized these developments into eight academic departments in the Faculty of Arts and four in science. There was also the College of Business Administration, the Faculty of Education, the Faculty of Law, the School of Social Work, and the University Extension programmes. Within a decade of its existence the University College of Addis Ababa had produced a total of 421 graduates - 235 of them with Bachelor Degrees and 126 with Certificates and Diplomas. This in itself was a remarkable achievement considering the fact that the University College did not enter into any kind of special relationship with any other University. It charted a new course, experimented with several options, made mistakes and learned the bitter way from those mistakes.

## University College of Rhodesia and Nyasaland

The initiative for the establishment of the University College of Rhodesia and Nyasaland was taken by the European settlers of Rhodesia who wanted higher education for their children locally and at a cheaper price, while doing everything to limit facilities for education, especially secondary education, to the Africans. They formed an Association called Friends of the University, later changed to The Rhodesia University Association (RUA). On May 29 1947, the Governor responded by establishing a Trust Deed for the Rhodesia University Foundation Fund with the Minister and the Secretary of Internal Affairs and L.M.N. Hodson, Member of the Legislature and President of the RUA, as Trustees. The Legislature in 1948 accepted a 250 acre site, offered by the City of Salisbury, at Mount Pleasant, adjoining the northern residential suburbs of the City. The Legislature passed an Act in 1953 constituting a University College in Salisbury. Queen Elizabeth, the Queen Mother, laid the foundation stone and accepted to be Chancellor. (Fletcher, 1962).

It was only then that the British Government began to see the University College as one of the possible instruments in the attempt to develop the Federation of Rhodesian and Nyasaland on a multi-racial basis as counterpoise to the racialism of South Africa. The Africans were extremely suspicious of the attempt at Federation and the European settlers had no intention of being faithful to the ideals either. The suggestion that the University College be located in Zambia had been rejected. The British Government however pushed the idea of the University College project, voted £1.25 million for the capital costs, while the Government of the Federation voted an annual recurrent cost of £150,000 for five years. A Royal Charter establishing the University College of Rhodesia and Nyasaland was incorporated in February 1955 as the last of the Asquith Colonial University Colleges in Special Relationship with the University of London. The first Principal was named later that year as Dr. Walter Adams.

The University College was to operate as an institution of learning, "open to all races"; it was to serve "not only the higher education requirements of Rhodesia but also contributing to the advancement of knowledge, science and research in Central Africa within the international community of universities". But the experience of Africans with the University College fell far short of this ideal. They were discouraged for instance from taking up positions at the University College as academic staff. Entry was fixed at the "A Level" and the expectation was that very few Africans would qualify to enter, and no thought was given to the possibility of African female students. It was a big embarrassment when one African woman student, Sarah Chavunduka, showed up for registration. For, while there were separate Halls of Residence for white male students and black male students, and another for white women students, none had been provided for African women. She had to live in the servants' quarters of the women's warden's house.

**Colonial Legacy**

Thus, the Colonial University Colleges were established partly in response to African demand, especially in West and Southern Africa, partly in response to the demand of European officials and settlers, especially in Central and Eastern Africa, but generally in pursuit of laid down colonial policies and objectives. They were colonial universities in the sense defined by John Hargreaves of an institution which "paid greater attention to its standing in the eyes of foreigners than to the relevance of its activities to the needs of its own country". (1973, p.35). The two essential characteristics of the Colleges, therefore, were the search for equivalence with European university standards and the attendant control of both curriculum and personnel by the colonial authorities acting in partnership with the metropolitan universities. The Colleges introduced a new age of higher education in Africa. As such, they were welcomed and widely appreciated. Eventually, they were recognized as part of the colonial legacy put in place in the period of decolonization. They began to be criticized, and attempts were later made to reform them; but they left a permanent imprint on the African experience with higher education. The patterns that they laid down became the norm, with their own vested interests, and every effort to depart from them had to be contested against expected opposition.

Each colonial power imposed its own pattern on the Colleges it sponsored. The British who, in the 1920s and 1930s cooperated with the Phelps-Stokes Commission, the Carnegie Corporation and other US agencies, seemed to have distanced themselves from such external influences during the period of decolonization. Such peculiarly British prejudices as the distrust of philosophy as an academic discipline, the notion that "it is an unhappy nation who is governed by specialists" and the consequent preference for General degrees in Arts and Science for would-be administrators, rather than Honours or Specialist degrees in Economics, Banking, Engineering, or Law, were imposed on the Asquith Colleges. The only exception was the professional course in Medicine, but this was geared more to produce doctors for specific government appointments than for private practice. For the French, on the other hand, philosophy was basic to all higher education, and jurisprudence was essential for all public administration. The Academic staff were employees of the Ministry of National Education, initially of France, later of the individual countries concerned. The Belgian system was closer to the French than to the British, and encouraged the incorporation of African Studies within the degree structure. The requirements for the degree took longer and were more rigorous than those in the French or British sponsored universities. As noted by Ashby in 1965, the degree programme at Lovanium involved a "pedagogic marathon, in which the student is exposed to more than twice as many lectures as he would have in Ibadan or Makerere, and, in science subjects, to about the same amount of laboratory work ... In level of achievement, a licence from Lovanium is probably somewhat higher than an honours degree in an English university ... In quality of teaching, in standard of achievement demanded for graduation, in content and range of curriculum, in the amount and sophistication of its research work, Lovanium stands very high indeed among African universities". (Ashby. 1966, p.362).

The Africans for their part had fought so often and for so long against colonial institutions that awarded local Diplomas which had no currency outside the locality and which, even locally, provided no access to the really significant policy-making jobs. The African members of the Council of Achimota in December 1938 "insisted most strongly upon their demand for opportunities for the African to obtain the very highest academic qualifications and the fullest participation in University life, in order that highly qualified Africans might be as eligible as Europeans for direct appointment to higher posts in Government. No provision of University classes at Achimota can secure anything like this ..." They preferred to send students abroad on scholarship. It was therefore necessary to overcome such skepticism and assure African opinion that the new set of colonial University Colleges would offer degrees that were not merely equivalent to those of European universities, but were, in fact, to be degrees granted by European universities.

Furthermore, the Colleges had, even in their physical appearance, to be comparable with European universities. They were conceived as small municipalities on the suburbs of existing urban centres. Because it was thought that there was not enough space in the capital, Lagos, Nigeria's first University was located in the northern suburbs of Ibadan. Lovanium was built some 12km. away from the centre of town. So was Dar-es-Salaam. Makerere was in the immediate suburb of Kampala. Of the older universities, only Nairobi is in the middle of town, and that is because it started as a College of Technology and not built as a university from the start. Even Lagos sought for a remote part of the city. The Colleges had to provide accommodation for all students, academic, administrative and technical staff and the bulk of the workers. They had to provide their own pipe-borne water, electricity, transportation, telecommunication, and other municipal facilities. The provision of such facilities became a factor limiting the number of students that could be admitted, or the range of disciplines that could be provided. It also made the per capita running cost of the Colleges much higher than comparable institutions in Europe. These facilities were provided as part of the responsibilities of government to the people. The colonial governments had been slow in accepting responsibility for elementary, secondary and teacher training institutions pioneered by missionaries. They became involved, often in partnership with the missionaries, and gradually began to take the initiative in regulating and demarcating spheres of influence. Higher education was an area where the initiative of the state was predominant.

As such, the University Colleges were viewed as aid or technical assistance from the colonial powers. The University Colleges became part of the status symbols conferred on the new states in anticipation of the granting of political independence and international recognition. Except in a few cases as in Ghana and Sierra Leone, little of the capital cost of the Colleges came from the territorial budgets. Even the recurrent budgets came mostly from abroad. From the start, higher education in Africa depended largely on external financing and, as the external funding agencies withdrew, most of the African countries found it difficult to absorb the total cost of the universities into their budget. It is the familiar story of the modernization approach to the development project in Africa, in which foreign assistance succeeds more in increasing dependence than in promoting the capacity for self-reliance.

The academic, administrative and technical staff began initially as staff seconded from overseas universities. In some countries, African staff was difficult to find, even for administrative, not to talk of technical and academic posts. The terms of secondment of expatriates were generous. Overseas colonial Colleges thus became an avenue of opportunities for younger staff particularly from Britain, France and Belgium, to spend some time in Africa and become an expert in African Studies, Tropical Medicine, Agriculture or Technology. The facility provided in the Asquith Colleges for younger staff to register as internal postgraduate students of the University of London encouraged such staff to do research and write up their material as doctoral theses. This was one of the most widely recognized advantages of the Special Relationship Scheme. It was so successful that it became a way of discouraging the recruitment of African staff. It was easier for expatriates with first degrees to show potential for higher education and be recruited into the scheme than for Africans with first degrees. Africans usually had to stay on in universities abroad and complete their Ph.D. to get recognized. This, coupled with differentials in salary and living conditions created for the young African academics a clear impression that the colonial University Colleges operated virtually the same system of racial discrimination that characterized the colonial civil services. And yet it was agreed that the policy of accelerated Africanization which was to end discrimination in the Civil Services could not apply to the University Colleges.

One result of this was that while the Colleges as institutions enjoyed a high degree of autonomy, the African staff for the most part regarded this institutional autonomy as a cover for undermining their own academic freedom. They welcomed the Special Relationship Scheme and the desire to maintain high academic standards. However, the scarcity of African Staff, especially at the professorial level, meant the absence of African opinion in the running of the Colleges. This was one reason why the Colleges, generally, and the Asquith Colleges in particular, were not able to make the degree of adaptation of the curricula that was expected. As two Kenyan academics later put it in 1964:

> Europeans who now run our [University] affairs for us cannot undertake any major reforms because they are prisoners of their own irrelevant and out of date prejudices. (cit. Southall, 1974 p. ix).

Some of the governments began to set up Provisional Councils for the Colleges, and to appoint senior African professionals - lawyers, medical officers, or educationists - into the Councils. Such Africans began to voice the concern that too few students were being admitted, the failure rate was too high, and many who were not admitted or who were weeded out were able to make good in European or US universities. This was the main area of complaint at the Jamaican Conference of Heads of the Asquith Colleges organized by the Inter-University Council in 1955, where Africa was represented by the Principals of Ibadan, Legon and Makerere. In that year, their seventh year, Ibadan had only 527 students and Legon 349 students, while Makerere had 448 in its ninth year. In the circumstances, the African staff were the first to approach nationalists, to question the degree of institutional autonomy and seek political intervention to reform the University Colleges and redress their grievances.

**Apartheid in South Africa**

For South Africa, the process of 'decolonization' of higher education may be said to have begun with the University Acts of 1916 enacted by the Union Government to establish the University of South Africa, and the Universities of Cape Town and Stellenbosch. By 1957 the University Colleges had become independent universities, granting their own degrees - Natal in Durban, Orange Free State in Bloemfontein, Pretoria, the Potchefstroom University for Christian Higher Education (*Universiteit vir Christelike Höer Onderwys*), and Rhodes in Grahamstown. (Only the Huguenot University College had failed to become a university). The University of Port Elizabeth was later founded in 1964 as a bilingual institution, while the Rand Afrikaans

University in Johannesburg founded in 1966, helped to redress the balance in favour of the Afrikaner population. These were famous universities with a wide range of courses. In addition, the UNISA then concentrated on examining candidates for external degrees by correspondence, a programme embarked on in 1945. Even after the post-World War II expansion of universities in the U.K., South Africa had a much higher proportion of university age white students attending universities, next only to the US in the world.

Such achievements only showed up the disabilities of the Africans and other non-Europeans in South Africa. Out of about 5,000 students in Cape Town in 1959 on the eve of the enforcement of Bantu higher education, there were 461 Coloured, 133 Asian and only 39 Africans; out of a little over 5,000 at Witwatersrand (Wits) there were 193 Asians, 74 Africans and only 30 Coloured. The value of the education of even those few for the development of their ethnic communities and in providing non-European leadership for the future of South Africa, should not be underrated. Nelson Mandela points to two other aspects of his life as the only African student in the Faculty of Law. Both staff and students contributed their quota to what he calls "the steady accumulation of a thousand slights, a thousand indignities, a thousand unremembered moments" which produced in him "an anger, a rebelliousness, a desire to fight the system that imprisoned my people". At the same time, he was able to make friends with some whites, including one or two Afrikaner who, out of human decency or radical ideology, were prepared to fight the system and became valued allies later. (1994, pp. 78-83). The Afrikaner universities never admitted blacks; Rhodes and Natal hardly ever. After a lot of pressure, Natal began in 1936 to admit a few, mostly Asians, to special classes, only at weekends and at Adams College during the long vacation. After World War II, the Natal Medical School for a few Africans filled an important gap. Even at Cape Town and Wits, campus facilities, including sports, were all segregated though teaching and examining took place together. Thus, the facilities of Fort Hare, such as they were, were all the Africans could look up to. The white universities even used them as an excuse to refuse admission to Africans.

There is thus some truth in the assertion of the Holloway Commission, set up in 1953 to enquire into the modalities of implementing apartheid, that "the Bantu do not object to the establishment of segregation as such, but to enforced segregation". (White Paper, 1957) There is a cruel irony in the fact that Bantu Education was enacted by a law entitled the "Extension of University Education Act". It established four new University Colleges of UNISA for specific ethnic groups:
- University College of the North at Turfloop, near Pietersburg in north Transvaal,

for the Sotho-Tsonga and Venda
- University College of Zululand, at Ngoya in Natal, for the Zulu and Swazi
- University College of the Western Cape, at Bellville, for the Coloured, and
- University College of Durban for Asians.

Fort Hare was taken over and made a University College exclusively for the Xhosa, and the Sotho of Ciskei. All these took degrees and Certificates of UNISA. But they were under the control of the Minister for Bantu Education. It required the permission of the Minister for non-Europeans to be admitted to even the "Open" Universities of Cape Town, Witwatersrand, Natal or Rhodes in subjects not available in the University Colleges, such as engineering and medicine. He controlled appointments and promotions of staff, including academic staff. Since even the presence of non-whites with whites on the Senate or Council of the University Colleges was considered undesirable, provision was made for Advisory Senates and Councils on which non-whites could sit, but they did not work, and appointment of non-European staff or Council member was thus discouraged. Therefore, the staff remained predominantly white, largely Afrikaner who were enthusiastic about the idea of ethnic universities. In the end, the ethnic communities had to rally round the universities to the best of their abilities, while the university authorities promoted growth through linkages with foreign universities. But as at Fort Hare, missionary philanthropy and private sector donations remained important.

The international community was shocked by the policy of apartheid. In defence of it, South Africa quit the Commonwealth and became a Republic. The English-speaking South African Universities kept up a fight in defence of academic freedom. To the non-Europeans, this sometimes appeared to be merely gestures in defence of their own rights and privileges, by people who were not prepared to make any substantial efforts to redress the disabilities of the Africans. The campaign to boycott South African universities, including even the `open' ones of Cape Town and Witwatersrand, culminated in their being barred even as observers from the Association of Commonwealth Universities and the International Association of Universities, since African members of these associations refused to sit with them. For the `open' universities and the international academic community, apartheid was an affront to academic freedom:

> To exclude black students from a university is an insult to their human dignity; it is inhuman. To force them into native reserves under the supervision of white authorities is oppressive. To pretend that this is done in order to preserve their native culture is intellectually dishonest. To demand the participation of universities in a programme of inhumanity, oppression and intellectual dis-

honesty is a violation of academic freedom". (Polanyi, 1974, p.11).

To the Africans, Asians and Coloureds, especially the Africans who were the dispossessed majority, and who had to bear the brunt of the inhumanity and oppression, it was a crime:

> Apartheid education had as its deliberate objective the systematic underdevelopment of intellectual skills and human potential ... what apartheid education has done - not as an incidental effect but as deliberate policy - is criminal. (Jakes Gerwel in Unterhalter, 1991, p.125).

Chapter 4

## THE POLITICS OF INDEPENDENCE
## AND HIGHER EDUCATION,
## 1960-70

### Critique of Colonial Education

As the countries approached or attained political independence, many African leaders began to point at the inadequacies of colonial University Colleges. They sought ways of ending affiliation of the Colleges to metropolitan universities, diminishing the degree of dependence on and control by the metropolitan countries or donors, and Africanising the staff especially in policy-making positions. Thus, the colonial University Colleges moved to become autonomous degree-granting universities, admitting a larger number of students and covering a wider range of disciplines. The politics of independence induced reforms in the management and curricula of the universities, and widening access to institutions of higher education. In the larger countries, the demand for geographical spread led to the establishment of new universities or of new campuses of the national university. In other places, attempts to create "Regional" universities serving a number of independent countries generally failed as each country wished to have and control its own university, virtually as part of the symbols indicating sovereignty. In the process of exercising this sovereignty African politicians, and even some of the African academics trying to take control of the universities from expatriates, had to rediscover to what extent the autonomy and academic freedom claimed by the expatriates were part of the colonial legacy that should be swept away or essential aspects of universal traditions necessary for the African university to make its due contribution to national development.

Criticisms of the colonial University Colleges and the legacy of colonial higher education crystallized around four main issues:

(i) That the colonial universities deliberately set out to train an elite who would merely step into the shoes of outgoing colonial rulers and become exploiters of their own people. The basic weapon against that was to widen access to higher education, reduce emphasis on the wholly residential system and full municipal facilities. In order to widen access, some countries decided to expand secondary education to include Sixth Form work and admit students at the "A" Level for 3-year Bachelor's degree at the university, while others preferred to admit students at the School Certificate level for a 4-year Bachelor's degree.

(ii)That the curricula of the Colleges were very narrow, and needed to be broadened. Instead of merely educating an elite to occupy government positions, Universities should seek to offer liberal education including subjects like philosophy, religion, African and modern European languages which colonial prejudices or inadequate funding had hitherto excluded. Even more, various disciplines that in European universities were not normally taught at undergraduate levels but were essential in developing economies needed to be introduced into the content of undergraduate degrees. These included education, banking, finance and insurance, and other practical subjects. Indeed, in the spirit of the American Land Grant philosophy, no subject needed for practical living can be excluded: journalism, home economics, hotel management and catering, nursing, etc.

(iii) Various controversies in the metropolitan countries had been part of the colonial legacy, for instance in the structure of university management or structure of the degrees. In the British system, there was controversy between the relative balance between students taking single honours specialist first degrees, and those with General degrees, and which of these was most relevant to the needs of developing countries. There was need for reform to evolve new degree structures more relevant to the needs of each country. The American system of a wide range of term or semester courses from which students could select with varying levels of concentration in one discipline or dispersal in a number of inter-related subjects, seemed eventually to offer a solution.

(iv)The Ivory Tower nature of the Colleges underlined their separation from the wider community. The basic weapon was not merely to discourage the physical location far from centres of urban life, but also to emphasize social responsibility through adult education, Institutes for extension classes in education, agriculture, health, public administration etc., and African studies, particularly African languages, history, oral traditions, music, drama, art, and culture generally.

## The International Factor

One notable feature of the politics of independence was the international factor. Whereas most colonial powers were able to insist on monopolizing the control of the process of decolonization - to ensure transition to its continued colonial or neo-colonial influence - such monopoly became difficult after independence. This was partly because of the post-World War II growth of internationalism, the United Nations and its various agencies, especially UNESCO and the International Association of Universities (IAU); but it was perhaps due even more to the growing intensity of the Cold War which became quite hot not only in the Korean War but also in the Congo crisis. The Cold War certainly enhanced the position of the USA in the leadership of the Western World and, consequently, the American factor in African higher education.

We noted above how a few students from West and South Africa acquired tertiary education in the US, largely through the influence of missionary organizations not only in the 19th century, but also in the 1920s and 1930s. The initial effect of this contact with America was the spread of the influence of the Tuskegee Institute through the visits and the Reports of the Phelps-Stokes Commissions to Africa, and other channels. The return of J.K. Aggrey to Achimota College encouraged a new generation of Africans like Kwame Nkrumah and Nnamdi Azikiwe to seek higher education in America. Thus, even during the period of decolonization, while the official policy was to discourage much contact with American higher education, there was a group of African leaders, whether beneficiaries of American education or not, who saw in American higher education the elements necessary to reform the colonial legacy inherited from the colonial university institutions.

Two notable examples need to be cited. One was Nnamdi Azikiwe who, by 1955, had become one of the three most notable leaders in Nigeria, and Premier of one of the three Regions. In the tradition of pan-Africanism pioneered by Edward Blyden, J. E. Casely-Hayford and others, Azikiwe in his 1937 book, *Renascent Africa*, as we mentioned earlier had demanded for "an indigenous university sustained through African initiative". (cit. Fafunwa, 1971, p180) He was very critical of the University College at Ibadan and he wished to found an American type land grant vocational university: "not only cultural, according to the classical concept of universities, but it should also be vocational in its objective and Nigerian in content." The World Bank Report of 1954 on development in Nigeria, stressing the need for many more graduates and greater diversification of courses, strengthened his hand. In 1955, the Government of the Eastern Region enacted the University of Nigeria law and arranged for the Produce Marketing Board to set aside half-a-million pounds each year for ten years towards the capital expenses of the university. He received no encouragement from Britain and his tour of America did not yield the massive financial support that he expected. It was not until he had secured the support of powerful British academics who were themselves using the American experience to pursue reform of universities in Britain that he succeeded better in the U.S. The Colonial Office referred his proposal to the Inter-University Council (IUC) which nominated J.W. Cook, Vice-chancellor of Exeter University, to join H.W. Hannah, President, and Glen Taggart, Dean of International Programmes of Michigan State University, to visit Nigeria and advise. Their report argued that American higher education could make a great contribution to Nigeria provided it "established a university of unquestioned academic standards interested in Nigerian problems". With this Anglo-American support, Azikiwe was able to go ahead to establish the University of Nigeria, Nsukka, (UNN) in 1960 with the cooperation of the USAID and Michigan State University.

Another example was Tom Mboya, the articulate trade unionist and Pan-Africanist leader in Kenya. When the colonial government in the struggle against the Mau Mau rebellion proclaimed an Emergency, they closed down Kenya Independent schools and tried to replace them with a government controlled system that was calculated to slow down the pace of education. Through his trade unionist connections, Mboya visited the United States in 1957 and was able to lobby for a number of scholarships in various Colleges for Kenyan students. He persuaded an African-American businessman, William X Scheinman, to pay the fares of 17 Kenyan students to benefit from the scholarships. In 1958, Scheinman paid for 38 others. (Makerere graduated 40 students in 1957 and 36 in 1958). In 1959, Mboya again visited the United States and, with Scheinman and others, formed the African American Students Foundation. Together they raised funds to charter an aircraft to airlift 81 students to New York. About 40 of them were on scholarship, selected by Mboya himself and a few friends; the rest had private resources. This was all done in a hurry, and matching students with available places was not an easy task. Arrangements for the reception, care and counselling of the students were inadequate for coping with the problem cases. The colonial government criticized the scheme as amateurish and politicized, diverting good students from more relevant facilities available locally or in Britain. There was improved planning in 1960. Mboya took advantage of the Presidential elections in the US and raised 100,000 US dollars from the Kennedy Foundation. The Kenya Education Trust, which he founded in Nairobi, was thus able to airlift 295 students in four DC aircrafts, 240 from Kenya, the others from Tanzania and Central Africa. In 1961, with Kennedy in the White House, the State Department gave 100,000 US dollars and involved the African-American Institute, the Council for Educational

Cooperation with Africa, and the African Scholarship Programme of American Universities (ASPAU) in the management of the scheme. 322 students were airlifted. With this indirect involvement of the US Government, the Kenya Government contributed £5,000 (Smith, 1966; Mboya, 1970; Goldsworthy, 1982). Apart from meeting the hunger of many students for higher education, Mboya's scheme helped to arouse interest in African higher education in the US. The Tom Mboya initiative was later broadened into an Africa-wide Scholarship scheme managed by the Association of African Universities in cooperation with various US and Canadian Agencies. It thus helped to institutionalize American involvement in African higher education.

International technical assistance and development aid was a feature not merely of American domestic politics and inter-party rivalry. In the context of the Cold War, development aid in the field of education, next to military assistance and arms supply, became the major arena for the rivalry between the US-led NATO countries and the USSR-led Warsaw Pact Alliance. African countries sought ways of exploiting this international rivalry to help finance the expansion and reform of their higher education and, if possible, to minimize dependence on any one country. Germany and the Soviet Union joined the former colonial powers in providing personnel and resources to teach English, French, German, Russian and Portuguese languages and cultures within Departments of Modern Languages. In addition, the Soviet Union and East European countries tended to concentrate on scholarships to invite African students to study in their countries. The Soviet Union even established the Patrice Lumumba Friendship University specifically for the reception and training of students and working class people from the developing countries, majority of them being from Africa.

In several places like Guineé-Conakry, the Portuguese-speaking countries, Ethiopia and Congo-Brazaville, the socialist countries assisted Ministries of Education with curriculum development and had a significant impact on the teaching of science and the training of technicians. At the university level, personnel was made available not only to teach Marxism-Leninism but also to assist with staff development, especially in the Faculties of Science, Engineering and Medicine. A notable example is the contribution of the German Democratic Republic (GDR) to the development of the Gondar Medical College in Ethiopia. The Americans offered fewer scholarships, but sent university teachers and advisers, peace corps personnel and assistance not only from the official USAID but also from various philanthropic American Foundations. Canada as a bilingual country played a significant role bridging the language divide in Africa. The Scandinavian countries concentrated their assistance largely on East and Southern Africa.

## The Ashby Commission in Nigeria

The Commission on Post-School-Certificate and Higher Education in Nigeria, otherwise known as the Ashby Commission, illustrates how the international factor began to interact with the politics of independence in expanding and reforming higher education in Africa. With the independence date set for October 1st, 1960, the Federal Government of Nigeria decided to review the development of all post-secondary education against expected manpower requirements over the following two decades. They got the Carnegie Corporation of America to finance the study. As the Chairman of the Commission, they selected Sir Eric Ashby, then Master of Clare College, Cambridge, a leading reformer of British higher education in the Post-World War II period and a vocal critic of the transplantation of Classics-based literary secondary and higher education from Europe to Africa. There were two other British members, Sir John Lockwood of the University of London, a crucial member of the IUC who personally played prominent roles in the development of the University of East Africa, and the University of Zambia, and G.E. Watts, Principal of Brighton Technical College. There were three American members: R.G. Gustavson, former Chancellor of the University of Nebraska and President of the Fund for the Resources of the Future; H.W. Hannah, former Associate Dean of Agriculture and President of Michigan State University that was preparing to establish the UNN; and Frank Keppel, former Dean of Graduate School of Education at Harvard and later Secretary for Education, Health and Social Welfare in the US Government. The three Nigerian members were just as distinguished: K.O. Dike, Vice-Principal soon to become Principal of the University College, Ibadan; Sir Shettima Kashim, former Federal Minister of Education, and later Governor of the Northern Region, and Chancellor of the University of Ibadan; and S.D. Onabamiro, Senior Research Fellow at the University of Ibadan and later Minister of Education in Western Nigeria. In addition, an American, Frederic Harbison of Princeton University, was commissioned to study manpower needs for university graduates and professionally qualified personnel. His study entitled "High level manpower and Nigeria's future" formed Part II of the Commission's Report.

The keynote of the Commission's Report was that the development of higher education should be guided not by what the Commissioners thought Nigeria could afford to pay for but by what they thought Nigeria needed for its development. As such, they regarded education not merely as a social service, but as an investment vital for development for which external funding could justifiably be sought. They were critical of the elitism and rigidity at Ibadan and advocated improved access and a wider range of courses:

there must be more diversity and more flexibility in university education if it is to be relevant to the needs of the Nigerian people ... A much greater diversity of demand is likely to be made on Nigerian universities than on their British counterparts. We believe that Nigerian universities should meet this demand on one condition: that what is required of them is indeed greater diversity and not lower standards. (p. 22).

This diversity should be both in terms of the range of courses available in the university and also in terms of a variety of institutions of tertiary education. They argued that while Nigeria needed professionals at the graduate level, Nigeria also needed even more complementary staff at the sub-professional level. They recommended therefore that while the universities continued to admit students at the Advanced level, a variety of other institutions admitting students at the School Certificate level should be established to train teachers, and technicians of different types. The universities should "sponsor" these institutions and guarantee the quality of their Diplomas and Certificates. The universities should themselves maintain diversity in the sense of undergraduate courses for a variety of professional training: bachelors degrees in education which incorporated pedagogy into the content of arts and science subjects; degrees in applied social science such as in business, banking, insurance, transportation, labour relations, and social work; in agriculture, veterinary medicine, forestry, agricultural economics and rural sociology; and in applied science such as fisheries, microbiology, industrial chemistry, technology and other vocational courses.

In what they regarded as a bold proposal, they recommended the establishment of three new universities, based in Lagos, Zaria and Enugu. Even though they were aware of the initiatives of the Governments of the Eastern Region in the proposed UNN, and of another by the Government of the Western Region, the Commission felt that the Federal Government should retain overall control, that all the universities should be federal, and be centres of national unity. They proposed that the Federal Government should become involved in the UNN which should take over the Enugu campus of the Nigerian College of Arts, Science and Technology (NCAST), while the Zaria campus of the College should become the nucleus of the University of Northern Nigeria which should incorporate existing tertiary institutions like the Institute of Agriculture in Samaru. They proposed that these should be degree granting universities from the start, but that, in starting each of them, international advice should be sought and the sponsorship of major world universities so as to give "currency" to their degrees. S.D. Onabamiro signed a Minority Report in defence of Regional initiatives in the expansion of secondary education and establishment of universities recommended by the majority. The Federal Government welcomed the Report and decided that the targets recommended by the Commission be treated as minimum, to be exceeded in many areas within the first decade. They endorsed proposals for massive expansion of secondary education and the accelerated training and recruitment of teachers for elementary, secondary and higher education. They bowed to the logic of federalism in Nigeria and the demand for geographical spread. They decided on three Regional universities and a new Federal University in Lagos, besides Ibadan. They did not follow up the Ashby Commission's advice to seek the sponsorship of major world universities, but each was obliged to use external examiners, and they sought the services of the IUC, Association of Commonwealth Universities, IAU and philanthropic Foundations in the recruitment of staff and specialist advisers.

Thus, the international factor interacted with the politics of independence to usher in a new age of higher education in Nigeria. The UNN, as the first degree-granting university in Nigeria, decided to adopt new courses in accordance with the American land-grant philosophy. It acquired a large plot of land, some 90km away from the Regional capital. It opened its doors in October 1960 as the climax of Independence celebrations, with 220 students and 13 academic staff. In December 1961, Azikiwe was installed 'life' Chancellor of the University. He was not only Chairman of the Council, he controlled appointments to both academic and non-academic positions, as well as the finance and programmes of the University, and many of the functions normally performed by Senate and the Development Committee of Senate. He was the University's landlord and he personally endorsed each of the 8,000 books that he donated to the University Library. By June 1963, the University graduated its first 150 students, 118 in Arts, and 32 in the Social Sciences and mathematics. By the 1964-5 session, the University had 2,500 students, and 250 academic staff, in 35 departments including agriculture, law, music, business management and engineering, as well as Institutes of African, Extra-Mural and Economic Development Studies. In 1962-3, 37% of the academic staff were Nigerians. In 1966-7, 69% were Nigerians. In January 1966, with the military coup, Azikiwe was removed as Chancellor and replaced by the Emir of Kano. The University was brought under the National Universities Commission to conform more with the pattern of governance pioneered at Ibadan, but the University's land grant philosophy, the course system of instruction, and continuous evaluation began to spread to other Nigerian Universities. The University suffered much physical damage during the Nigerian Civil War, and had virtually to begin afresh in 1970 after the War.

The Government of the Northern Region, following the recommendation of the Ashby Commission, requested the IUC to send a delegation to advise on the scope and activities of the University to be established in Zaria.  The Carr-Saunders Commission visited Northern Nigeria in April 1961 and issued a brief Report which formed the basis of the Ahmadu Bello University (ABU) Law of 1961, revised in 1962.  Sir Ahmadu Bello, the Sardauna of Sokoto and Premier of the Northern Region became the Chancellor.  Norman Alexander, professor of physics at Ibadan, was appointed the first Vice-Chancellor.  The University was inaugurated in October 1962 with 421 students and 89 academic staff taken over from the pre-existing tertiary institutions.  Departments of Arts (History, Geography and English) and Science hitherto teaching "A" level courses in the Nigerian College became the nucleus of the Faculties of Arts and Science.  The Institute of Administration was developed into Faculties of Law and Administration (including Accountancy and Business Administration).  The Nigerian College had previously taken over courses in Engineering of the University College, Ibadan, hitherto awarding degrees under the Special Relations scheme of London.  This, and the degree programmes in Fine Art, were taken over by the University and developed into Faculties of Engineering and Architecture.  The Institute of Agricultural Research at Samaru was developed into a Faculty of Agriculture with separate departments in Plant Science, Animal Science, Soil Science, and Agricultural Economics.  Later, Departments of Crop Protection and Agronomy were added.  The Islamic Centre in Kano was developed into the Abdullahi Bayero College with a Faculty of Arts and Islamic Studies, including Shari'a Law.  A Department of Education in the Faculty of Arts was developed in 1968 into a separate Faculty of Education.  The Faculty of Medicine was established in 1970.  The first Chancellor was assassinated in the military coup of January 1966 and the Vice-Chancellor also resigned during the ensuing national crisis.  He was replaced by Ishaya S Audu an Associate Professor of Paediatrics from the University of Lagos under whom ABU became recognized as a model multi-campus developmental university, responding to a variety of demands at both the professional and sub-professional levels. (Audu, 1976) Staffing remained a major problem.  The initial staff were largely expatriates avoiding the Nigerianization policy of other universities and tended to be older and rather conservative.  They were then joined by younger more radical staff, often directly from abroad and becoming even more radicalized by the polarization against the conservatives.  The pace of Nigerianization was slow.  In 1963-4 only 17% of academic staff were Nigerian; 19% in 1966-7 and 37% by 1969-70.

The Government of Western Nigeria set up a University Planning Committee in 1961.  The Chairman was Obafemi Awolowo himself, leader of the governing

Party who had retired as Premier and was then Leader of the Opposition in the Federal Parliament. The members were drawn from the University of Ibadan and from academically inclined top civil servants. They were all Nigerian, though some members of the Committee were sent to visit the UK, USA, and some Latin American countries. The blueprint was therefore wholly Nigerian-crafted. Oladele Ajose, Professor of Preventive Medicine and the first Nigerian appointed professor at Ibadan, was named the Vice-Chancellor, and Ife was selected as the seat of the University. It, however, started in October 1962 at the Ibadan campus of the former Nigerian College. It was not until January 1967 that it was able to move to its 13,000 acre site outside Ile-Ife.

The University opened with 244 students and 51 academic staff, growing by 1966-7 to 1,200 students and 200 academic staff of whom 57% were Nigerian. It was plagued by political problems almost from the beginning. The Governing Party was split in 1962. The Federal Government intervened on behalf of the minority faction, keeping them in power and later sending Awolowo, leader of the majority faction, to jail on a charge of treasonable felony. The majority of the academic staff tended to side with the Awolowo faction. The Deputy Vice-Chancellor, Saburi Biobaku, a former Registrar of Ibadan and Secretary to the Government of Western Nigeria, read an official statement that the credo of the University was to support the Government of the day and whichever staff did not like it should resign. This was resisted, among others, by the Dean of Agriculture who was then dismissed on a charge of insubordination. Eight other staff, both Nigerian and expatriates, resigned in protest. The University did not settle down until after the 1966 coup when funds were provided to accelerate the development of the Ife site and to effect the relocation there. Ife became well-known for its attention to Yoruba culture and innovative programmes in areas such as physical and health education, food technology, chemical technology; computer science, electronics, and electrical engineering; estate management; pharmacy and pharmacology, and health sciences in place of the conventional Faculty of Medicine.

The Ashby Commission, in its advocacy of diversity in University experience, recommended an urban non-residential university in Lagos, emphasizing business and commercial subjects, and running evening classes and correspondence courses. The Federal Government approached Unesco to advise and they sent an international team which included a Frenchman and a Russian. The Unesco Commission which reported in September 1961 advocated a city university with a limited range of courses - medicine, law, business administration and social studies, arts linked to education, science, applied science and technology - but with a variety of modes of teaching - formal full time classes, part-time evening programmes, correspondence courses.

The Lagos University Act was passed in April 1962 providing for an autonomous Medical School and Teaching Hospital, with its own Council, linked to the Ministry of Health, but awarding degrees of the University. The University started in temporary quarters in October with 100 students and 24 academic staff in Medicine, law, business and social studies. Within a year, evening courses were started in law and business administration. Work was initiated on the permanent site. By the 1964-5 session, there were 338 students and 75 academic staff (excluding the Medical School). Although almost 60% of the staff were Nigerian, all 6 Deans were expatriates and only the Medical School had a Nigerian dean and vice-dean. Thus expatriates dominated the Senate while Nigerians dominated the Provisional Council.

As a result of the Federal elections in December 1964, there was a re-alignment of parties resulting in a change of Federal Minister of Education. The initial three years of Eni Njoku, the First Vice-Chancellor, was due to expire in May 1965. The Council, which had the power to appoint, called on the Senate to propose three or more names for their consideration. The Senate insisted that Eni Njoku, an Igbo, was doing a good job and he should be re-appointed till retirement age. The Council considered Senate unwilling to cooperate and proceeded to appoint Saburi Biobaku, a Yoruba, probably more with an eye to the distribution of major federal appointments among different ethnic groups than with the consideration of the immediate best interests of the University. (The Visitor, Minister of Education, and Vice-chancellors of the two Federal Universities were Igbo, and the Visitor had also insisted on appointing as Chairman of the Council of Ibadan a discredited former member of staff, also an Igbo.) The Senate decided to resist. They appointed a Committee to take over the functions of Vice-Chancellor. Council dismissed five of the expatriate Deans as leaders of the resistance. A substantial number of the staff resigned. The students rose in revolt, and one of them later made an attempt on the life of the new Vice-Chancellor. The University was closed down for three months and it took a while to recover from the disruption. Full recovery was delayed by financial constraints until after the Civil War.

The University College of Ibadan contributed senior academic staff and ideas into the development of all the new universities. In its turn, it was affected by the new developments, in the search for liberalization, diversity and relevance. The University College in Special Relations with London was transformed in 1962 into a degree-granting University. With the support of major US Foundations - Ford, Rockefeller, Carnegie, etc. - a vigorous staff-training and post-doctoral research programme was undertaken. Innovative programmes in African Studies, Agriculture, Forestry, Human Nutrition, Nursing were undertaken. Research was given a new boost in both basic and applied sciences, medicine and diverse areas of African studies, giving a high international visibility to Ibadan. In 1962-63, Ibadan had 1,688 students and 252 academic staff, 30% of whom were Nigerians. In 1966-7, the number of students had risen to 2,729 (compared with 3,482 at UNN) and 320 academic staff, of whom 54% were Nigerian. The staff rose to 442 in 1969-70 and the percentage of Nigerians was 67. The intense ethnic rivalry going on in the country sharpened the competition for personal advancement and achievement. The dwindling number of senior expatriate staff who dominated the College in the 1950s brokered the process of Nigerianization, and ensured that the ethnic rivalry was kept under some control until the crisis of 1966 which culminated in Civil War, and which led to the resignation of K.O. Dike as Vice-Chancellor and of the majority of the staff from Eastern Nigeria, particularly the Igbo.

In the period 1962-3 to 1969-70, Federal Government subvention to Nigerian universities amounted to about 25 million pounds. From 1966-7 under the military administration, the Federal Government assumed responsibility for 75% of the costs of ABU, and 30% of UNN and Ife, leaving the Regional/State Governments to provide the rest. It is estimated that in 1960-64, almost 10 million pounds was committed by external donors, and actual disbursement in Nigeria amounted to 4.265 million pounds. Major external support included over 2 million pounds by Ford Foundation for building, research and personnel at Ibadan and another major grant to develop the Faculty of Education at UNN; over 1 million pounds by USAID through MSU for UNN - the initial principal and first two Vice-Chancellors (G.M. Johnson 1960-64, and Glen Taggart 1964-66) and 30 professors and teachers biennially, with equipment and technical assistance especially in the central administration and agriculture; Rockefeller Foundation support for Agricultural and medical research and staff development at Ibadan; Nuffield Foundation for research facilities; Carnegie Corporation support for education projects and Institutes of Education at UNN, ABU, Ife; the Netherlands Government grant to develop the Faculty of Engineering at UNN; the USAID contract for Wisconsin to develop Agriculture at Ife and ABU; and UNESCO for general assistance at Lagos, especially the School of Business Administration in collaboration with USAID; scholarships provided by West German Government at various Nigerian Universities and a professor of History for three years provided to UNN by East Germany. (Fafunwa, 1971, chapter xi). This gives some measure of the interaction between the international factor and the politics of independence in the development of higher education in Nigeria in the 1960s.

## New Initiatives in Ghana

The Pan-African philosophy and commitment to the total liquidation of colonialism in Africa constituted an ideology that placed Kwame Nkrumah and the ruling Convention Peoples Party at logger heads with the colonial University College of Ghana at Legon. Perhaps also because of this ideology, the overt impact of the international factor was initially marginal, operating largely as pressure groups advising the Chancellor; the politics of independence was, therefore, the major factor propelling the development of higher education in Ghana.

Criticism of the University College focussed on the slow pace in the growth of student numbers, and the College's insistence on an entrance examination over and above the School Certificate including a pass at credit level in the English language; teaching classics but not African philosophy and religion; as well as some privileges of staff such as paid leave in Britain annually. However, the real issue was the refusal of authorities of the College to be dictated to from outside. Ghana became a sovereign nation in 1957, anxious to take control of all organs of the state to push its policies; but the government appeared powerless to make changes it wanted in the University College. It decided in 1961 that the affiliation of Legon to London should be broken. It therefore established an International Commission on Higher Education, with two members from the US, four from Britain, one from Sierra Leone, and one from the Soviet Union under the chairmanship of Kojo Botsio, the Minister of Agriculture. The Commission upheld the principle of University autonomy, but also stressed the need for relevance. It then advocated the establishment of two new University institutions along innovative lines: (i) developing the Kumasi College of Science and Technology into a vocational University and (ii) establishing at Cape Coast an urban University College affiliated to the new University of Ghana, admitting not only fresh school leavers on full time courses but also working teachers, civil servants, bank clerks and others to be trained on a part-time basis.

Thus, the **University of Ghana** was constituted in October 1962 and Kwame Nkrumah was installed the Chancellor and head of the University. With Nana Kobina Nketsia, a prominent Ghanaian leader as interim Vice-Chancellor, the Chancellor invited Dr. Connor Cruise O'Brien, an Irish left-wing scholar and foreign affairs officer who played a prominent role as UN Representative in the Congo crisis of 1960-61, to be the Vice-Chancellor. At the same time, the Chancellor arranged for the establishment of an Institute of African Studies, with another radical scholar, Thomas Hodgkin, Fellow of Baliol College, Oxford, and former Secretary of the Oxford University Delegacy for Extra-Mural Studies, as Director. (Ashby 1966, chapter x; *Annual*

*Report, 1973-4)*. The University grew more rapidly, though constrained by the small scale on which the main buildings were originally designed. Many innovative programmes were started, often assisted by external funding. The M.A. programme and research publications of the Institute of African Studies, no less than the Music and Dance Troupe, became well known. The Institute's publications were also providing material for improving the content of various courses in African Studies within the degree programmes of the University. Other innovative Institutes included Statistical, Social and Economic Research; Population Studies, and Adult Education. Agriculture started Home Science; Arts a Language Centre; Social Studies started Nursing and Psychology.

Yet in spite of this steady expansion and development, and the appointment of close associates of the Chancellor to key positions in the University, the Government was set on a collision path with the University. It decided to use the transition from College to University to remove expatriates and Ghanaians too vocal in their opposition to policies of the Government. The University resisted. No one responded to an initial letter asking members of staff to reapply for posts in the new University. A later circular indicated that people would be re-appointed without their having to re-apply. In the process, six people were not reappointed, including M. Dowuona, the Registrar, a vocal advocate of university autonomy and maintenance of standards. The Government continued to press unpopular measures on the University - category of "special professor", instituted by and directly responsible to the Chancellor, which the Government wanted to use to reward loyal Ghanaians, irrespective of their status in the University; attempt of Government to control appointment of Heads of Departments; transfer of the University's Faculty of Agriculture to the new University in Kumasi, and the Institute of Education to the new University College in Cape Coast without adequate consultation; expulsion of six expatriate teachers in 1964, etc. As the University resisted, pro-government demonstrators staged confrontation with students or mounted attacks and personal abuse on the Vice-Chancellor and other University officials. Connor Cruise O'Brien resigned at the end of 1965 and was succeeded by his deputy, Alex Kwapong, a distinguished Ghanaian Professor of Classics who seemed to have been more adroit in dealing with the situation. The coup of February 1966 removed Nkrumah but the problem of relations with the Government remained perennial.

The Kumasi College of Science and Technology was constituted as the **Kwame Nkrumah University of Science and Technology**, in the centre of political opposition to the Government. Starting out afresh with a Ghanaian Vice-Chancellor it did not suffer from any colonial hang-ups: no Latin grace or gowns at dinner; rather national dress on formal occasions; residential hostels rather than collegiate Halls of Residence. It soon became well-known for its vocational programmes in Agriculture, Architecture and Building Technology, Pharmacy and Pharmacology, School of Mining and Technology, and the Consultancy Centre, with due attention to appropriate technology. It drew international recognition, co-operation and funding. (Anfom, 1976). Yet it operated within the academic traditions and respect for standards pioneered by Legon. After the overthrow of Nkrumah, its name was changed to the Kumasi University of Science and Technology.

Contrary to the proposed urban community-based university in Cape Coast emphasizing evening programmes for serving teachers and workers, and using existing classrooms and laboratories suitably upgraded, the Government decided on a more ambitious wholly residential **University College of Science Education**. Its purpose was to train large numbers of teachers, for all levels of education - elementary, secondary, teacher training, vocational, agricultural, technical - particularly teachers of science and technology. It acquired a 10 sq. km land, 5 km away from the city. It started classes on the site in temporary buildings with 155 students in 1962 and embarked on elaborate building plans. An Egyptian, an uncle of Mrs. Nkrumah, was appointed Principal. Funds were made available and work started on the project in 1965. A few months later, with the coup that overthrew Nkrumah, funds dried up. Rational development of the campus has remained a problem in view of its distance from town and the separation of residential areas for both staff and students from the classrooms, library, laboratories, administrative buildings and cafeteria, all scattered widely over the enormous campus. It was necessary to carry out drainage and land reclamation in order to provide axis for communication. Seven village communities remain on the campus, posing problems of relations with the University community.

**Cautious Nationalism in Francophone Africa**

Independence made itself felt on higher education in Franco-phone Africa in three principal ways: (i) the independent countries began to make some contribution to the cost of higher education and as a result began to demand some Africanization of the content and management of higher education; (ii) Partly as a result of this, individual countries began to demand from France the establishment of their own institutions, even if they also had to be making some contribution to the cost. Thus Dakar, from the initial concept of a Regional University for all of Francophone West Africa, gradually became the University of Senegal; (iii) Probably because of the strong impact of Unesco in Francophone Africa, the leaders of Francophone universities were particularly active in schemes of inter-university cooperation in West Africa and in Africa as a whole. As a result, those universities probably made more effort than English-speaking universities to facilitate co-operation through language study and exchange of students. However, since expatriates remained firmly in control of the universities throughout the 1960s, the pace of change was rather controlled. The interaction with Anglo-phone universities obviously had some effect. However, in most cases, reforms aimed at Africanising the curricula and decolonizing the structures of control and management did not come to the fore until the 1970s.

**The University of Dakar** began to shed its colonial status from 1966 when the Senegalese Government agreed with France to share in the running costs. The number of students grew from 94 in 1959-60 to 2139 in 1965-6, and 4,163 in 1970-71. Attention was beginning to be paid to the recruitment and training of African staff. Of the initial 106 teachers in 1959-60, only 7 were African, and only one of them had even a Master's degree. In 1970-71, of the 206 academic staff, 45% were African; namely, 30% of the more senior teachers and 60% of the Assistants. The Medical Faculty considered it more important to retain direct equivalence of their degree to that of the Sorbonne than to seek any adaptations in their curricula. However, the Faculty was promoting relevance and reaching out to the wider society through its research institutes of Applied Tropical Medicine, Child Care, and Public Health, and the Centre for psycho-pathological research.

The School of Legal and Economic Studies began to undertake local research, getting ready to offer postgraduate research (third cycle) in the 1970s and professional training in the practice of law. The Faculty of Science introduced courses for teachers and technical people leading to the Diploma in Science. Most of the Africanization of the content was, of course, in the Liberal Arts School, in Philosophy, Classical and Modern Literature, Arabic and Islamic Studies, History and Geography, especially within an innovative degree in Education for teachers. The Institute of Black African Studies (IFAN), the Centre for Research Studies and Documentation on African Institutions and Legal structures, and the Institute of Applied Linguistics were providing relevant material for adapting curricula to African realities. There were postgraduate courses in Linguistics, Philosophy and Sociology, leading to the award of the third cycle degree. The University, in cooperation with the relevant Ministries, also developed a number of vocational schools for the training of people at the sub-professional level: a Training College for Teachers and Inspectors of Schools; an Institute of Technology with several departments, not only in engineering but also in applied biology and chemistry, meteorology, marketing, management, and eventually a data processing centre; an Institute of veterinary science and medicine, school of librarians, archivists and documentalists, and Centre for information studies and sciences, Institute of dental and stomatological science, and a French language and civilization course. (Unesco,1986).

Of particular importance was the growing political significance of the students, as their numbers grew rapidly and they began to exert political pressure through demonstrations; such that political leaders in Senegal began to resent the considerable role of non-Senegalese students in such demonstrations. The Government had moved to consolidate its support in the University among loyalist students and academics, since the trade unions and the bulk of the students and left-wing academics became the focus of opposition to the regime. Against the background of students unrest in France and other places, the years 1968-70 were particularly turbulent in Dakar. At the height of it, in 1969, the Government air-lifted the bulk of students from Côte d'Ivoire, Togo and Benin back home, without prior consultation with the students or governments concerned. That event led to the expansion of university education in the affected countries, as the various national Governments, in consultation with the French Government and French universities, had to take emergency measures to send the more advanced of the deported students to France while accelerating plans for establishing national universities locally.

The Government of Cote d'Ivoire had expressed the desire to have its own university as early as 1958 and had established a Centre for higher education in 1959 with courses in Law, Science and Liberal Arts. However, it was not until January 1964 that arrangements for technical assistance and cooperation with France were concluded. Work began on the University Library and other buildings and a presidential decree established the **University of Abidjan** with schools of law, science, liberal arts and medicine. These were upgraded to Faculties, science in 1966, medicine in 1967, law in 1969 and liberal arts in 1971. As at Dakar, the curricula followed closely the pattern in French Universities, but research institutes tried to explore African realities and provide material for adapting the content of courses. In 1966, the research centres in ethno-sociology and tropical geography were developed into institutes. Other research centres/institutes followed in Applied Linguistics, Audiovisual, History, African art and Archaeology, and Social and Economic Research. These were later constituted into the University Centre for Research and Development (CURD). There was also a vocational Institute of Technology for training technicians. The number of students grew steadily from 66 in 1960 to almost 4000 in 1970-71, with an academic staff of about 250.

Because of its status as a Mandated Territory, the international factor was more prominent in the Republic of Cameroun than in other Francophone countries. This was further heightened when, after a UN plebiscite, Southern Cameroon, hitherto part of the Eastern Region of Nigeria, opted to join the "Federal Republic of Cameroun" in 1961. Tentative steps had been taken between 1959 and 1962 to establish a variety of institutions of higher education: a National School of Administration and Magistracy; a University preliminary studies centre in law and liberal arts, an Institute of the University of Toulouse, managed and taught by professors from Toulouse, sometimes taking turns three weeks at a time, with a class of about 350 in the Certificate course for Proficiency in Law; the UNDP/UNESCO assisted Advanced Teacher Training College; the National School of Agriculture; and the School of Business Management. Unesco was requested in December 1961 to send a team of experts to survey the development of higher education in the Federal Republic of Cameroun and advise. As a result, the Federal University, later renamed **University of Yaounde**, was established in July 1962, as an umbrella institution, to coordinate all the existing sub-professional institutions. The degree programmes of the University were in three Faculties: Science, Arts, and Law and Economics. To these were added the University Centre for Health Sciences (CUSS) in 1969, and the International Advanced School of Journalism in 1970. Student numbers rose very fast: 497 in 1962-63; 788 in 1963-64; 2027 in 1967-8, and 2572 in 1970-71. The number of academic staff rose even more rapidly: 16 in 1962-3; 36 in 1962-3; 51 in 1963-4; 101 in 1967-8; and 200 in 1970-71. The percentage of Cameroonian members rose from none in 1962-63 to 29% in 1965-66, 31% in 1967-68; and 44% in 1970-71, as the students - staff ratio declined from 31 in 1962 to 20 in 1967-8, and 13 in 1970-71.

In Zaire, independence was accompanied by political turmoil, attempted secession, outbreak of civil war, and the full impact of the Cold War which the efforts of the UN were unable to contain. The secessionist Government led by Tshombe closed the State University of Lubumbashi; while the Free University of Kisangani, whose campus was destroyed in the civil war had to move temporarily to the campus of Lovanium. Eventually peace was restored but with the ascendancy of the US which was felt as much in higher education as in other fields. This was manifested in the pattern of technical assistance from USAID and various US Foundations, especially Rockefeller; the gradual restoration of academic life on the three different campuses, of Lovanium, Kisangani and Lubumbashi, and plans for the integration and rationalization of courses in all three to constitute a National University. But again, the reforms belong largely to the 1970s.

## Attempted Federation in East, Central and Southern Africa

The attempt to develop Makerere as an inter-territorial University for all of East Africa at least had a more solid basis than the similar proposal for Ibadan as a University for all of West Africa. Since the de la Warr Commission Report of 1937, Makerere had been viewed as serving and, in fact, had served the needs of the whole of East Africa. The British were determined to decolonize East Africa as a "Community", with an inter-governmental Authority and Assembly managing common services - railways, telecommunication, Airways - co-ordinating tariffs and trans-border trade, and using not only English but also Kiswahili as lingua franca. The inter-territorial University was to be one of the common services. We have noted, however, how the ambition of the European and Asian settlers in Kenya led to the establishment of the Royal Technical College, not only for technology, but also for economics and commercial subjects. The position of Makerere became threatened when the RTC registered its students for the external degrees of London. The Carr-Saunders Working Party of 1955 gave de facto recognition for the RTC to develop into a University College in special relations with London, and took note of the ambition of Tanzania to establish a University College in Dar-es-Salaam. The Lockwood Report of 1958 tried desperately to rationalize courses between the three Colleges within a proposed Federal University of East Africa, with a single Vice-Chancellor, common Senate and Council. The Federal University was established in 1963 but, like the East African Community itself, it did not long survive the attainment of political independence.

In spite of common boundaries, utilities, and shared colonial legacy, internal pressures and policy orientations in each of the territories generated divergent developments which fractured the will for the concept of Community. In particular, the role of European settlers in Kenya politics and economy produced negative reactions in both Uganda and Tanzania. As for the University itself, the transition from a University College of East Africa to Makerere University College at par with the former RTC of Nairobi and a proposed University College of Dar-es-Salaam produced inevitable tensions. It was frustrating, perhaps more so for the long established Makerere, but hardly less so for the still to develop Nairobi and Dar-es-Salaam. Planned expansion and developments at Makerere had to be retarded or truncated. Nairobi could not keep to the allocated disciplines of engineering, architecture and basic Arts and Science, nor could Dar-es-Salaam agree to concentrate on Law. A Committee chaired by Davidson Nicol of Fourah Bay College, including an American, a Canadian and a British, was called in to advise on priorities and allocation of resources and responsibilities, but it was not an easy task. Planning of development and allocation of resources within the Senate and Council was made impossible by the rival political pressures of three independent countries, each with its own political and developmental ambitions. Tanzania declared for village-based African socialism, Uganda of the Common Peoples' Charter moved in the same direction of socialism and centralized planning, while Kenya was for a capitalist approach to development. Tanzania moved in 1966 to involve the students in the life of the village communities through compulsory national service. The students resisted and 323 of them were expelled.

The University was autonomous, granting its own degrees, but it remained under the tutelage of the IUC which had to be consulted over appointments of staff, external examiners, and expert advisers. The Vice-Chancellor, most Deans and senior academics were expatriates. In 1963 only about 10% of staff were East Africans, and the pace of Africanization was slow, partly because of the competing demand for qualified people in the Civil Service and within the private sector. The politics of independence dictated that as soon as the concept of the East African Community lost its attraction, the University Colleges developed into separate Universities, with the President of each country becoming the Chancellor of his own university. (Southall, 1974).

Malawi and Zambia became independent countries on the ashes of the Federation of Rhodesia and Nyasaland. The failure of the University College of Rhodesia and Nyasaland to become a non-racial or multi-racial institution, serving the needs of African peoples no less than those of the European settlers who were only a small minority, was itself one of the factors justifying the breakup of the Federation. It followed, therefore, that both Zambia and Malawi would seek each to establish its own University, as a matter of priority as soon as it achieved independence.

Zambia sought the advice of a joint Anglo-American Committee selected by the IUC and the American Council on Education, under the chairmanship of John Lockwood, and financed jointly by the U.K. Ministry of Overseas Development and the Carnegie Corporation . They advised the establishment of an autonomous University in Lusaka, granting its own degrees, responsive to the real needs of the country, but which at the same time should win the respect and gain proper recognition of the university world. In view of the long neglect of secondary education, the University was to admit students from the School Certificate for a four year degree programme, so as to open access to a wider range of students and offer both degrees and diploma courses. Its priority was to produce personnel to replace Europeans particularly in the Civil-Service and as teachers. A Provisional Council, including Eni

Njoku, then Vice-Chancellor of the University of Lagos, was established to plan the initial courses. The Council selected another Nigerian, Saburi Biobaku, then Deputy Vice-Chancellor, University of Ife, as the first Vice-Chancellor but, after accepting, he changed his mind and opted to go to Lagos instead. Douglas Anglin of Canada was then selected, with a Zambian, Lameck Goma, as his Deputy. The University was inaugurated in 1966.

Malawi sought advice from the American Council on Education. Funded by the USAID, a Committee chaired by Eldon L. Johnson, an American, with John W. Blake of Britain, Arthur Porter of Sierra Leone and Twum Barima of Ghana, visited Malawi and advised on the establishment of an autonomous University. They also favoured admission at the School Certificate level. They envisaged a small University, integrating all post-secondary institutions in the country, granting both degrees and diplomas, and avoiding at least for a long while such expensive faculties as Medicine, Architecture and Engineering since it was cheaper to send the few candidates in those fields to study abroad. The University thus had four constituent parts: (i) Bunda College of Agriculture, near Lilongwe, granting both diplomas and degrees in Agriculture; (ii) Chancellor College, the seat of the Vice-Chancellor, in Zomba, offering diploma and degree courses in Education, basic Arts and Science, and Public Administration; (iii) the Kamuzu College of Nursing; and (iv) the Polytechnic in Blantyre for diploma and degree courses in Business Studies, Technology, Commerce, and Management.

The attempt to create a Federal University for the three High Commission territories in Southern Africa was viewed, not as a matter of planned deliberate choice, but of necessity because each territory was regarded as too small to sustain a university. Secondary education was little developed. The few candidates seeking University education were content to study in South Africa until the rise of Bantu Education barred the way, and encouraged the development of Pius XII College as a Roman Catholic sponsored university college like Lovanium, without the direct linkage with a more established university. The College then began to cater for students from all three territories, though the vast majority were from Lesotho. Decolonization and approach towards independence brought international assistance, notably from the US, Canada, and the UK, to build up a credible federal university, to strengthen the will of the three territories to resist incorporation into the apartheid system of South Africa. Thus, the University of Basutoland, Bechuanaland and Swaziland (UBBS), later Botswana, Lesotho and Swaziland (UBLS), was inaugurated in 1964 with John W. Blake, a professor of history from Keele University, as the first Vice-Chancellor. The problem was that the University was never fully federal, since it had virtually no physical presence in Botswana and little in Swaziland. In 1966, the Swaziland Agricultural College became the location for some University activities, and in 1970 the College was formally handed over to the University. Funding and staffing were difficult and, even in Lesotho, there were questions being asked as to how much impact the University was making on the manpower and other needs of the country. It was obvious that the federal structure of the University could not long survive such strains as each country consolidated its achievement of political independence and sought ways of accelerating its development programmes.

**Conclusion**

The 1960s, the decade of independence, made a significant impact on the development of higher education in Africa. This was most noticeable in the increase in the number of institutions and of students, as well as the increasing variety of courses, especially vocational and professional. The newly established independent governments made their impact felt in asserting their sovereign rights to own and to control their universities. This was made manifest in the failure to sustain attempts to create inter-territorial or regional centres of higher education. The intention of governments in seeking to control the universities was usually stated as being to make them more responsive to development plans. In fact, the governments cared much less about the curricula than about administrative control - the appointment of the Chancellor, members of Council, Vice-Chancellor and, if possible, Deans and Heads of Departments. They interfered more with institutional autonomy than with academic freedom. The aim was to ensure the political support or, at all events, to eliminate opposition within the university community.

To some extent, the politicians regarded the universities, dominated as they were by expatriate staff, as part of the apparatus of imperialism, comparable to multinational corporations, which had to be decolonized. (Mazrui, 1978). To that extent, the politicians had the support of many African academics in their struggle to control and direct the universities. In what has been called "a destructive conflict", it was the expatriate staff defending their established privileges who called for the defence of university autonomy and the maintenance of universal standards while the African staff, many of whom felt alienated and discriminated against, tended to seek the intervention of the politicians to give the universities a national character and ensure rapid Africanization. (Mamdani, 1993). This failure of many African academics to fully appreciate the necessity to defend autonomy in the long-term interest of the academy was one of the most enduring legacies of the colonial situation.

In pursuit of policies of Africanization, university staff training and development schemes were actively promoted through postgraduate work locally and link arrangements with overseas universities. Government scholarship programmes were sometimes also extended to include scholarships for postgraduate work. However, once the main administrative positions in the universities were Africanized, the Africanization of academic positions was not a priority for the politicians. Their priority was to get the universities to produce the graduates and professionals to replace expatriates in the civil service and the parastatals, and reduce the dependence on expatriate teachers in the schools. They were content, in the meantime to leave the bulk of the teaching and research to expatriates, if necessary. It was assumed that if the replacement of expatriates would not lead to a lowering of standards, the African graduates should possess qualifications equivalent to those of the expatriates they were replacing.

Thus, the external factor remained important in the development of African higher education. Indeed, it was enhanced by the politics of the Cold War and US/USSR rivalry in the field of technical assistance programmes. African governments and the universities tried to exploit this in order to dilute the over-dependence on the former colonial powers in the recruitment of funds and personnel. To some extent, this external factor remained a constraint in the desire of government functionaries to exercise control over the universities. The theme of giving an African identity to the universities was harped upon from time to time. Institutes of African Studies were established and more attention given to African languages and oral traditions. But, in practice, the issue of African identity was not yet on the priority agenda. Promoting it through inter-university cooperation was one of the main objectives of the newly founded Association of African Universities.

Chapter 5

# THE ASSOCIATION OF AFRICAN UNIVERSITIES

## Antecedents

The Association of African Universities (AAU) which was inaugurated in Rabat, Morocco on November 12, 1967 was the product of several initiatives. The colonial powers establishing pioneer university institutions in Africa, especially the British and the French, often held inter-governmental meetings to discuss the pace of development and the nature of university institutions most appropriate to the conditions in Africa. The Ministers of Education of newly independent African countries met under the auspices of the UN Economic Commission for Africa (ECA) in Addis Ababa in May 1961 to discuss the importance of education to economic development. During the meeting, a committee of six African states was asked to prepare "a synthesis of the educational goals, targets and qualitative attainments during the next twenty-five years decided by the African states". This became known as the 20-Year Addis Ababa Plan. The Ministers of Education met in Paris under the auspices of UNESCO in April 1962 and decided to constitute themselves into a standing committee to implement the Plan.

From within the university institutions themselves, expatriates-dominated as they were at the time, there was felt the need for cooperation in adapting the foreign model to suit African conditions. Davidson Nicol, a distinguished African scientist and Principal of Fourah Bay College, conscious of the historic role of FBC in Africa, convened a meeting of the heads of West African Universities at an International Seminar on Inter-University Co-operation in West Africa in Freetown, in December 1961. The prevalent view was that adaptation would come partly from increased attention to African studies in research institutes and in using the results to Africanize the curricula, and partly in the collective response of African universities to shared problems of Africa which distinguished them from their European models. They thus moved tentatively through various proposals for committees and commissions working across the English/French divide, establishing regional centres, pooling resources and sharing facilities, towards the idea of an Association of (West) African Universities. This became more explicit at the UNESCO/IAU sponsored conference on Higher Education in Africa in Tananarive in September 1962. Apart from such expected tasks as "to teach and advance knowledge through research; to maintain adherence and loyalty to world academic standards; and to train the `whole man' for nation building", the conclusions and recommendations of the Conference were that the role of higher education in Africa must include a commitment "to ensure the unification of Africa; to encourage elucidation and appreciation for African culture and heritage, and to dispel misconceptions of Africa through research and teaching of African Studies; and to evolve over the years a truly African institution of higher learning dedicated to Africa and its people, yet promoting a bond of kinship to the larger human society". (UNESCO, 1963)

Although the majority of the participants at Tananarive were expatriates, the few Africans present were very active. A committee of four African scholars, chaired by Rochefort Weeks, President of Liberia University and Rapporteur of the Conference, prepared the Tananarive statement on targets and recommendations on Higher Education in Tropical Africa. It was the Committee that decided to convene a meeting of heads of African institutions of higher learning in Khartoum in September 1963, hoping that the presence of heads of North African institutions would ensure that a sizable proportion of the group would be Africans. The Khartoum meeting, chaired by El Nazeer Dafaala, Vice-Chancellor of the University of Khartoum proposed a draft constitution for adoption at a planned inaugural meeting. That meeting was twice postponed due to the political climate prevailing in both Nigeria (Ahmadu Bello University, Zaria) and Egypt (University of Alexandria) which had offered to host it. It was finally held at the University of Rabat in Morocco on the initiative of the Rector, Mohammed El Fasi, a former Minister of Education and Chairman of the UNESCO Executive Board.

On the level of ideology, the AAU was seen as part of the evolving Pan-African organizations under the general umbrella of the Organization of African Unity (OAU). Thus, the Report of the Executive Vice-President to the Second Conference of the AAU in Kinshasa, 1969, saw the AAU and its scholarship programme as an attempt "to create the type of students, of future leaders, who through their assimilation in more than one African social scene, will develop an awareness of the realities and aspirations, of the traditions and ideals of their peoples in Africa and hence a sense of belonging not to one tribe or nation but to Africa as a whole, and this is the unity of Africa which we like to see and are out to achieve."

The scholarship programme was the specific project used to actualize inter-university cooperation. The programme as noted earlier, went back to the initiative of Tom Mboya, the Kenyan Trade Unionist and political leader and his scholarship project in 1958-61. In order to regularize, broaden and institutionalize the programme, the USAID agreed to fund the African Scholarship Programme of American Universities (ASPAU) through the African-American Institute (AAI). To meet the objection that ASPAU was undermining the development of higher education in Africa by drawing the best students away from African universities, AAI started organizing an INTERAFrican scholarship programme, to channel qualified African students to different African universities outside their own countries because of the lack of either space or of the desired discipline in their own countries. Thus the INTERAF began to focus attention on undergraduate studies leaving ASPAU, and the later AFGRAD, for postgraduate and staff development. The AAI and the USAID welcomed the formation of the AAU as the body best placed to take over the running of INTERAF and recommending students for ASPAU. The offices of the African-American Institute were thus available to provide initial secretariat support. The overheads built into the Scholarship Programme was also important revenue for the AAU. In 1969, the budget of the AAU was $63,000 and expected income from subscriptions by member universities was only about $30,000. The gap was to be filled partly from the scholarship programme and the rest from appeals to the governments, OAU and other possible donors.

## Early History

The objectives of the Association were stated in the 1969 Constitution as follows:
(a) To promote interchange, contact and cooperation among university institutions in Africa;
(b) To collect, classify and disseminate information on higher education and research, particularly in Africa;
(c) To promote cooperation among African institutions in curriculum development and in the determination of equivalence of degrees;
(d) To encourage increased contact between its members and the international academic world;
(e) To study, and make known the educational and related needs of African university institutions and, as far as practicable, to coordinate the means whereby those needs may be met;
(f) To encourage the development and wider use of African languages;
(g) To organize, encourage and support seminars and conferences between African university teachers, administrators and others dealing with problems of higher education in Africa.

The administrative structure established consisted of three organs: The General Conference, the Executive Board and the Secretariat. The General Conference meets once every four years to elect a new executive board and to approve programmes and budgets for the next four years. The Executive Board which meets annually has the responsibility of ensuring, on behalf of the General Conference, that the Association is being run as approved. The Secretariat, headed by a Secretary-General who should, preferably, have headed an African university, ensures the day-to-day running of the Secretariat. The Secretariat reports to the Executive Board. The Constitution was amended during the Eighth General Conference in 1993 to include an Executive Committee of the Executive Board that would meet every six months and thus be in a position to keep more closely in touch with the activities of the Secretariat.

When in 1963 leaders of African institutions of higher education decided in Khartoum to form the Association of African Universities, follow-up action was entrusted to Dafaala who helped organize the inaugural meeting in Rabat. The University of Khartoum then seconded him, as Executive Vice-President, with salary, to the Association's office which was in Khartoum until a decision on a permanent location was taken. A subsidiary office, within the AAI offices in Lagos, was opened to operate the scholarship programme supervised by a Sub-Committee of the Executive Board, under the chairmanship of the Vice-Chancellor of the University of Lagos.

Meetings of the Executive Board were held in Rabat November 14, 1967; Accra January 22-23 1968; Kampala 21-22 October 1968; Cairo 6-7 April 1969, and 13-15 November in Kinshasa, just before the Second General Conference, 19-20 November. The decision on the permanent location of the Association's headquarters was taken at the sixth Meeting of the Executive Board at the University of Lagos, Nigeria from June 15 to 17, 1970. A total of seven offers had been received and Ghana, Sudan and Uganda had been short-listed. Ghana was chosen upon presentation by the then Vice-Chancellor of the University of Ghana at Legon, Professor A. Kwapong, of a formal letter from the Government of Ghana indicating the facilities and immunities that would be accorded to the Association. These included offices, 6 units of housing, diplomatic status and exemption from local taxation for the senior international staff, and a contribution to the Endowment Fund.

Tidiane Sy was appointed Assistant Secretary-General at the same meeting and was to ensure leadership until Y.K. Lule, a former Principal of Makerere University College was appointed the first Secretary-General of the Association at the end of 1972. The two-year delay is explained by the fact that the position had been offered to, and turned down by, Saburi Biobaku, then Vice-Chancellor of the University of Lagos, Nigeria. The highlight of Tidiane Sy's tenure was the organization of the

1972 Accra Workshop on *Creating the African University: Emerging Themes of the 1970s*. The aim was, through inter-university cooperation, to seek collective ways of making the university models inherited from the colonial past more African and more relevant to African realities. It was a major effort to respond to the objectives of the Association concerning co-operation in tackling the educational and related needs and other problems of African universities, importance of African studies and languages, etc. The Proceedings of the Workshop has remained a major landmark in the evolution of the African university.

Lule organized the Third General Conference of the Association in Ibadan in 1973, and put the Secretariat on a firm footing, including the establishment of a Documentation Centre. He left the Association in 1976 to become actively involved in the politics of Uganda and, later, albeit briefly, its Head of State. He attended the 5th General Conference of the Association in that capacity at Khartoum, thus "demonstrating clearly that his heart (was) still with the academic world and more particularly with the Association of African Universities". Levy Makany, Rector of the Marien Ngouabi University, succeeded him as Secretary-General in 1977. In May 1983, he concluded a report entitled *Fifteen Years of Inter-university Cooperation in Africa* as follows:

> [Our] successes and failures relate to an epoch. In this world of constant change we should not be overly proud of our successes nor be overwhelmed with disappointment over our failures. We should face the future boldly, keeping our aims in view and making a firm resolution to attain them, and seeking the ways and means of attaining them.

> It is an obvious truth that the Africa of tomorrow, united and prosperous, will bear the mark of what we do today. That the Africa of tomorrow will be stamped with the politics of our governments is certain, but it will also bear the indelible mark of the seal of the education and the training that the universities will have provided on the continent. (Makany, 1983).

The post INTERAF days were difficult and, at the time Makany was writing, the AAU was traversing its lowest period yet with the period from 1981 to 1983 being dubbed "the crisis years". Communications on the continent were still very difficult and yet one of the objectives of the AAU was "to encourage increased contact between .... members and the international academic world". The AAU cooperates with Unesco and the International Association of Universities (IAU). It also maintains close links with the Association of Commonwealth Universities (ACU), the Association of Partially or Wholly French-speaking Universities (AUPELF), Association of Arab Universities, and others. However, the lack of an adequate communication structure also implied inadequate visibility to universities and to potential donors. The increase of AAU's visibility and enhancement of communication structures between universities and between them and the Association was to become one of the principal recommendations of the Management Review commissioned by Professor Donald Ekong, Makany's successor.

Donald Ekong, former Vice-Chancellor of the University of Port Harcourt in Nigeria, joined the Secretariat as Secretary-General in September 1987. This was at a time when the international community showed more interest in African education which culminated in the formation of the Donors to African Education Task Force whose mandate is to look at issues at all levels of African Education and seek ways of giving support whenever possible. In 1991, the idea of a cohesive programme as opposed to a series of projects became a reality and has attracted interest from various quarters. The emphasis on regional cooperation, whose aim is to maximize the use of available resources has been acclaimed as the future path of Africa's development. In this connection, two regional groups are most noticeable: the Association of Rectors and Vice-Chancellors of West Africa (i.e. of ECOWAS countries), and the Association of Eastern and Southern Africa Universities (AESAU).

**Student and Staff Exchange**

In the twenty-six years since the founding of the Association, the successive Secretary-Generals have attempted, within the limits of the human and material resources available to them, to implement the stated objectives. During the first few years of the Association, emphasis was laid on the first objective: "to promote interchange, contact and cooperation among university institutions in Africa". During the first decade, the (INTERAF) Scholarship Programme was utilised to facilitate the sharing of university-level training facilities available in some countries with those countries which did not have them, or enough of them. African students who would have otherwise gone to the more developed countries of Europe and North America for undergraduate courses were thus enabled to take these courses in conditions approximating more nearly to the conditions under which they would work. By agreements with the universities and respective governments, INTERAF Students paid only the subsidized rates payable by the nationals. Each receiving university and country thus made substantial contributions to the Scholarship Programme.

INTERAF was designed in such a way that after the initial years of co-management with the AAU, the AAI would pass total responsibility for it to the AAU. The program was eventually phased out as most African countries established institutions of higher learning and those who did not, made bilateral arrangements with other countries. AFGRAD, a staff-development program was then initiated by the AAI but this involved smaller numbers and lasted a shorter time. It does not appear that the overall achievements of this programme were evaluated. However, from what can be gleaned from the files, it made an impact at the level of staff development in African countries.

Since INTERAF was the first major project to be managed by the AAU it might be useful to see what lessons were learnt from the experience. First, it appears that there might have been some misunderstanding as to the respective roles that AAU and AAI officials were to play in the co-management. Secondly, although from time to time, others contributed funds to the scheme, for example the UK Ministry of Overseas Development, and Canadian AID, the USAID funding of the order of 1m dollars annually was predominant. Thus, when the AAI withdrew, it left a gap in the finances that took the AAU several years to fill, - hence underlining the need for diversified sources of funding in order to ensure some measure of stability.

The AAU has maintained, in the spirit of that first objective, a staff exchange programme over the years though on a low-key basis. In 1991, however, subsequent to recommendations from an AAU Management Review, the Ford Foundation gave a grant to revitalize this programme that is perhaps the most requested and appreciated of all AAU's projects. In addition, a number of donors have given funds to the AAU to run a student exchange programme, notably the German Academic Exchange Service (DAAD).

## Information and Documentation Centre

The second objective: "To collect, classify and disseminate information on higher education and research, particularly in Africa" seems to have been one of the most discussed and perhaps the most controversial. It was one of the main programme activities adopted at AAU's first General Conference in Rabat, Morocco from 9th to 13th November, 1967. Dafaala, the Executive Vice-President, reported at the second General Conference: "other schemes which the Association is either handling or hoping to handle are exchange of information which it has started, the building of a documentation centre which is being done...."

By the time the third General Conference was held at the University of Ibadan

(Nigeria) from 9th to 14th April 1973, considerable work had gone into the establishment of the Association's documentation centre. At that conference, the Secretary-General, Y.K. Lule, reported that assistance had been sought from, and given by, the West German Government who provided the services of an expert documentalist, Dr. H. Lass, who visited Accra in August 1971 and, after consultation with headquarters staff, produced a set of recommendations. These recommendations were accepted by the Secretariat which then proceeded to solicit for funds to set up the Documentation Centre. The French Government responded with a grant with which the secretariat was able to make a start by appointing an Assistant Documentalist. Work was started on establishing contact with university libraries and others throughout Africa and collecting material. In February 1972, the Ford Foundation announced a two-year grant for the Documentation Centre. The Centre had already established a procedure for processing, classifying and cataloguing information from various universities and research organizations and disseminating it. A list of post-graduate studies offered at most African universities had been compiled and circulated. Plans were under way to start collecting material on current research in different fields and to distribute it to all universities. In addition, the Secretariat was regularly advised by a number of universities about vacancies on their staff, compiled the information thus received, and disseminated it to member universities and other interested bodies. Lule indicated in his report to the Third General Conference at Ibadan that,

> The Documentation Centre is destined to play a very important role in the future in the co-operative efforts of our universities. Lines of communication must be kept open between scholars with common interests in research and study. This is essential in order to avoid duplication of effort and to enable research workers and others decide on the areas of cooperation which would be beneficial to all concerned. The Documentation Centre must therefore be developed further and kept alive ... It is therefore imperative ... to keep this essential line of communication between African scholars open and alive.

In 1974, the Documentation Centre published the first edition of the Directory of African Universities, which is a listing of African universities with names of Chief Officers and a list of constituent schools, colleges and faculties. Although originally planned as a two-yearly publication, the second edition was published only in 1988 and the third in 1993. The centre also introduced the Bulletin of African Universities which was published biennially and which was meant to disseminate information on higher education in Africa and, later, a Who's Who in African Education. In 1980, the Documentation Centre published the first edition of the Association's Newsletter. It was "favourably received by the public". Also, in 1980, the first hint of wishing to computerize the Documentation Centre was made with reference to the PADIS (Pan-African Development Information System) Network. In 1984, the Centre acquired a publishing unit which was disposed of in 1993. In subsequent years, regular mention is made of the expected role of the Documentation Centre within the framework of AAU's objectives.

Two review missions of the Documentation Centre were undertaken, the first by J.K.T. Kafe and G.F. Daniels in 1982, and the second by Dejen Abate. In December 1991, at the request of the Secretary-General, James J. Murray III, of the American Council on Education, undertook a review of the Information/Documentation Programme of the AAU and recommended that the role of the AAU as a depository of documentation on higher education in Africa and elsewhere be minimized, and that the Association concentrate on improving the quality of internally produced documents such as the Newsletter, the Directory of African Universities and other documents. He further recommended the enhancing of the AAU's visibility in member universities as well as improved communication with them. A Communications Officer and a Documentation Officer have been appointed to help rationalize the operation of the Information and Documentation Centre and to explore the possibilities of electronic linkages between member universities and between them and the AAU.

The objective of the AAU to serve as a clearing house for information has therefore evolved over the years and is still evolving hopefully in a way that will prepare the Association to meet the communications challenges of the 21st century.

## Programmes

As has already been indicated, INTERAF and AFGRAD constituted the major programmes during the first two decades of the Association. Other projects fitted in as financing became available. The Association followed up the Accra Workshop on Creating the African University with others on more specific areas of the curricula requiring adaptation in African Universities. These included:

- The Teaching of History in African Universities, Lagos, 1977.
- The Teaching of African Languages in African Universities, Lagos, 1981.
- The Teaching of Biology and its Impact on the Development of Africa, Brazzaville, 1983.

In addition, meetings of Deans and Heads of Departments of specific areas of concern in the universities were held: Directors of Institutes of African Studies, Deans of Medicine, Deans of Engineering, etc. As underfunding and the crisis of African universities deepened in the 1980s, attention was shifted from curricula reform, partly to issues of relevance of the universities to development, partly to improving the internal management of the universities. The Association organized two seminars:

- Administration and Management in African Universities, Arusha, 1984
- University Resources and Financial Management in Universities of West Africa, Lome, 1987.

In collaboration with the ECA, the AAU organized a series of activities in connection with the African Priority Programme of Economic Recovery, 1986-90 (APPER). This included the "2,000 Scholarships for Women Project"; Staff Exchange Programme, and assisting participation in international meetings. The AAU also commissioned a number of studies, including (i) Cost Effectiveness and Efficiency in African Universities; (ii) University-Productive Sector Linkages; and (iii) Graduate Education in Western and Central Africa. Similarly, the AAU cooperated with UNESCO in the Priority Africa Programme Seminar Series on Restructuring the African University, the first of which, in Accra in 1991, on Planning, Management and Governance of Higher Education in Africa, the AAU helped to organize.

In 1991, however, during negotiations for funding with IDRC, it was suggested that the time had perhaps come for the AAU to have a more holistic approach to its activities and the concept was mooted of four-year Core Programmes, around which would be articulated the major preoccupations. The 1993-1996 Proposal divides AAU activities into two major components: Membership Services and Regional Cooperation to revitalize Higher Education in Africa. Among programmes planned under Membership Services were: Staff Exchange, Fellowships and Scholarships, and Information Exchange. The wider area of Regional Co-operation to Revitalize Higher Education in Africa is covered under four sub-headings: Regional Co-operation in Graduate Education and Research; Improvement of Teaching and Learning in African Universities; Strengthening Leadership and Management of African Universities; and Emerging Issues in Higher Education and Development.

**Financing**

At the time of the inauguration of the AAU, there were forty-six (46) institutions of higher learning that qualified for membership of the AAU; thirty-eight (38) of them joined in 1968, a further three in 1969, bringing it to a total of forty-one (41) by 1969. In April 1994, the number of member institutions had risen to 120. During the 8th General Conference in Accra from January 18 to 23, 1993, the by-laws were changed to allow for associate membership of the Association and the International Centre of Insect Physiology and Ecology (ICIPE) became AAU's first associate member.

Membership dues depend on the category of membership and the number of students an institution has, and are currently as follows:-

| | |
|---|---|
| 500 students and over: | US$ 3,000 |
| less than 500 students: | US$ 2,500 |
| Associate Member: | US$ 1,500 |

Although non-payment of dues by members remains one of the most difficult issues with which the AAU is confronted and the current debt owed to the AAU by member universities is well over one million US dollars, it is nevertheless important to point out that those universities that do pay their subscriptions have faithfully sustained the Association over the years. Of the secretariat's current annual general administration budget of approximately $300,000, subscriptions account for two thirds. Further, as efforts at the secretariat are made to strengthen communication between the AAU and member universities, it can be expected that universities will become more and more aware of AAU's activities and therefore more inclined to pay. On the whole, participation in AAU's activities is limited to those institutions which are financially in good standing although exceptions are occasionally made in order to ensure a more equitable distribution of activities both geographically and linguistically. Enough emphasis cannot be laid on the importance of African universities assuming financial responsibility of the Association. That the African countries themselves are confronted with multiple financial and other problems is a well-known fact; further, contributions are paid in hard currency and it is not only to the AAU that African countries are indebted. They are no less in arrears in their contributions to the UN and the OAU organizations to which their political commitment is certainly not in doubt. Yet, if universities perceive the Association as a useful organ for articulating their concerns, then their financial and other obligations should be met so as to boost the Association's credibility.

Donor Agencies have rallied to the support of the AAU from its inception. Cooperation at given historical moments depended on whether AAU's objectives coincided with those of specific Donor Agencies. The formulation of a well thought-out Core Programme has led to a perceptible mobilization of donors around the AAU with multi-year grants so that it is now possible to plan three or four years ahead. In addition, as a result of informal consultations between the AAU and the donor community during the 8th General Conference (Accra, January 1993), it was mutually agreed that regular consultations be arranged so that donors can be up-dated on AAU's activities and, in turn, make comments and suggestions. The first two such meetings were organized in Dar-es-Salaam (September 1993) and Dakar (May, 1994). They are usually organized to coincide with other meetings that both the donors and some staff members of the AAU would normally be expected to attend so as to minimize expense.

From the outset, it was expected that African governments would regularly support the Association and, indeed, a number of countries did give or pledge to give grants to an Endowment Fund. However, as they themselves have been faced with increasing financial and political problems at home, not to mention the many international and regional organizations that they have to contribute to, this support has dwindled, with Nigeria being the only country that still makes a regular monetary contribution to the Association, along with Ghana, the host country, which continues to contribute generously in kind. Efforts are currently being made to sensitize African governments to the need to support this apex Association that is being more and more recognized as the mouthpiece for higher education on the continent.

There have been close links between the Organization of African Unity (OAU) and the AAU since the inception of the latter. The AAU was given observer status at meetings of the OAU. As noted earlier, it would appear that the AAU's founding fathers envisioned the AAU as an Association that would bring together African universities in the same way that the OAU had brought together newly independent African countries. As expressed in the Preamble to the Constitution, "We, the Heads of Universities and University institutions in Africa ... have resolved to establish a corporate body to achieve our aims and objectives in harmony with the spirit of the Organization of African Unity". The OAU was therefore supportive of the AAU and has regularly given it financial assistance although the amounts have decreased over the years as its own financial situation has been adversely affected by the financial crisis on the continent. In addition, the OAU has always given, and continues to give, unwavering political support to the Association.

## AAU Evaluation

An Association of the stature of the AAU can only progress through a continual process of both external and internal evaluation. The first evaluation of the AAU on record was undertaken by the Canadian International Development Agency (CIDA) in 1987, aimed at assessing AAU's capacity for managing a CIDA-funded scholarship programme. The outcome must have been positive since CIDA entrusted to the AAU the management of Africa 2000 Scholarships Programme for Women which enabled 19 women students to undertake studies in 10 countries. The last of the beneficiaries of this scheme are expected to complete their studies in 1996.

Soon after that, the second review was undertaken by Harvey E. Curtman and Hamidou Haidara of Management Consultants Development Associates on behalf of the USAID with a very specific purpose: "to have a look at AAU's capability/capacity to perform certain tasks/functions which might be requested by AID to support the implementation of mutual interests in developing African human resources utilizing African organization(s) for the placement of Africans in various African institutions. (Letter from James Washington, Human Resources Development Adviser, USAID, March 1988).

The reviewers stated that "today's (September 1987) AAU is a weak organization with few if any links to the old INTERAF programme. The principal cause for AAU's decline since the phase-out of INTERAF is its reduced budget. This forced major cut backs in staff and activities which in turn translated into a loss of prestige among member institutions and other organizations". (USAID Review, September 1987, page 19) The AAU Secretariat was of the opinion that the reviewers had not interacted with a sufficiently large number of decision-makers from African universities to warrant the many statements about the AAU contained in the report. In a detailed response to that report, the newly-appointed Secretary-General explained the decline of the AAU as follows:

> The beginning of the decline of the AAU followed the discontinuation in 1980 of the external (mainly USAID) funding for the programme. With the change in AAU leadership by the assumption of office of a new Secretary-General in August 1987 [renewed efforts are] being made to restructure the Secretariat for increased efficiency, to achieve greater cost-effectiveness in the activities of the Association and give them a new impetus, and to expand the funding base of the programmes. The response of the universities to these efforts has been very encouraging. (February 1988, p. 12).

Though this review did not recommend further immediate collaboration between USAID and AAU, it seems to have prompted, from the newly-appointed Secretary-General, not only a lucid and articulate statement of AAU's mission, past activities and future perspectives, but also a re-thinking of the structuring and management of review missions if these were to be beneficial to all interested parties. In October 1991, the Secretariat commissioned a Programmes and Management Review whose terms of reference were: to review all areas of the AAU with particular emphasis on personnel, financial and programmes management and communication. The review was financed by the Ford Foundation and carried out by Gallium T.G. Mohamedbhai and James W. Trowdbridge. In their report, they recommended that more specialized reviews be carried out in the areas of financial management and communications. These were carried out by John P. Doran and James J. Murray III, respectively. The findings of these reviews were discussed by the Executive Board and their gradual implementation is already leading to the emergence of a stronger, more efficient Secretariat. This, in turn, has led to increased interest by Donor Agencies, an ever-increasing budget and more complex Core Programmes. It was only a matter of time before the issue of programme monitoring and evaluation would be raised to enhance the overall programme management and to fulfil the reporting requirements of the various Donors. After discussion in the Secretariat, with Donors and with monitoring and evaluation specialists, a monitoring and evaluation plan was set up. Two consultants are scheduled to work closely with Secretariat Staff to establish evaluation criteria and mechanisms. When this plan becomes functional, it will also serve as an internal tool for continual assessment of programme activities.

**Conclusion**

The AAU has been confronted with specific problems at each stage. But lack of sufficient funds and adequate communications structures can be said to have consistently bedevilled the Association. The launching in 1968 of the Endowment Fund and its re-launching in 1993 could be seen as a possible long-term solution to the first problem. If sufficiently endowed, the resulting yield in addition to contributions from member universities could finance the administrative costs of the Secretariat and such basic programmes as staff and students exchange. Other programmes would still need to be financed by grants from interested donors. In these days when the keyword in project management is sustainability, enhanced endowment is an option worth exploring. The second problem of communications is currently being addressed through the exploration of electronic linkages between member universities and between them and the AAU. So much interest has been shown in this area that one can safely predict that by the year 2000, this problem will have been resolved.

On the section on the Association of African Universities in his study entitled *A Consultation on Higher Education in Africa* (1991), Trevor Coombe wrote:

> There was universal support for the African Association of Universities from the African academic community, from other international university associations, and from donors to African higher education. Under its present leadership, the organization has won respect for its capacity to articulate the interests and needs of its member universities, set an agenda for debate on university reform, and facilitates investigations for a range of important questions in academic planning and management.

> If the AAU did not exist, it would be necessary to invent it. It is difficult to exaggerate the need for a continental body to represent and defend the interests of the African university community, especially at a time of unprecedented privation, when the fortunes of most African states are at a low ebb and their international influence is diminished.

Chapter 6

# HIGHER EDUCATION AND AFRICAN DEVELOPMENT
## (1970s and 1980s)

**Introduction**

In many ways, the Workshop which the AAU organised in 1972 set the agenda for African universities in the following two decades. Creating the African University, which was the theme of the Workshop, had a dual meaning, one stressing the issue of identity and links with the African cultural past, the other responding to the practical needs of the moment, for high level manpower as well as knowledge and skills to create wealth and modernise African societies. While in the colonial period, and even in the Decade of Independence, the issue of African identity was predominant, for the period 1970-90 the emphasis was on relating to the needs and aspirations of the rural communities. As T.M. Yesufu, an economist and manpower planner, who edited the proceedings of the Workshop, put it in his Report, "A truly African University, it was submitted, must be one which, while acknowledging the need to transform Africa into the twentieth century, must yet realize that it can best achieve this result by completely identifying itself with the realities of a predominantly rural 'sixteenth century' setting, and the aspirations of an unsophisticated but highly expectant people..."

It follows that an emergent African university must, henceforth, be much more than an institution for teaching, research and dissemination of higher learning. It must be accountable to, and serve, the vast majority of the people who live in the rural areas. The African university must be committed to active participation in social transformation, economic modernization, and the training and upgrading of the total human resources of the nation, not just of a small elite. (Yesufu, 1973, p. 41).

The politics of independence continued throughout the 1970s to encourage the expansion of higher education in terms of the opening of new universities and increasing both the number of students and the variety of courses available in the existing universities. Attempted inter-territorial universities were broken up into national universities. National systems of higher education, consolidating centralized control by government, were established. Higher education was accepted by the governments as necessary and worthwhile investment in development. The goal of development was seen as modernization of the social, economic and political institutions and processes, bringing them in line with those in the industrialized world, whether capitalist or socialist oriented; and the importance of the role of education, particularly higher education, was not questioned. To begin with, foreign experts generally supported this view of higher education linked to development which encouraged centralized government control, and heightened popular expectations of, and demands on, the universities. The establishment of national universities raised issues not only about ownership but, even more, about the structure, management, definition of goals, and who was to determine these. It therefore also involved the issue of university autonomy and academic freedom, the relationship between government and the academic community of staff and students, and the creation of the atmosphere in which the university could best flourish.

Throughout the 1970s, various overseas donors supported university expansion and institution building, assisting specifically with research programmes and seminars aimed at helping the universities to adapt foreign models of higher education to African realities. After the Accra Workshop, the most sustained effort was probably that of the Rockefeller, Ford Foundation and other donors funding the Higher Education for Development Project of the New York-based International Council for Educational Development. This was a world-wide project under the direction of Kenneth W. Thompson, former Vice-President of the Rockefeller Foundation, comparing how universities in the various developing countries adapt to their role in development. The African Regional Report, and a summary of the Reports from the Asian, Latin American and African task forces, who were all indigenous scholars and university administrators, represent the high-level mark of the external support for African university development. By the 1980s, the World Bank and other influential foreign experts began to see higher education more like social welfare satisfying the needs of the individual than as investment for the common national good. They lost faith in the earlier belief that the universities were the most important instruments of social change, even in the sense of modernization, achieving equality, income redistribution, etc. They imposed measures of structural adjustment on the economies, involving devaluation of currencies, reduction of public expenditure, and shifting resources from higher education to elementary and secondary education. The universities were told to generate funds, and the governments were urged to encourage private universities.

As long as the economies of the African countries continued to grow, the governments made resources available to the universities. The sudden increase in the revenue accruing from the sale of crude oil in Nigeria fuelled one of the most spectacular rates of expansion in higher education. This expansion continued into the 1980s. The rate of opening new universities slowed down, except perhaps in Nigeria and Kenya, but the demands on the existing universities continued to grow. Population growth and improvements in secondary education produced more students who were qualified and anxious to enter the universities than the universities could cater for. Admission to Francophone universities was open to all students with the baccalaureate or the equivalent of the "A" level, and the universities had to try to cope with an unpredictable number of students. Yet in several countries, expansion of universities came more from the political ambitions of politicians, manifested particularly in the pressure for geographical spread of universities. As a result of expansion, the award of bursaries, and the rate, became bones of contention between governments and students organizations. In developing national systems of education, the governments tried to emphasize training in professional schools and institutes where admission and the award of scholarships could be more selective and better controlled.

Resources available to the universities began to dwindle as the economies ceased to grow and even declined; prices of primary products plummeted, the high cost of petroleum products made inflation and the price of imported manufactured goods gallop, and the burden of servicing external debt became unmanageable. For this reason, the relationship between university communities and governments became more troubled. It was as if the governments, having created the universities and nurtured their expansion, and not being able to provide for them so they could become functional, became afraid of what they had created. Many governments, because they lacked legitimacy, shook at the slightest movement of their own shadow, and tended to exaggerate the potential of organized students to initiate revolution. Sometimes, the governments sought control of the universities not because they wished to, or thought that they could, improve their responsiveness to societal needs, but rather   with the hope of destroying the right to criticize and to protest.

## National Universities in East Africa

In the era of de-colonization, while the rest of Africa were struggling to free themselves or consolidate their achievement of political independence, the Portuguese in their African colonies, especially Angola and Mozambique, were pursuing a contrary policy. In imitation of South Africa and Southern Rhodesia, they tried to build up the white settler population ostensibly as a way of discouraging African dreams of self-government. Between 1940 and 1960, the settler population of Angola rose from 40,000 to 250,000, and of Mozambique from 27,000 to 130,000. Developments in education, especially higher education, were meant more for the settlers than for the Africans. Both in Luanda and in Maputo (Lorenço Marques) Centres of General University Studies were established in the 1960s, in affiliation with the University of Coimbra in Portugal, which supplied curricula, staff and technical assistance. These were upgraded to Universities in 1968 as part of the propaganda to combat the liberation movement that broke out into armed struggle in 1964.

By the same token, support measures for the various liberation struggles, in Angola and Mozambique, in Zimbabwe and Namibia, required not only military training and supplies but also higher education for qualified youths and future leaders of the movements. And whenever independence was achieved, existing institutions of higher education received immediate attention in reorganization and nationalization. On the attainment of independence in Angola and Mozambique in 1975, and with substantial assistance of foreign aid, the universities were developed as essential tools of national development. In 1976, the University of Maputo was renamed **Eduardo Mondlane University (EMU)** after the leader of FRELIMO, himself an outstanding intellectual, who was assassinated in 1969. Similarly, the University of Luanda was named **Agostinho Neto University(ANU)** after the leader of MPLA and first President of Angola who died in office prematurely in 1979. The unstable political situation in both countries, however, bedevilled sustained development in the universities. These universities had been trying to develop at the height of the Cold War and in the midst of civil war fostered and financed from outside. In their wars of liberation against Portugal, a staunch member of NATO backed up by the US, they were obliged to seek support from Socialist countries. With their economies already tied to the West during the colonial period, thorough-going socialism was bound to have pockets of resistance. After independence foreign powers, notably the US and South Africa, continued to encourage armed struggle by opposition parties - RENAMO and UNITA - against the socialist governments of FRELIMO and MPLA.

Courses at the EMU were carefully planned and monitored to meet the immediate needs of the Government for relevant manpower. Many of the courses in the previous University of Lourenço Marque were suspended. In 1976 the emphasis was on the Faculties of Law and Economics. In 1980, the Faculty of Education was reorganised for the rapid production of secondary school teachers. In 1984, some of the courses in Science, especially biological and agro-pastoral were restored: An innovative Faculty catering for war veterans and workers was established. By 1986, there were 2,106 students in the university, 1,630 pursuing degree programmes, the others varieties of diploma and certificate courses. 952 or 46% were on bursaries, including 66 non-Mozambicans. There were 365 teachers, of whom 188 were nationals and 177 expatriates, mostly on Technical Assistance programmes. While only 11 of the nationals had doctorate degrees, approximately two-thirds of the expatriates had doctorate degrees. There was no Faculty of Arts, but a well organized Historical Archives of Mozambique and an active Centre of African Studies. Another notable feature of higher education in Mozambique is the number of institutes for the training of middle level technicians and technologists, mostly run by the Ministries. The Ministry of Health has one national Centre and 7 schools for the training of nurses, midwives, pharmacists, para-medical staff, laboratory technicians etc. The Ministry of Agriculture has a 3-year programme for training topographers and land surveyors. Similarly the Ministry of Ports, Railways and Marines has several technical and nautical schools. (Lopes, 1989, pp.70-73).

The ANU is located on three campuses but by far the largest and the oldest is at Luanda - where 3,100 of the 3,900 students in the University are distributed among five Faculties (622 in Economics, 533 in Medicine, 528 in the Sciences, 636 in Law, and 760 in Engineering. The Huambo campus had 465 students, half of them in Agriculture, and the rest shared equally between Economics and Medicine. The campus at Huila was devoted to Education, with 336 students, and 600 others in the Social Sciences studying by correspondence. Political Economy and Marxism - Leninism were compulsory in every Faculty. A major problem was the great diversity of the training and orientation of the 422 teachers, most of them being expatriates - Cubans, Portuguese, Zaireans, Vietnamese, Russians and Latin Americans. Another feature in the dearth of national teachers, was the use of 119 assistants chosen from the most advanced students. As in Mozambique, there were several technical schools at the Intermediate stage, covering a wide range of courses in health, agriculture, technology, accounting, planning, industrial. There were 11 Institutes established by different socialist countries according to different agreements of technical assistance. (Lopes, 1989, pp.23-27).

The Federation of Rhodesia and Nyasaland was formally dissolved in 1963 and the University College of Rhodesia and Nyasaland became the sole responsibility of Britain and the white minority regime of Southern Rhodesia. When the settlers declared Unilateral Declaration of Independence (UDI) in 1965, Britain pulled out, and the settlers later constituted the College as an autonomous University of Rhodesia in 1970. The main development in that period was a Faculty of Engineering with the capital cost raised by public appeal, and with substantial contributions from South Africa, so as to enable the University play an active role in defeating international sanctions imposed on the minority racist regime by the United Nations. It was not until independence was achieved by the African majority, after a long armed struggle and following the elections of April 1980, that the University came into its own as the **University of Zimbabwe**, Harare. Thus, throughout the 1980s, when other universities in Africa were beginning to experience underfunding and structural decay, the University of Zimbabwe flourished within the exhilarating politics of independence until 1990-91 when the Government amended the Act of the University, granting more powers to the Minister and the Council for Higher Education. This politicized the administration, opening the door for the interplay of ethnicity, provoking staff and student resistance, and the eventual resignation of the Vice-Chancellor. That was just when the star of Namibian independence began to rise. Overseas scholarships for higher education had been a significant element in the support measures the UN Council for Namibia organized for SWAPO (South West African Peoples Organization). In the active preparation for independence, the United Nations Institute for Namibia located in Lusaka, Zambia, was organized, ready to transform the Bantustan College in Windhoek into the **University of Namibia** when independence finally came in 1990. In like manner, on the achievement of independence by Eritrea, the **University of Asmara** became one of the important symbols of the sovereignty of the new state, and its development a priority item on the agenda.

The three national universities that grew out of the federal University of East Africa in 1970 illustrate the diverse effects of nationalization on higher education. The most significant was probably the role of the Head of State in his position as the Chancellor (or Visitor as he is known in Nigeria), that is, the proprietor of the University. There was already tension in Dar-es-Salaam between the University College and Julius Nyerere who, as President of Tanzania, had caused the expulsion of 323 students in 1966 for resisting compulsory national service. Nyerere was at the time Visitor of the College and Chancellor of the University of East Africa. There is no doubt that the role of the Head of State as Chancellor of his own national University brought national politics to the University campus with much increased immediacy, and endowed university domestic issues with an uncomfortable measure of national significance. The universities became "political institutions". (Court, 1974). Every students' demonstration or academic strike became a matter for deliberation at the level of the national cabinet.

In setting up **Dar-es-Salaam** as an autonomous **University**, Nyerere had appointed a Commission of Inquiry to advise on reorganization. Being himself an intellectual and an ideologue, he kept the university under very close observation. Its location on one campus at some distance from town seemed only to have facilitated the process of centralized control.  Nyerere was insistent that in a socialist economy, such as he was building within the ideology elaborated in the Arusha Declaration of 1967, there was no room for a university trained elite who looked down upon and had no understanding of the villagers they were meant to serve.  The problem was how to reorganize the University so as to inculcate the new values of vocational commitment to public service.  Direct involvement during the long vacation in developmental projects and sharing the life of the manual workers in the agricultural villages or factories was one way.  Another was to alter admission requirements and demand not merely performance in the School Certificate but also an attestation of character from the village party leaders, and performance in pre-university compulsory national service.  At the University, compulsory subjects like 'East African Society and Environment' or 'Development Studies' are taught in a way to shape orientation and inculcate socialist ideology.

In the end, the basic solution offered was to bring the University community more directly under the control of the ruling and only recognized party.  The former Principal of the University College was appointed an ambassador, and the Executive Secretary of the Party was made the first Vice-Chancellor of the new University.  The Youth Wing of the Party was accorded privileges on campus, and the staff were encouraged to join the Party.  Party control of the day to day life of the University was institutionalized.  On the Council of 28 members the Chancellor appoints the Chairman, the Vice-Chancellor and 7 other members, 2 of them in consultation with the Vice-Chancellor.  The Ministers of Education, Finance and Planning appoint 5 members; the students, 5 members; the National Workers Union and Cooperative Union, one member each; and 3 members by the National Assembly.  The Senate appoints 3, and Convocation one member.  Committees of Council oversee students affairs and staff development, besides estimates and finance.  The budget of the University is presented to Parliament through the Ministry of Education; development plans are routed through the relevant ministries to government.  The University "operates like a Government agency attached to a ministry."  It orientates itself to development not only through changes in its curricula, especially in the social sciences, but also through service institutions located on campus, notably:

- Economic Research Bureau
- Bureau of Assessment and Land Use with specific research topics to be determined by government

- Institute of Kiswahili Research
- Institute of Adult Education, to reach the masses  through evening classes, correspondence courses, radio programmes and special lectures
- Computerization of school examinations of the Ministry of Education
- Consultancy to Government Ministries in various ways. (Mmari, 1976)

Above all, every aspect of university development is integrated into government centralized planning. The most important aspect of this concerned human resource development and allocation. Under this, the Government controlled university staffing and could second staff from government ministries or parastatals to the University and transfer staff from the University into government agencies.   Furthermore, "through its different organs, the Government decides on the national requirement for high-level manpower in the different professions, the civil service, the semi-government organizations and the national institutions".  This planning is detailed enough to break down requirements for B.Sc. Education into students with Mathematics and Physics, and those with Chemistry and Biology.  And the detailed planning reaches down to the schools.

As the new structures began to be unfolded, the students decided to mount resistance in July 1971.  The President of the Students Union was rusticated because of the impertinence of his letter to the Chancellor, and a further period of students unrest ensued. Eventually, Party elders intervened, found that the new Vice-Chancellor had not observed details of University rules of discipline, but refused to approve that the expelled student leader be re-admitted.  The matter was resolved when the student transferred to the University of Nairobi. (Gaidzanwa, 1994, pp.15-16; contrast Shivji 1976, p. 91).  The fears of staff and students were further allayed by the creation of a post of Chief Academic Officer, appointed from among the senior indigenous professors, possibly to make up for the Vice-Chancellor's lack of academic background. He had little power, but much potential for smoothening things over in the background. Dar-es-Salaam soon became known as the prototype of the Developmental University, truly responsive to its society.  Open forum and intellectual debates were encouraged and many radical young expatriate academics were attracted.  It also began to be obvious that the most able Tanzanians, as soon as they had built up some reputation in the University, preferred the more power-laden role of Consultants and Advisers in Government to that of university teachers per se.   Tanzania's second university, established in 1984, is the specialist Sokoine University of Agriculture located in Morogoro, some 200km west of Dar-es-Salaam.

Like Nyerere, Milton Obote similarly ordered a Commission to inquire into the workings of **Makerere** and offer advice on setting up the new University. The main result would appear to have been the replacement of Y.K. Lule, the former College Principal, with Frank Kalimuzo, a top civil servant and Secretary to Obote's Cabinet, as Vice-Chancellor. There was perhaps an ethnic factor involved as Lule, a Muganda and former Secretary to the Kabaka's government, was not acceptable in the climate of Obote's anti-monarchical crusade. Obote himself spent a year at Makerere, but was not a university graduate. General Idi Amin who replaced him in 1971 as Chancellor of the University did not even have the benefit of complete elementary education, and proved to be a capricious and ruthless tyrant. In July 1972, the Vice-Chancellor was kidnapped from his house in the boot of a car and was never seen again. Apparently, this was because the Chancellor had sent a message on the eve of the University Graduation Ceremony, demanding to be conferred with an Honorary Doctorate of Economic Science because of his contribution to the Ugandan economy by his order expelling the Asians. The Vice-Chancellor's reply to the effect that this was not possible because of the necessity to involve Council and Senate in the choice of candidates for such an award obviously made the Chancellor very angry. Other staff and students similarly disappeared and no one knew who was next and for which reason one might become a victim. Expatriate staff, and many Ugandans who could, found their way out. It was not the University alone that was crumbling but the whole state until 1978 when Idi Amin attempted a pre-emptive strike into Tanzania and failed, and Uganda was invaded early in 1979 by Tanzanian forces. Eventually Idi Amin fled, but the various factions of Ugandan exiles could not unite to establish a credible administration in the country. There were frequent changes of regime beginning with that of Lule who only lasted a few months as Head of State. There were civil strifes and coups d'etat. There was no stability in the country or peace on the University campus till the regime of Yoweri Museveni began the period of slow reconstruction in 1986. The most that the University as a corporation, and the individuals within it, could aspire to under the Amin regime was bare survival.

A more stable political order in Kenya protected the **University of Nairobi** from the kind of misfortune that befell Makerere. There was not the same degree of consensus behind a clear ideological position as in Tanzania. Instead of centralized planning, Kenya preferred the policy of laissez-faire and the operation of market forces. As David Court put it:

> Tanzania's deliberate attempt to reduce wage differentials within the society contrasts with Kenya's stress on the functionality of sizable differences as an inducement and reward for effort. The Tanzanian stress on self-reliance and

the search for locally applicable standards and criteria differs sharply from Kenya's concern to preserve 'international standards'. (Court, 1979, para.7).

For example, while in the 1960s both Makerere and Dar-es-Salaam appointed indigenous Principals, the College Council of Kenya, because of the politics of local versus expatriate staff at the time, was obliged to look abroad and appointed a Sierra Leonean historian, Arthur Porter. This might also have been to avoid appointing a Kenyan until a credible candidate from the preferred ethnic background was available. In 1970, a Kenyan diplomat was appointed the first Vice-Chancellor of the new University. Beneath the apparently stable political order was a ruthless struggle for power, first to eliminate the opposition from parliament, then for control of power or strategic positions within the ruling Party. As Jomo Kenyatta aged, and the ethnic factor came to the fore, the struggle for power involved political assassinations, one of the earliest victims being Tom Mboya in 1969. It should be noted however that the struggle within the party was the crucial issue of politics which affected conflicts within the University; but that the University had little effect on the party struggle. The location of the University's main campus on a mere 18-acre site in the city centre, with the rest of the University scattered on other sites, integrated the University staff and students effectively into the social and economic life of the city. There were hostels which provided a focus for students activities, but no housing for staff. The first few generations of Kenyans on the staff were like part of the ruling elite who, in spite of political rivalries, had access to loans to acquire some of the economic gains of independence, usually a house or apartment in the city, and a farm or other source of generating income. This also had a stabilizing effect on the University.

The University grew rapidly. In 1970, Kenyatta College of Education, also in Nairobi, was upgraded to the status of a University College affiliated to the University of Nairobi. The College continued to admit students at the 'O' Level, but gradually the Teachers Certificate course for elementary school teachers was phased out and the College concentrated on a 4-year B.Ed. Degree and a 2-year Diploma course for secondary school teachers in particular areas of need such as Science Education, or areas not at the time catered for at degree level such as Kiswahili, Music and Fine Art. This was followed by the gradual reconstitution of the rest of the University into Colleges - Agriculture and Veterinary Science; Health Sciences; Engineering and Architecture; Adult Education and Distance Learning. This was to decentralize the administration because of the physical separation of the location of the different Colleges. Each College was headed by a Principal. Kenyatta University College had its own Registrar and more autonomy than the other Colleges. In addition, there were the Institutes of African Studies, Computer Science and Development Studies, mostly supported by outside funds, and very active in the area of applied and social science research. By the 1980s, expansion of student numbers and the pressure for the geographical spread of universities necessitated the founding of new universities after a Commission had reviewed the development. The Kenya Council for Higher Education was constituted. Moi University, located at Eldoret, with special emphasis on Agriculture, Forestry and Wildlife Management, was founded in 1984. In the following year, Kenyatta University College was made into a separate University. Egerton University located at Nakuru was founded in 1987 to specialize in Agriculture, Home Economics and Education. Besides these state Universities, there were a number of small private universities, most of them established by American and religious foundations.

## National Universities in Southern and Central Africa

In contrast with the University of East Africa, the breakup of UBLS was more drawn out on account of the small size of the countries and the lack of resources for each of them to develop its own university. A Commission in 1966, chaired by Sir Roger Stevens, then Vice-Chancellor of Leeds University, advised UBLS to seek ways of devolving some of its activities to Botswana and Swaziland. Some courses in agriculture were begun in Swaziland and, as noted earlier, the Swaziland Agricultural College was eventually taken over by the University as its Swazi campus. Little devolution took place in Botswana. The Sir Norman Alexander and Pickard Report of 1969 further emphasized the need for devolution. An enlarged Commission under Alexander in 1970, with members from the US, Canada and the West Indies, recommended how devolution might be done: 2-year Part I courses on each of Botswana, Swaziland and Lesotho campuses, with Part II in all the Faculties on the Lesotho campus. The arrangement remained controversial within each campus and within each government, both on account of the expense and effectiveness, and the equity basis of allocation of resources. The Senate of the University then called for another Commission in November 1973, under the Dean of Education, and with representatives of each campus and government. Their 1974 Report recommended vertical instead of horizontal division, that is, sharing courses and Faculties (as East Africa tried to do) rather than the triplication of Part I courses. They recommended

- Botswana:   Engineering and Earth Sciences + B.A., B.Sc. and B.Ed. in Arts and Sciences,

- Swaziland:   Agriculture + B.A. and B.Ed. Arts
- Lesotho:      Law  + B.Sc. and B.Ed. Science.

This proposal obviously made the Government of Lesotho angry and, in 1975 they decided unilaterally to dissolve  UBLS and develop the Lesotho campus as an autonomous **National University of Lesotho**. Foreign advisers    and donors recognized the inevitability of the break and tried to support not only Lesotho in its effort to build its own university, but also the other two Governments to establish the **University of Botswana and Swaziland**, with its base in Swaziland. Representatives of donors sat on the Council of each University. Even then, it was realized that this could only be a temporary arrangement.  As the economies of both Swaziland and Botswana improved, and the fear of absorption into South Africa diminished, independent Universities of Swaziland and Botswana were established in 1982. (Wodajo, 1976a).

From the beginning the **University of Malawi** was planned as a national system, a 4-campus University embracing all post-secondary institutions, vocational in orientation, and avoiding expensive Faculties like Medicine, Architecture or Engineering beyond the level of the Polytechnic.  What needs to be noted in the 1970s and 1980s was the strict personal surveillance of the Chancellor and 'Life' President of Malawi, Kamuzu Banda; the predominance of expatriate staff, and the prohibition of political activism.  The state's close alignment with South Africa kept the agriculture-based economy relatively buoyant and the University benefited from the Cold War, pro-US/South Africa axis of the Chancellor.  There were four external members of the University Council nominated by the IUC of Britain and the American Council of Education.  Assistance for capital development at the Chancellor College in Zomba came from the UK Government and the Beit Trust of South Africa; and, for the Bunda College of Agriculture, from USAID.  So also the Polytechnic which got assistance from the UK, USAID, African Development Bank and the EEC.

In the face of expanding student numbers and the need to increase the range of academic and professional fields of study and research and in the interest of geographical spread, it was decided in 1975 to reconstitute the **University of Zambia** into a federal university comprising three constituent institutions: namely, "The University of Zambia at Lusaka", "The University of Zambia at Ndola", and "The University of Zambia at a rural campus" (later named Solwezi).  The University of Zambia at Ndola opened in October 1978 and was temporarily accommodated at the Zambia Institute of Technology in Kitwe, pending the physical development of its permanent site in Ndola.  The University of Zambia at Solwezi existed in name only.

The federal scheme proved unsatisfactory as it created difficulties and problems in the life and work of the University. Lack of funds made it impossible to develop the new sites at Ndola and at Solwezi. Eventually, in 1987, the federal scheme was abandoned and university education in the country re-organized into two independent universities: the University of Zambia as it was before 1975, located in Lusaka; and a new university, the **Copperbelt University**, in Kitwe on the premises of the Zambia Institute of Technology, which was itself incorporated into the University as the School of Technology. The Copperbelt University was to develop as a technical university and initially allocated responsibilities for only four Schools of Study: Business and Industrial Studies, Environmental Studies, Forestry and Wood Science, and Technology. By law, the President of the country was Chancellor of both universities. However, with the change of government in 1991, the new President, Frederick Chiluba, refused to take up the Chancellorships. The law was subsequently amended to have separate Chancellors for the two universities to be appointed by the President from among distinguished persons, so judged if they have held high academic or other public office or have attained recognition in their profession.

**The National University of Zaire**

The reform of higher education in Zaire in 1971 was part of the effort of Mobutu and the MPR (Popular Movement for Revolution) to establish hegemony over all the major sectors and institutions of the Republic. The guiding philosophy was the search for what was called "authenticity", basically a search for an African identity. Besides the three different Universities, there were 17 Institutes of higher education, established on different initiatives and with diverse policies. One particular problem was that a number of the Institutes, meant largely to train technicians at the sub-professional level, began to claim the equivalent of degrees. The National Institute of Mines intended to train geologists and mining technicians claimed on its Certificates to be training mining engineers. The National School of Law and Administration actually awarded degrees. Moreover by 1969, the students unions remained the major centre of organized opposition to the regime, since the labour unions had been re-organized as an ancillary of the MPR in 1967. The Youth Wing of the Party was without much influence on the campuses of the different universities. In April 1969, the student unions based on Lovanium, wrote to the government making several demands, including a share in the University administration, similar to students' demands in the US and Europe at the time, and threatening 'revolutionary violence' to back up their demands. A demonstration by the students on June 4 became violent and several dozen students were reported killed by the armed police. The Government dissolved all student organizations except the Youth Wing of the Party. In June 1971, the students, still defiant, tried to celebrate the anniversary of the 1969 demonstrations, resulting in a violent clash with the Army. Lovanium University was closed for 2 years, and all the students conscripted into the Army. (Young and Turner, 1985, p.62). Mobutu decided to consult a meeting of indigenous teachers from all the universities and institutes of higher education, most of them being still very junior. They met at the end of July and, on August 6, the Law establishing the National University of Zaire was promulgated.

Basically, the three universities and the 17 Institutes were merged into a single complex University system and brought under a Council which was under Party control. Initially, the Commissioner for Education was to be Chairman of the Council, but this was amended in January 1972. Instead, the Commissioner was no longer to be a member; he was above the Council, with the power of veto, and the channel of communication with the Party. He was to appoint up to 5 members of the 14 member Council. The Principal Secretary of the Ministry of Education was also a member. The Rector, an appointee of the government, became the Chairman, and 2 other members were to be appointed by the Political Bureau of the Party. The Pro-Rector was a member, but no other representative of the academic staff. The Rectorate established in Kinshasa, was to coordinate activities in the entire university system, with the support of its Departments of International Cooperation and Academic Matters, Finance, Building and Construction, Information and Protocol, Legal Matters, Research and Publication, and Programming. The three Universities became Campuses of the National University, each under a Vice-Rector with his own Board and Management Committee for the day to day running of each Campus. There were also Faculty Boards. Students were represented on Faculty and Campus Boards. The Youth Wing of the Party also had access to the Faculty and Campus Boards. There was an attempt to rationalize disciplines between the Campuses: Humanities, Mining, Agriculture and Veterinary Medicine in Lubumbashi; Social Sciences, Administration, Psychology and the Science of Education at Kisangani; Law, Economics, Engineering and Pharmacy at Lovanium, with Medicine and the natural Sciences available at each Campus. The Institutes were grouped into two, those dealing with Teacher Training, those dealing with Technology. The Directors of the Institutes constituted the Boards of the two groups of Institutes; the Chairman of each represented the group on the Council of the National University. (Ngobaasu, 1974).

The Reforms had substantial support and external funding. However, as the

Mobutu regime became more and more rapacious, external support dwindled and the economy declined. Student numbers continued to grow, the number of scholarships and the value in real terms also diminished. This brought a lot of hardship on students at a place like Lovanium, several kilometres away from town, and with public transport and even meals for non-resident students becoming increasingly expensive and uncertain. When it is realized that Lubumbashi is about 1,300km from Kinshasa, and Kisangani more than 1,000km, and that communication by road or even by telephone is very difficult, it is not surprising that the unified system proved unmanageable. By 1981, the status of University was restored to each of the campuses, but UNAZA and the Rectorate have remained to coordinate the system and maintain liaison with the Party and the Government. The major problem of the University has been the economic and political collapse of the state. There were no funds for research, equipment or books. The salaries became too small to maintain the staff, and each had to seek additional employment or other ways of earning extra income, or begin to drift abroad. The control by the Party has not been able to shield the University from collapse.

**The University of Madagascar**

The students of the University of Tananarive acted as catalyst to the popular uprising against the 12-year old government of Philbert Tsirinana in May 1972. The President was accused of rigging election and trying to perpetuate his unpopular rule. The students organised series of strikes and demonstrations in the capital and elsewhere which were joined by the populace, including university and school teachers, workers, etc. The government arrested some 400 demonstrators and deported them to an island, and tempers were further inflamed. The President called on the armed police to use force to disperse the crowd but the commander refused. He turned to the security police who fired on the crowd killing 40 people in the capital and seven in Mahajanga. Tsirinana found that he had lost all authority to rule and he surrendered power to the Army Commander, General Ramanantsoa. This was followed by the 1973 decree constituting the University of Madagascar as a national system of higher education in which all the institutions of higher learning were regrouped into five Faculties (Etablissments) of Law, Economics and Business Administration; Science; Agricultural Sciences; Letters; and Health Sciences. The regime remained divided and unsettled until 1975 when Lt-Comdr (later Admiral) Didier Ratsiraka took over and won a mandate in a referendum for a socialist programme of reform. It was in pursuit of this Charter of Revolution that the University was reconstituted in 1976.

The emphasis of the reform was on devolution, equality of access, geographical spread, and production of the graduates to implement the plan for socialist reform (Uwechue, 1981, p.790). As to the academic franchise which the university had hitherto enjoyed, Article 3 of Decree No.76-043 of 27 December 1976 guaranteed them, but added the important clause that they were to be enjoyed only where they did not conflict with the Charter of the Socialist revolution.

The University was organised into six regional centres or campuses to which were attached other institutions of higher education in the area so that the new University more effectively constituted a national university system to deliver higher education at both the professional and the sub-professional levels. Each University Centre was expected to be a focal point for development in the region. The centres were:

**Tananarive,** specialising in Science, Letters, Polytechnic, Health
   Sciences, Agronomy, and Advanced Teacher Training (ATTC)
**Antsiranama**, Polytechnic, Engineering, Mathematics, Industrial,
   Chemistry, ATTC
**Fianarantsoa**, Science, Informatics (Computer Science), Law, ATTC
**Mahajanga**, Pre-medical Sciences, Dentistry, and Science.
**Toamasina**, Economics and Business Administration, French studies,
   Philosophy and History-Geography.
**Toliary.** Science, Letters, ATTC.

The Rectorate and the central University offices were located in Tananarive. In 1983-4, the combined student enrolment on the 6 campuses was 34,162 of whom 58.3% obtained Government bursaries. For 1984-5 the enrolment had risen to 37,181, but the percentage of those on bursaries had fallen slightly to 57.2. Similarly, the number of academic staff rose from 960 to 1059, of whom expatriates were 233 and 238 respectively, representing a drop in the percentage from 24.2 to 22.4.

**Higher Education and the Ethiopian Revolution**

The University of Addis Ababa, formerly Haile Sellassie I University, prided itself on the traditions of service built into the Colleges which were regrouped into the University in 1961 - the extension services of the College of Agriculture at Alemaya; the concern of the Building Institute for low cost housing; the emphasis of the Public Health College at Gondar on community health, etc. Both staff and students showed initiative in projects of mass literacy, social work in orphanages and other forms of voluntary service. There was therefore broad consensus among staff, students and university administration when the Ethiopian University Service (EUS) was inaugurated in 1964. Even though many students thought it should have been voluntary, the statute required all undergraduates and specified Diploma students to spend one year of service among the rural communities as a condition for the award of the degree or diploma. The aim was partly to get the students to put their learning to practical use, and in addition, thereby contribute to social welfare, and partly to ensure that the student learnt, at first hand, something of the life of the village communities. The students on the scheme were to collaborate with the appropriate government ministries or agencies, but the overall administration was in University hands, in terms of the planning, orientation, assignment and logistics. (Habte, 1976).

While it may be argued that the students welcomed the EUS because most of them were from poor homes, identified with the poor, and desired change, there can be no doubt that their participation in the programme was a major factor in their radicalization. Other factors included their frustrations with their studies, trying to cope with a wide variety of expatriate teachers and study in English, a foreign language, with consequently high failure rate. As the numbers of students rose rapidly in the 1960s, hostels became increasingly overcrowded, with large numbers of non-resident students who had no satisfactory places to live. Their poverty and frustrations were compounded by government repressive measures - police brutality, killings, imprisonment, expulsion, university closures, etc. designed to break their spirit. Instead, they became more violent, their demands more specific, and their language less and less respectful of the person of the emperor, the founder and Chancellor of the University. The EUS did two major things: it widened the scope of the authorised National Union of Ethiopian University Students to embrace other students on a country-wide basis; and it provided them with a mission as they came in close contact with both rural and urban poor, and the problems of squatters and the imperative of land reform. With the EUS , the great famine of 1973 became a live issue on University campuses. (Balsvik, 1985). By the early 1970s, they did not merely desire change, they wished to do something to bring change about.

Ali Mazrui says that the Ethiopian students he met in December 1973 were the most radical in Africa and that, in the creeping coup d'etat of 1974, "the soldiers got radicalized partly in response to the students." The part that the students played during the coup in Addis Ababa which brought Mengistu Haile Mariam to power in 1974 remains forbidden ground. Publications which are usually silent on the matter stress instead their role in raising political consciousness, mobilizing and radicalizing the rural areas, largely through their participation in the EUS. But it seems unlikely that it was such participation in the EUS that led the Government to decree the *zemecha* programme, under which the University was closed for 2 years, to enable staff and students to embark on "development through cooperation". This was described as an expanded EUS programme providing "ample opportunity to our students and faculty to apply their technical know how to the basic needs of the broad masses of Ethiopia". More likely, the regime realized that the students, like many king makers, were likely to prove too independent minded, and they might resist the immediate imposition of Marxism-Leninism and, therefore, needed to be broken. Selected staff and East European advisers spent the two years redrafting curricula and entrenching compulsory courses in communist ideology. Not all the students came back in 1976. Some moved from *zemecha* to organizing guerilla war against the regime, the struggle that was to last till Mengistu was toppled in 1991.

The University had to be reconstituted after 1976. It was brought under the Commission for Higher Education (CHE) which operated through a Council consisting of the Minister of Education as Chairman, the Ministers of Health, Agriculture and Industry, the Commissioners for Higher Education, Planning, and Science and Technology. There was no academic on it, not even the President of the University. All institutions of post-secondary education were brought under the Commission in one National system of higher education so as to facilitate control by the Government. The University was reorganized, and its first objective, as for all institutions of higher education, was "to teach, expand and publicize socialism and formulate methods to carry out these functions". (CHE 1978, p.5). The University was now to consist of the main campus, College of Agriculture in Alemaya, and of Public Health in Gondar, Colleges of Pedagogical Sciences, and Colleges of Social Sciences on separate campuses in Addis Ababa; Faculties of Medicine, Science, and Technology; School of Pharmacy; Law School and the University Continuing Education Centre. In order to improve geographical spread, two junior colleges of Agriculture and one for Science Teachers were established, along with a number of research institutes. Because of the loss of several expatriate and Ethiopian teachers, special effort had to be made for staff training and development. A School of Graduate Studies was established to promote Master's Degrees in specific areas of need so that the students must have been in employment and be sponsored by their employers for the course. New arrangements were made for doctoral students to find sponsorship from abroad so that the student will spend some time with a foreign supervisor who would also come to visit at the early stages of the work and at the time of examination. At the same time, the regime carried its struggle against the Eritrean Liberation Front to dismantle the University of Asmara, seen as supporting the rebels against the Ethiopian regime. It was necessary on achieving independence to rebuild it as if from scratch.

## University Autonomy and National Identity in Khartoum

Far from avoiding the subject, the role of the students in the political life of the Sudan is openly acknowledged and debated. The University College of Khartoum had been constituted into an autonomous University as early as 1957. The University was very conscious that there were two different systems of higher education in the Sudan, the traditional Islamic, patterned after Al Azhar, and the modern Western, patterned after British Universities. The University of Khartoum was the exemplar of the latter and it had to struggle to remain so. To do this in an Islamic and partially Arab country, it had to act with conviction and determination, and without apology. That may be one reason why the University College, like Gordon College before it, took pride in its anti-colonial nationalist activities. The struggle to maintain credibility as an exemplar of the Western university, yet nationalist and completely Sudanese, has been central to the development of the University. Maintaining the autonomy of the University has therefore been a major concern (Hassan, Y.F., 1991).

The University Act of 1957 provided for a Chancellor appointed by the Head of State on the recommendation of the Council. In 1960, General Aboud, in an effort to curb the growing opposition of militant students, decided to appoint himself Chancellor. In 1963, he went further to place the Council and the University under the direction of the Minister of Education. This ensured that staff and students joined in the growing opposition to the regime. And it is generally acknowledged that, "the spark of the October Revolution 1964, was struck within the precincts of the University. In recognition of its political role, the National Charter of the October Revolution emphasized the independence of the University together with that of the Judiciary." (Hasan, Y. F., 1991, p. 178). The civilian regime that took over in 1964 soon became very unpopular. The university community were part of the progressive forces that Colonel (later General) Gaffar Nimeiri courted in his bid for power. However, soon after coming to power in 1969, he appointed himself Chancellor, with powers to appoint Vice-Chancellor, his deputy and even deans. A high powered Committee was set up to reorganize the whole system of higher education so as to achieve greater national identity, relevance of courses and efficiency. The upshot was the creation of the National Council for Higher Education (NCHE) in 1975, under Ministerial control, to be responsible for planning, financing and monitoring all higher education, with powers over curricula, admissions, etc. The University protested. The Association of Academic Staff, the Senate and others drafted alternative proposals to meet the declared Government objectives of relevance and national identity while re-establishing the autonomy of the University, but the Government refused to yield.

The aim of the NCHE was to bring the University of Khartoum within an integrated system of higher education which included universities both of the western and Islamic tradition as well as all the other tertiary institutions. This meant also that, contrary to the principle that the staff were employees of the Council of the University, they were brought under a unified national salary scale instead of one that was sensitive to the particular needs of the University. While in this and other ways treading on the autonomy of the University of Khartoum, the NCHE released the tertiary institutions training personnel at the sub-professional level from direct control of other ministries such as agriculture, health, justice etc. and centralized all under its control. The Council recognized the Islamic University of Omdurman, besides others like the University of Cairo, Khartoum Branch, founded in 1955, funded and staffed largely by Egyptians; and the Ahfad College for Women, a private institution which started as an elementary school, grew steadily and was now recognised as a University College; The Khartoum Technical Institute, founded in 1950, was reconstituted as the Khartoum Polytechnic with the status of a University College, to train technologists at both the professional and sub-professional levels, as well as in commerce, secretarial services and fine art. The Council then established two new universities, one in Gezira just south of Khartoum, the other at Juba, the first university in the South. Both were located in rural areas, and were expected to focus on vocational and developmental issues. This also improved the geographical spread of higher education.

The task of co-ordinating funding, admissions, curricula, and orientation for all the institutions proved very difficult and inefficient. The University of Khartoum sometimes had to bypass the Council and go directly to Government. This strengthened its case when at last the Revolution of April 1985 drove Nimeiri from power. The new University of Khartoum Act of 1986, based largely on recommendations from the University, restored its autonomy "within the framework of the national policy on higher education", as formulated by the NCHE. The Vice-Chancellor and his deputy were now to be elected by three electoral colleges, namely, the Assembly of staff, the Senate and the Council; Deans were to be elected by Faculty Boards, and Heads by the Departments, and ratified by the Chairman of Council or Vice-Chancellor as appropriate.

However, this victory of the University was shortlived. General Omer el Bashir seized power in June 1989 probably, as usual, with a number of university teachers as collaborators and advisers. The new regime had a definite political agenda in which the issue of cultural identity took precedence over development in terms of economic growth and modernization. In this regard, the role of education, and particularly higher education, was for the regime of central importance. They were determined to end the dichotomy between Western and Islamic within the educational structure by emphasizing Arabic language and Islamic studies. The powers of the NCHE over all institutions, and the subordination of the Acts of individual universities to the overall control of the NCHE were made clear beyond dispute. The first aim of the institutions of higher education was declared by the NCHE as "the indigenization of higher education so that it can express adequately the distinctive traits of the Sudanese people and which originate from their Islamic, Arabian and African beliefs and heritages". In fact, they declared a Revolution in Higher Education on three main counts:

> *Arabicization*: Arabic was now to be the language of instruction; Arabic and English are compulsory subjects of study; pass in Arabic and religious studies are required for admission to any institution of higher learning. No exception was made for the universities in non-Islamic areas, that is Juba and three new establishments.

> *Expansion:* Six new universities were created to ensure geographical spread and absorb all Sudanese studying abroad who were to be repatriated because foreign exchange would no longer be made available for overseas study. These were: University of the Quran and Islamic Studies, Kordofan, Wadi al-Nil (North), al-Sharq (East), al-Fatih (Darfur), Bahr al-Ghazal and A'ali al-Nil (Upper Nile). The Khartoum Polytechnic was reconstituted as the Sudan University of Science and Technology.

> The Egyptian-owned Cairo University, Khartoum campus, with over 9,000 students, was nationalized and added to institutions under the NCHE. At the same time the Government was to encourage approved private universities and bring them closer to the state universities.

> The annual intake of over 6,000 was to be doubled immediately, with effect from the 1990-91 academic year. Residential accommodation was therefore cancelled and all Sudanese students were to receive a monthly allowance. *Centralized Control Clarified:* In the event of conflict, the Act of the NCHE prevails over those of other institutions. Each post-secondary College or

School must be affiliated to a university so that the NCHE can reach all through the universities. (Hassan, Y. F., 1991; Forojalla, 1992).

The intellectual community in Khartoum, as we have seen, has been prominent in the political life of the country. Their political ideologies ranged from extreme Marxist/Leninism to fundamentalist Islamic orthodoxy. But, perhaps because of the tremendous achievements of the University of Khartoum in the national life, they tended to support its western traditions of liberalism, and rallied from time to time to defend its autonomy as essential for those achievements. The unified integrated National System of higher education abrogated that autonomy. It is open to doubt whether the six new universities established at the same time by the NCHE were expected to be of the same rank of quality as the University of Khartoum. Perhaps, instead of trying to force them all into the same mould, it should have been allowed to remain as an exemplar that could eventually help to raise the standards of the others. It is not surprising that what was seen as an attack on the University of Khartoum was resisted, but the new regime seemed determined to implement the new policy fully. It was meant to achieve cultural identity and unity. However, the very attempt to impose it over the diversity of opinions in the North and over the non-Arab non-Islamic peoples of the South, had as much potential to create political instability as it had to promote unity.

**National Systems in Francophone Africa**

We have noted how the University of Dakar was intended to serve all Francophone West Africa. When in 1962 the attempted Republic of Mali, incorporating Senegal and French Soudan (now Mali), broke down, Mali took steps to organize its own system of higher education. Côte d'Ivoire had the resources to start its own University even before the Government of Senegal began to deport non-Senegalese students suspected of joining in anti-government demonstrations. The University Centre of Benin located in Lome and Porto Novo, was meant to serve both Togo and the Republic of Dahomey (Benin) - Faculty of Science in Porto Novo, Letters in Togo. Soon the Centre had to be split so that Benin developed its own **Université Nationale du Benin,** and Togo **the Université du Benin, Lome.** The Central African Foundation for Higher Education located in Brazzaville was meant to serve Congo-Brazzaville, Gabon, Chad and the Central African Republic. It was dissolved in 1970 and each of the four countries tried to build its own National system of higher education. Similarly, the mandated territories of Burundi and Rwanda which had hitherto been served to a limited extent by the universities in Zaire, especially Lubumbashi, had to develop their own systems of higher education after the abrupt independence of Zaire. These efforts raised two main issues: the question of national identity in view of the continuing predominance of French cultural influence and financial support, and the particular problem of organizing universities in small countries with limited financial resources.

Cameroon even preceded Côte d'Ivoire in organizing its own national system. Cameroon was not typical of Francophone countries because of its German background, the international attention derived from its status as a mandated territory, and the inclusion of a sizable English- speaking territory. From the start, the Unesco Advisory Commission of December 1961 had advised that a Federal University of the Cameroon should incorporate all the post-secondary institutions in the country, with the exception of the School of Administration and the Military School. This was to facilitate manpower planning and effective co-ordination of the total national effort in the development of higher education. Thus, an all-embracing University was established in 1962 on the basis of functional bilingualism, and with the mission of reconciling the French and British colonial legacies of education, law and political order so as to promote national unity. The French tradition indicated that higher education had to be under the control of the Minister of Education. The British tradition indicated the need for an intermediary between the University and Government. Thus was created the post of Chancellor who is virtually a member of the Government but is also the overall head of the University on a full time basis, like the Executive Chairman of a corporation. The Vice-Chancellor/Rector was then like the Managing Director responsible for day to day administration, but directly responsible not just to Council but to the Chancellor who presided over the University Council as well as the Boards of the University specialist Institutes, Schools and Centres. The University Council included the Rector, Deans of Faculties, Directors of the Institutes, Schools and Centres, representatives of government ministries, and of academic staff and students. In 1972, the Republic was declared no longer federal but unitary. The name of the University was consequently changed to the **University of Yaounde.**

The University grew rapidly in the 1970s, as facilities for secondary education improved, especially in the Francophone areas. The rise of student numbers, especially in the Faculties of Law and Economics, Human and Social Sciences, and Science where admission was open to all holders of the baccalaureate, was phenomenal. The respective enrolment in the three faculties in 1963-4 was 564, 39, 73, total 676; in 1980-1: 4826, 1550, 1424, total 7,800; and in 1984-5: 6324, 2297, 3263, total 11,884.

The total enrolment in the University in 1984-5 approached 14,000. There were research centres attached to the Faculties: African Documentation Centre attached to the Faculty of Law and Economics, established in 1970, and African Studies, attached to both Humanities and Law and Economics. As the University was exploding, new University Centres for vocational training were established partly as a form of decentralization, and partly for a wider geographical spread: Buea for Languages and Interpretation, in 1977; Douala for Business Administration, in 1982; Dschang for Agriculture and Forestry, in 1982; and Ngaoundéré for Science and Technology, in 1985. From 1977, the University Centres were granted autonomy, so that their Directors presided over their own Boards, recruited their own staff, conducted their own admissions, and were responsible directly to the Minister.

The specialist Centres, Schools and Institutes for training professionals remained under the Chancellor: Health Sciences, Journalism, International Relations for training diplomats, the Polytechnic, and the Advanced Teachers College on three different locations at Yaounde, Bambili and Douala. Admission into these specialist institutions, unlike admission into the faculties, is competitive and selective. Sometimes, candidates spend a year or two in the faculties before gaining admission into the schools. The International School of Journalism, established in 1970, served not only Cameroon but also Central African Republic, Gabon, Rwanda and Chad. The University Centre for Health Sciences (UCHS/CUSS) soon became well reputed for its innovative and exemplary approach to medical education in Africa. The aim of the Centre is to train professional and ancillary personnel for health services, deliver comprehensive health care and undertake operational research. The idea is to train medical doctors, nurses and other paramedical staff and technicians within the same establishment and to a common purpose, and to achieve proficiency in three interrelated branches of Medicine: Medical Science, Clinical Science, and Social and Preventive Medicine. This approach has exerted much influence on developments in other parts of Africa, and has received significant financial support from the UN Agencies, and Aid organizations of France, Canada, US and the UK. (Monekosso, 1976).

The significance of the French cultural presence and financial support in the average Francophone country can perhaps be best illustrated from the example of Guinea and Mali. Guinea was the only country that said "No" to the proposed French community in 1958. It was joined by Mali in seeking a Russian or Vietnamese, rather than French, approach to the establishment of "higher education for development". Guinea developed the Conakry branch of IFAN which it inherited as the State Research Agency to administer the National Archives, National Library and Museum; conduct research in the Social Sciences and Natural Sciences; and supervise the Pasteur Institute and two agricultural research stations, one for citrus fruits, the other for rice. It also housed the offices of UNESCO. The main institution of higher education has therefore been the **Conakry Polytechnic**, built, equipped and financed by the USSR, to train engineers and teachers, at the professional and auxiliary levels. With the financial support of advisers from the USSR and other socialist countries, Mali established a number of vocational institutes attached to respective ministries, teaching at different levels from upper secondary to sub-professional, to degrees and even Masters level. The emphasis was on production of manpower tailor-made to specified jobs prescribed by the ministries. There were five main post secondary institutions: Advanced Teacher Training College, the Rural Polytechnic Institute, the National School of Engineering, the National School of Public Administration, and the Medical School. While in 1963 70% of Malians with the baccalaureate went abroad on scholarships - about 1,400 were abroad, 300 of them in France - this figure was reduced to 38% by 1970 and 20% by 1976. However, the demand for teachers even for the Institutes necessitated the creation in 1972 of the Centre for Advanced Training at the doctoral level. This was replaced in 1981 by an Institute for Advanced Training and Applied Research under a Director of Higher Education. Eventually, it was decided in 1986 to incorporate all these into a **University of Mali**. Meanwhile, it was clear that in spite of all the detailed planning, there was unemployment; and attempts to control the award and the value of bursaries provoked constant conflicts between students and the state. Thus Mali and Guinea were able to experiment with different national models of development-oriented higher education because of their rupture with France. Their example might also suggest that other countries need not try to follow them. (Tidiane Sy, 1976; Unesco, 1986).

By contrast, not only Togo and Benin but also Burkina Faso, Niger, and Chad established university centres and other post-secondary institutions in the 1960s which were developed into national systems of higher education in the 1970s. Mauretania did not establish the University of Nouakchott until 1981. Gabon established the Omar Bongo University in 1970 and a second one named the **Masuku University of Science and Technology** in 1986. Marien Ngouabi University in Brazzaville; University of Bangui in Central Africa, and the University of Chad in Ndjamena were all established in 1971.(AAU, 1988) Even with French co-operation, these universities in small countries with limited funds, had to study how best to get a university to meet a good proportion of their national needs. Mali and Guinea were able to experiment with different national models of development-oriented higher education because of their rupture with France and leftward inclination towards the Soviet bloc. In spite of their being held up as possible models for small countries with limited financial resources, no other country has been tempted to follow their example. Another country held up as a possible model was Mauritius, an island country of under 1 million people, with an economy based up to 90% on the planting and processing of sugar cane. The state spends three fourths of the education budget on elementary education and almost 90% of children of school age are catered for. Secondary education is in private hands, and the state tries to keep the budget on higher education to the minimum. **The University of Mauritius**, incorporating the former College of Agriculture, was established in 1971. It has three faculties: Agriculture, Public Administration, and Industrial (including Sugar) Technology. The basic purpose of the University is to train people at all levels and of all varieties required within the Sugar industry. Only 10% of the students in the University pursue degrees, the rest are trained at sub-degree levels. Admission is strictly regulated by anticipated vacancies in the sugar industry. It should be noted also that the whites who dominate the island and the industry, and the Asian middle class are usually able, when necessary, to send their offsprings to universities abroad. (Wodajo, 1976b).

Meanwhile, Senegal proceeded to develop the University of Dakar as the University of Senegal. It retained the French structure of a university consisting of Faculties open to holders of the baccalaureate, possibly with some research or documentation centres attached, a number of Grands Écoles and Institutes for specialist professional studies for which admission is competitive and selective. There was no attempt to create a unified national system bringing all institutions of higher education under one umbrella. The University was renamed **Cheikh Anta Diop** in 1987 in honour of the prodigious Senegalese physicist and philosopher, former director in IFAN who died in 1986. Student numbers continued to rise rapidly, reaching 14,789 in 1988, including 2,474 non-Senegalese, mostly from other Francophone African countries. It was against the background of such numbers that a decision was taken to establish the **University of St. Louis** in 1990, restricted only to the four Faculties of Law, Economics and Business Studies, Applied Mathematics and Informatics, and Humanities.

The situation at the **University of Abidjan** was similar, except that the National Schools (ENS) working directly with government ministries were even more pronounced at Abidjan: Agronomy, Public Works, Statistics, Administration and Teacher Training. The numbers of students were galloping as at Dakar: about 6,000 students and 268 teachers in 1972-3; 14,217 students and 778 teachers (of whom 620 or almost 80% were Ivoriens) in 1988. The numbers were to reach 21,356 students in 1993. The students in Abidjan thus became a political force whenever they allied with the Union of Teachers and other workers. The Government decided in 1991 to re-organise the University, changed its name to the National University of Côte d'Ivoire, with the Faculties and Institutes shared among three Campuses, each under the direction of a Vice-Rector: Cocody and Abobo-Adjame on the outskirts of Abidjan, and Bouaké, some 450km to the interior.

## Sierra Leone and Ghana

Fourah Bay College continued to award the degrees of Durham University until 1965 in its restricted three Faculties of Arts, Economics and Social Studies, and Pure and Applied Science. It was with difficulty that it embarked on a Faculty of Engineering. This meant that for its needs in Agriculture, Medicine and other fields, Sierra Leone had to send students abroad. This gap was particularly felt in the areas of Agriculture and Education. The Government had approached USAID and the University of Wisconsin to offer technical assistance and funding to upgrade the Njala Agricultural College, 125km from Freetown, into the Njala University College specifically for Agriculture and Education. It was then possible to move towards a national **University of Sierra Leone** in 1967, with a Charter to award its own degrees. At first the Vice-Chancellorship rotated between the Principals of the two University Colleges, within a sort of federal system. The University was reconstituted in 1972 into a unitary system in which the Office of a full-time Vice-Chancellor was separated from that of Principal. The former Colleges became Campuses of a single University, each under a Principal. The two faculties at Njala, and the four at Fourah Bay made up the University. A seventh Faculty, Law, was added to Fourah Bay. Some departments were duplicated between Agriculture in Njala and Applied Science in Fourah Bay. Every care was taken to relate the courses both in Agriculture and Education to the Society and involve leaders of the Society in the work of the Faculty Boards. The problem of the University has been shortage of funds to pay adequate salaries, train staff, buy equipment, support students, and conduct research. While Njala has been relatively protected by its distance, Fourah Bay students have frequently been confronted by government or supporters of the ruling party.

Throughout the 1970s and 1980s, **Ghana** did not establish any new university. Student numbers increased steadily, but not dramatically from 5,380 in 1970 to 8,500 in 1985. Most of the increase was at Kumasi which rose from 1394 to 3,600, compared with Legon which rose from 2730 to 3554. Cape Coast which could have expanded to take the students enrolment for all the universities hardly rose at all from 1256 to 1476 (including part-time students). A number of factors were responsible such as the nature of the initial buildings at Legon which were planned for 800 students, instead of for 5,000; but the two principal factors were shortage of funds owing to the collapse of the economy, itself partly the cause and partly the result of political instability. Funds for research dried up. Many Ghanaian teachers emigrated. Books and equipment were short. Students' living conditions deteriorated and the value of bursaries in real terms declined. The staff and the students were bound to be concerned about the political instability that so much affected their life. Students confrontations with the changing regimes were frequent, provoking university closures, sometimes for more than a whole year. The relationship with Jerry Rawlings has been typical. The students were a prominent part of the popular support that propelled him to power in 1979, and gave him enthusiastic welcome at his second coming in 1981. But relationships soon became sour and the record of attempted repression has not been different from that of earlier regimes.

## The Nigerian Federal System

We have seen how, in reacting to the Ashby Commission Report in 1960, Nigeria had established the principle that each Region or State was entitled to establish its own University. By 1962, there were three Regions, with three Regional universities and two Federal ones in Ibadan and Lagos, Ibadan capital of the Western Region and Lagos just outside it. The universities enjoyed a large measure of autonomy inherited from the colonial past. Universities even maintained liaison offices in London for staff recruitment, training, etc. The Mid-West Region was carved out of the Western Region in 1963, and it soon began to dream of its own University. This was delayed because of the Civil War (1967-70). Meanwhile, on the eve of the Civil War, Nigeria had been reconstituted into 12 states. After the war, the Mid-West tried to get Ibadan to adopt the Mid-West College of Technology and develop it into a University College. When that did not work out, the Mid-West turned to the Federal Government for help, which it eventually got in 1972. Ibadan then went to open a new "Campus" in Jos. Thus, the fever for the establishment of new Universities already existed in terms of demands from the States even before the sudden boost in oil revenues. These were demands for federal universities on the grounds of geographical spread, because most states did not at that time believe they could afford the capital costs of establishing a university.

It was the oil revenues that incited the Federal Government to create not only a national system of higher education, but also of education as a whole, under federal control as a factor of reconciliation and unification after the Civil War. In 1974, the National Universities Commission (NUC) was reconstituted from an Advisory body in the Cabinet Office to an autonomous statutory body. In 1975, the Federal Government took over the four State universities - Nsukka, Benin, Ife, ABU - so that all the six universities in the nation could be under the direction of the NUC. In 1976, the Government announced the establishment of four new universities and three university colleges. The difference was unclear and in 1977 all were made universities - Sokoto, Maiduguri, Jos, and Calabar; Ilorin, Port Harcourt, and Kano. There was no prior planning and the NUC was charged with the responsibility of overseeing the establishment of all the seven universities, which were endowed with identical Acts and structures handed down from above, a process which greatly enhanced the powers of the NUC and constituted a major erosion of the autonomy of the universities. Other steps in the process of this erosion included the following: The Committee of Vice-Chancellors were planning a University Community Service along the lines of the EUS; in 1973 the Government stepped in and made it the National Youth Service under government control, not during university studies, but in the year after graduation; the academic staff were incorporated in 1974 into the Civil Service pensionable salary scales, thus undermining, if not completely abrogating the role of University Councils as employers; then admissions were centralized under a quasi-government agency. The NUC took over the function of external representation of the Universities, recruitment and purchasing, and as such the liaison offices of the Universities in London. The erosion reached the point in 1978 when the Government transferred a few Vice-Chancellors round from one university to another without consulting them or the universities concerned.

The Constituent Assembly had insisted in 1979, contrary to the wishes of the Military Government, that higher education should be restored to the concurrent list of issues on which both the State and the Federal Government could take the initiative. This set off a fresh round of opening new Universities. The 12 states had become 19 states. The new Civilian Federal Government announced the establishment of 7 new Universities of Technology - Bauchi, Makurdi, Yola, Akure, Owerri, Abeokuta and Minna - so as to have a Federal University within each State. (There were already two, Ibadan and Ife, in the Western State). At the same time eight states decided to establish State Universities as essential to maintain the spirit of federalism and pursue development programmes. Thus from six universities in 1975, Nigeria was to have 28 universities by 1982, that is twenty-two new universities within the space of seven years. An Open University and a University of Abuja, both in the new federal capital, were being planned. There were also indications that the Nigerian Defence Academy and the Police College were to become additional universities, besides demands by private entrepreneurs and religious bodies asking for license to open their own universities.

Later, the number of states was increased to 21, and then 30, further spurring on the demand for new universities - to fulfil federal government commitment to provide each state with a university and to allow any state that wished to open its own university. One additional problem was that some of the states wishing to establish universities often resolved controversy as to the location of the university by creating multi-campus universities so as to achieve geographical spread even within the state. A related problem was that when a state had a university, and the state was then split into two, a multi-campus university then became two universities, or the problem of sharing the assets of the university could become so contentious that a possible solution might be for the Federal Government to take over the university.

The Military regime in 1984-5, weighing the economic consequences of the spate of new universities, tried to curb the expansion by cancelling the Open University -probably the one that should have been allowed; converting three of the Universities of Technology into Campuses of the nearest Universities - Abeokuta, Makurdi and Yola; discouraging multi-campus universities and prohibiting the establishment of private universities. The regime that took over power in 1986-92 weighed political reasons and loosened the reins: Yola reverted to a University of Technology, Abeokuta and Makurdi into Universities of Agriculture and Abuja allowed to proceed. A number of national heroes were honoured by naming universities after them: Sokoto became Usumanu Danfodio; Bauchi, Abubakar Tafawa Balewa; and Ife, Obafemi Awolowo. Nnamdi Azikiwe refused to have the University of Nigeria, Nsukka, changed to his name, but had accepted that the Anambra State University of Awka be named Nnamdi Azikiwe. The Head of State was known to announce off the cuff the establishment of universities which were not even mentioned in the prepared speeches. It was therefore sometimes uncertain just how many universities have actually been put into operation: as of 1993, probably 32 Federal universities and about 10 state universities. Student enrolment rose from 14,500 in 1970-71 to 92,000 in 1982-83, and 135,670 in 1985-86, and near 200,000 by 1992. The number of teachers rose from 2,255 in 1970 to 7,980 in 1983, of whom the percentage of non-Nigerian teachers fell from 28.9 in 1970 to 20.5 by 1983.

In the meantime, the price of crude oil fell sharply in 1980-81. What with over commitment and too much hurry in trying to build everything at the same time, including a new federal capital, inflation was rising rapidly, and the burden of external debt increased. Eventually the creditors imposed structural adjustment and devaluation in 1986, enjoining reduction of public expenditure and privatization,and the Supreme Court eventually ruled that there was no law to back up the prohibition of private universities.

Severe problems have arisen from this unplanned massive expansion of the university system, as is fairly well documented in the Report of the Longe Commission of 1992. The most obvious problem has been underfunding and the direct consequences, such as decline of research activities, shortage of books and equipment, emigration of staff into industry or universities abroad, and general deterioration of the quality of education. Probably, just as severe are the consequences of inefficiency within an over-centralized system which have compounded the problems of underfunding.

Neither the NUC nor the Federal Ministry of Education has the infrastructure or the management to look after 32 Federal universities, not to say all the 42 within the national system. Yet the NUC has continued to prescribe uniform constitutions, and even uniform curricula in the name of maintaining minimum academic standards. The Head of State as Visitor tries to behave like the Chancellor in other countries, using the same group of advisers to appoint Vice-Chancellors, Pro-Chancellors, members of Council, and honorific Chancellors to all the Federal universities. Confrontation with students over economic and anti-democratic policies, arrest and detention of student leaders, closure of universities disrupting academic calendars, are frequent. Government efforts to divide the students and undermine student unionism seem only to have heightened the degree of student violence, drug-taking, and students' secret cults which engage in gang warfare on and off campus. (Ojo, forthcoming).

## Conclusion

No attempt has been made here to evaluate in detail the contribution of the universities to African development, either in terms of cultural identity or of responsiveness to the immediate needs and aspirations of the majority of the African people. It was obvious that the universities had gone a long way to providing the manpower to indigenize the civil service and parastatals in most countries, and the crying need for indigenous teachers at all levels, including Advanced Teacher Training and other institutions of higher learning had, to a large extent, been satisfied. All these had effects on secondary and elementary education in terms of trained teachers and textbooks. Some of the universities also made important contributions in the applied social sciences, tropical medicine, agricultural extension, chemical analysis of the properties of local materials, etc. Some studies, mostly in the 1970s, indicate how well many of the universities were responding. It is because of such contribution that the collapse of some, and decline of most of them is now acknowledged to be a tragic setback to African development. As indicated above, many of the governments imposing control over the universities with the declared intention of making them more responsive to the needs of the people were themselves far from being responsive to those needs. In many cases, the imposition of such controls have aided the decline of the universities more than their responsiveness, or capacity to respond more.

By the end of the 1980s, it was clear that the universities and national systems of higher education were in a crisis. Nowhere, except in newly independent Namibia and Eritrea, could one find governments carefully nursing up the universities as vital agents of development. Rather, attempts at brutal control and suppression were far more common. The worst example was possibly that of Zaire where in 1992 the military invaded university campuses, first Louvanium and then Lubumbashi with more devastating effect, raping and killing several students. Similar incidents happened in Burkino Faso in 1987, Niger in 1989, Côte d'Ivoire in 1992, and Kenya also in 1992. Pressure began to come from outside to curb the excesses of governments and support the processes of democratization and, at least, an end to the reign of the military and one-party autocracies. The appraisals of the 1980s suggesting that the importance of the universities to national development, or renewal, had been exaggerated began, therefore, to be revised. This led to a re-examination of the nature of the crisis, a review of the history and the mission of the universities in the changed circumstances of the 1990s, a critique of the management of funds, personnel, students affairs, relations with government, the gender issue, strategies for raising and generating funds, etc. An attempt will be made in the succeeding chapters to review these issues as they have arisen from our brief survey of the history of the African experience with higher education.

## PART II: ISSUES AND PROBLEMS OF THE 1990s

Chapter 7

## THE PROBLEMS OF THE 1990s

**Introduction**

In the 1990s and beyond, institutions of higher education in Africa, especially the universities, must contend with several interrelated major problems, whose combined effect threatens to strangulate them. But this should not invariably lead to complete collapse. The universities have shown remarkable resilience so far. As one commentator has said,

> Despite the brains that have been drained out of them over the years, and the compromises they have been compelled to make with their own standards, [these] universities remain great national storehouses of trained, informed, inquiring and critical intellects, and the indispensable means of replenishing national talent. They have considerable reserves of leadership and commitment on which to draw. Impoverished, frustrated, dilapidated and overcrowded as they may be, they have no substitutes. (Coombe, 1991).

It is, therefore, important to understand the nature and complexity of the problems and attendant crisis which they confront in order that proper and effective measures and strategies can be sought to reduce their severity.

To say that higher education in Africa is in crisis does not mean simply that the funds available to run higher education institutions are grossly inadequate, thereby making them subsist on a "starvation diet". More than that, African countries and societies are going through a period of economic uncertainty, political and social upheavals, plus other contortions, and higher education has become a victim of the prevailing state of affairs (UNESCO-BREDA, 1992). The situation is likely to remain so, well into the twenty-first century.

A number of African countries have been plagued by civil wars, even before the 1990s. Outstanding examples are Liberia, Ethiopia, Somalia, Eritrea, Rwanda, Burundi, Namibia and South Africa. In most of these countries, higher education has suffered, and continues to suffer, considerable if not total destruction of infrastructure and facilities. In many cases, the campuses have had to be abandoned since the sheer survival of persons dictated the flight of students, academics and other staff into exile or safe havens within the countries. Under such conditions, the provision and management of higher education has become extremely difficult, if not impossible. The problems that have arisen include the rescue and rehabilitation of both staff and students in the asylums or countries of refuge. There are also issues of absorbing the refugee staff into available universities, fitting refugee students into other institutions and training programmes, and preparing both staff and students for eventual return home when circumstances permit. Equally, the reconstruction of damaged institutions poses its own problems, in the conditions of privation.

The cruel "winds of stringency", consequent upon the severe economic recession of the past two decades or so, and the prevailing unjust international economic order, continue to blow unabated across the African continent with devastating consequences for the universities and other institutions of higher education in most African countries. The consequent contraction of resources to the universities, coupled with increasing demand, constitutes the most critical problem and greatest challenge for Africa's higher education. In the words of Kenneth Berrill, in the foreword to a publication on *Resources and Higher Education*, "the alternative to adequate resources is a starvation diet which may possibly begin by stripping off surplus fat but will in the end debilitate and ruin". This is the fate which many African institutions of higher education face in the continuing harsh economic circumstances afflicting various African countries.

The damage sustained by under-resourcing the universities during the years of economic decline, in almost all Sub-Saharan African countries, has been massive generally and, in some areas, debilitating (Coombe, 1991). In fact, the first impression one gets of an African university campus in the 1990s is one of an all-pervading state of physical, managerial, and intellectual dilapidation (UNESCO-BREDA, 1992). For the concerned Africans anywhere and the most senior academics in the older African universities, there is indeed an unmistaken sense of loss, amounting almost to grief, as they compare the present state of their universities with the vigor, optimism and pride which these same institutions displayed twenty or thirty years ago (Coombe, *op. cit.*).

**Diminishing Financial Resources**

The resources of the university include the financial, physical, and human resources which it has at its disposal, to carry out its functions. Over the years, a combination of factors has conspired to worsen the crisis of resources (AAU, 1991; Coombe, 1991; Goma, 1989; Saint, 1992; Sentenza-Kajubi, 1992; UNESCO-BREDA, 1992; World Bank, 1988). The woeful economic situation of most African countries during the 1970s and 1980s has meant a steady dwindling of both externally- and internally-sourced financial resources for the universities, resulting in funding levels which cannot match, in real terms, the requirements of critical inputs - equipment, books and journals - to sustain acceptable standards of instruction, research and service.

The constraints on resources produce consequences at various levels and of several dimensions: visible and as yet invisible effects on the systems of higher education as a whole, on the progress of science, technology and scholarship; on the kind and quality of individual academic work, and on the teaching and training of students (Goma, 1989). This is manifested in most African universities in the squeeze on student accommodation, the collapse or decline of municipal services, crowded classrooms, teaching reduced to chalk and talk, frustrated teachers who must hustle for additional income, libraries whose acquisition votes have been nominal for years on end, and impoverished research. (Coombe, 1991).

The foreign exchange needs of Africa's universities cannot be satisfied in the prevailing economic circumstances. The bulk of the goods to run the universities in Africa is imported from outside the continent. This applies especially to scientific equipment and other manufactured materials since the industrial base of most of the countries is not sufficiently developed to provide the kind of technological devices required for teaching and research. (ESAURP, 1987). Thus, even when government block grants make generous provisions for the purchase of material, there may be no allocation of convertible currency, for its procurement. Similarly, substantial amounts of foreign currency are required to cover the cost of expatriate staff, the foreign training of indigenous staff, and staff travel to conferences abroad, not to mention the purchase of library books and textbooks.

The situation also affects access to facilities for publishing the indigenous scholar's works. Many African academics find themselves in a predicament. Publishing abroad is not easy, and can be subject to agonizing delays. At the same time, African university presses have been victims of the economic squeeze, and home universities that do not have their own publishing facilities are not prepared to handle publication.

(Assie-Lumumba 1993). "Faculty members' chances of promotion suffer accordingly. At a more basic level, the circulation of ideas and research findings slows down. Where an embryo research community with research traditions may have been starting to develop, potentially capable of producing an impact on the country and the region, the process has been virtually arrested".

There is real danger that financial stringency can make, and, indeed, *has* made, it difficult for many African institutions of higher education, particularly the universities, to meet the requirements of modern science and technology. Many institutions and, in some cases, even their governments, have been forced to begin to urge concentration, in the meantime, on the less expensive branches of the natural sciences and the humanities and social sciences. (Goma, 1989). A gap may thus be created in the quality of work between the technical studies and the humanities and social sciences. Financial constraints may, therefore, frustrate desirable expansion in the curricula intended to meet the developmental needs of the countries concerned.

### Stagnation and Deterioration of Physical Resources

A number of universities in Africa have been at a standstill for new construction and capital development. In the Eastern and Southern African sub-region, Makerere University is a classic case; but such constraints are also felt, for example, by the Universities of Addis Ababa, Dar es Salaam, Eduardo Mondlane and Zambia (ESAURP, 1987). These universities are in countries where the economies have not fared well in recent times. Many others continue to operate from temporary premises since their establishment, awaiting the construction of their permanent location.

Not merely has capital development been arrested, African universities have also suffered serious deterioration of their facilities, thereby undermining opportunities for excellence in the performance of expected tasks. Lack of a maintenance culture, insufficiency of funds to carry out repairs, and poor procurement procedures have led to a steady running down of existing facilities - buildings, equipment, and other infrastructure. (UNESCO-BREDA, 1992). Indeed, some buildings have deteriorated to the point where universities might end up losing present structures. At the same time, unplanned expansion, in response to increasing demand for higher education, has led to an overstretching of physical resources.

There are other sets of problems besides those connected with the deterioration of existing physical facilities. One is that many of the older universities were planned when much smaller numbers of students and staff were envisaged. Expansion has required not merely the addition of one or two classroom blocks, but an increase to facilities available in several buildings. Another is that a number of the universities were built at a time when centralization was still fashionable, but recent trends by universities and/or faculties to decentralize - for example, to create Colleges or Schools - now require additional support structures in terms of new buildings and building annexes. (ESAURP, 1987).

It is clear that the deterioration and shortages of physical facilities - lecture rooms and laboratories, staff and student housing, staff offices, equipment and supplies - constitute the most limiting factor for extending university capacity in most African countries. In the development and provision of physical resources one constant, namely the inadequacy or unavailability of financial resources, remains central and hampers the quest to meet the university's needs.

Thus, while the demand for higher education continues to increase unabated, the present capacities of African universities cannot meet the demand by those qualified to enter university. Given the current economic crisis, it is unrealistic to contemplate constructing a sufficient number of much needed new buildings, let alone new universities, on the traditional lines, with an adequate supply of qualified teachers and the pedagogical infrastructure and student support services to meet the increasing demand for higher education (Assie-Lumumba, 1993). The best that can be hoped for, therefore, is rehabilitation and revitalization of the existing infrastructure. There is also need to seriously reconsider present policies regarding the university's role or responsibility in providing residential accommodation for students and staff. This is not easy in view of the location of several universities away from centres of urban settlement where staff and students might have been able to find alternative accommodation and adequate public transportation to university facilities. But universities can no longer afford to lock up a very high proportion of their financial resources in the provision of such municipal facilities. Because of the commitment to provide housing, universities are sometimes obliged to incur high costs in accommodating staff in commercial hotels while waiting for vacant university housing. Universities need to reach agreements with government, municipal authorities and entrepreneurs to undertake the provision of these facilities.

## The Impact on Human Resources

Financial and physical constraints can and do lead to reduced or impoverished academic performance of individual members of the faculty which could, and does indeed, contribute to deficient teaching and research in the course of time. Many African academics suffer a loss of professional self-esteem. (Coombe, 1991). Of all the casualties of the years of austerity in the African universities, the damage to morale is particularly serious. Many individual academics make every possible effort to try and cope as best they could with the hardship and frustration of contemporary African academic life. "But one should not romanticize the scholarly community in Africa. Inevitably, energy is sapped, compromises are made, and productivity falls. The extreme erosion of working and living conditions on many campuses has driven some academics to seek refuge in cynicism, venality, actual or psychic truancy, dereliction of duty and opportunism. The wonder is, when so many have to hustle to survive, that serious intellectual and pedagogical activity persists even in African universities which have been most hard pressed". (Coombe, *op. cit.*).

There can be no doubt that "much of the malaise which many African scholars suffer arises from the sense of being out of contact, and of being denied the means to be up-to-date as scholars and teachers. Many university people, who are already isolated by geography and national borders, dread the prospect of falling irretrievably out of communication with the international academic system. ... They have suffered for years the shortage of foreign exchange for library books and journals, personal subscriptions to international scholarly associations, up-to-date scientific and computing equipment for teaching and research, spare parts, reagents and other consumables including paper, reprographic facilities, travel to conferences, professional contact visits, research attachments and sabbatical leaves. The proliferation of electronic databases and networks, and the conversion of many international bibliographic and research abstract services to micrographic and     CD-ROM technology, seems about to relegate most African universities to a communication and information backwater". (Coombe, 1991).

Staff retention has increasingly become more difficult. Indeed, the loss of talented staff - the "brain drain" - is one of the most critical problems currently faced by African universities. Studies commissioned by UNESCO-BREDA on the brain drain phenomenon have shown that it is the most highly trained, and the most experienced personnel in areas of dire need in Africa (medicine, engineering, the natural sciences, computer science) who tend to get out of the universities. (UNESCO-BREDA, 1992). The burden of these losses is all the heavier for the universities and related institutions since migrant doctors, engineers and scientists tend to leave their countries during the most productive period of their lives. (UNESCO, 1978). Although a number of African countries have achieved tremendous success at training nationals under their Staff Development Schemes to meet their staffing needs, they have not met with corresponding success at retaining those whom they have trained. The trend has been and continues to be that very substantial numbers of highly qualified indigenous academics leave the universities shortly after their return from postgraduate studies abroad financed by or at the instance of the universities. The overall attrition rate for a number of the universities is frightening.

It may be argued that as long as the emigrant academics remain within Africa, their action constitutes merely a "brain circulation" for the benefit of Africa or the individual recipient African countries; and that only when or where their destinations are overseas does it amount to a "brain drain". (Goma, 1989, 1990). Many of those who have fled the universities and taken up employment elsewhere in their countries, are now in occupations in which they are not directly practising their particular highly skilled professions: accomplished academics - scholars, scientists, engineers, researchers and generators of original thought and innovative ideas - can be found seeking to become renowned managers of routine administration in the public, parastatal or private sectors. This may be said to constitute a "brain haemorrhage". (Goma, 1990). At all events, the flight of academics from the university - whether it is called "brain drain", "brain circulation", or "brain haemorrhage" - can only have a harmful impact on the individual losing institutions.

The strong pull is from outside sources located in the industrialized countries of Europe and North America and, more recently, in the Gulf states. There has also been a considerable brain drain from some Eastern and Southern African countries to universities in other African countries where hard currency may be earned, such as the erstwhile Bantustans of South Africa, and Botswana, Lesotho and Swaziland.

Higher salaries and better fringe benefits offered by other institutions and sectors within the country or elsewhere abroad have often been cited as the major factor in attracting academic staff away from the African universities. But this is an over-simplification of a complex problem. Many young lecturers leave because they are unable to advance themselves by research and publications or by acquiring advanced degrees; while senior lecturers and professors have obligations to growing families, and may have suffered sharp declines in real income. (Coombe, 1991). Many can exploit their seniority and academic records in the labour market, at home or abroad. The unsatisfactory working environment prevailing in many African universities is certainly a major factor contributing to the exodus of academic staff from these institutions. (Goma, 1990). Thus, while the chance to earn a higher salary and better conditions of service are important, many of those who are committed to their professions or specializations have migrated, and are migrating, because they can see no professional future at home; because they believe that they can use their professional training more effectively and thus work more productively elsewhere; because they cannot secure much-needed research funds and/or other resources for their work at home; or because they do not have professional colleagues to stimulate and help them (*Education and World Affairs,* 1970). They cannot keep abreast of developments in their own fields and maintain active contacts with their peers in other countries, because the lack of foreign exchange has made it difficult, if not impossible to keep up subscriptions to much-needed journals and other publications, or to attend important and relevant symposia, conferences and similar meetings abroad. Senior university staff, after several years of work and experience, like to work in a conducive environment where there is enough infrastructure, equipment and money for research, (ESAURP, 1987) the kind of support which is inadequate in most African universities in the present economic circumstances.

The other causes of the brain drain are mainly social and political. Civil wars and ethnic conflicts and, until recently, liberation wars, and lack of academic and political freedom in some countries, have threatened sheer physical survival of person, family and property of many African academics. Thus, finding that they can no longer carry on their scientific or scholarly work with any degree of professional integrity, many are forced to seek safe havens elsewhere, (UNESCO-BREDA, 1992; World Bank, 1989). On the social plane, there seems to have been, within most African societies, clear evidence of social devaluation in the status of the scholar and other intellectuals vis-a-vis, for example, politicians, military personnel and bureaucrats. (Adekanye, 1994).

The effects of the brain drain range from serious to devastating for many affected universities. Staff losses generate additional work loads for those that remain, produce a continuing need for costly staff development programs, and negatively influence university teaching and research: the combined effect is to undermine the quality of the university enterprise. (Luhanga, 1993). There can be no doubt that, in many cases, the staffing position of such institutions as University Teaching Hospitals, and other key faculties and research institutes/units has deteriorated. As a result, the training and production of such essential manpower as doctors is grossly impaired; the task of the universities to produce and supply graduates of good quality and adequate numbers necessary to cope with the needs of national development, is being seriously frustrated; expensive infrastructures remain idle and deteriorate due to disuse; badly needed research remains undone, while promising research has had to be abandoned. At a time when governments are, or should be, according adequate importance to science and technology, such frustration in the work of the universities and relevant research institutions kills the promise and hope expected from the intervention of science and technology in the development of African countries.

The existence of senior academic staff contributes immensely to the quality and quantity of teaching and research in the universities, as well as to their administration. A university that fails to keep its senior academic staff is likely to lag behind in innovation and creativeness, and hence perpetuate dependence on external sources for generating new ideas. (ESAURP, 1987; UNESCO-BREDA, 1992). Regrettably, Africa's universities and research institutions continue to be robbed of senior academics who should be providing intellectual leadership for the development of new areas, advanced research and postgraduate supervision. The institutions are, thus, deprived of men and women that could advance significantly the cause of scholarship, science and technology and the opportunity to contribute to the establishment and consolidation of African universities as eminent seats of learning, research and scholarly excellence. Instead, many African universities are left with young, inexperienced and insufficiently trained staff who lack the necessary mentors and role models to guide them. (Saint, 1992).

Apart from staff who resign their positions and move elsewhere, African universities also suffer significant qualitative losses as staff resources are drained away by a combination of secondary employment, extended leaves, and secondments. (Blair, 1993). With regard to secondary employment, the economic crisis has motivated many academics to seek private teaching work or other paying activities outside the university, while others seek for extra work within the university. (Assie-Lumumba, 1993). Some staff also operate small business enterprises. Improved personnel management may ensure that such secondary employment does not unduly impair the efficiency of the staff concerned, but many universities lack the necessary personnel management policies. (Blair, *op. cit.*). It is therefore necessary to establish personnel management systems which give clear guidance on issues such as career development, promotion procedures, leave and outside employment policies.

African universities and other institutions of higher education will not be in a position to attract, recruit and hold together good staff, adequate in numbers, expertise, and morale if all they can offer are poor salaries, deficient working conditions and insufficient opportunities for research and academic advancement. (Goma, 1989). However, many committed academics still show a strong preference for university life. They place a high priority on research and publication opportunities, and generally plan to stay and seek promotion within their current institutions. (Blair, 1993) Others demonstrate growing interest in consultancy and contract research possibilities. Staff retention requires institutional packages which provide a satisfying professional environment. (Court, 1993). Among these, priority should be accorded to efforts to improve academic working conditions, particularly through the provision of more resources for teaching and research and related facilities. (Blair, 1993).

Experience elsewhere has shown that one key to retaining exceptional people and to repatriating those who go abroad is to identify and support such highly trained and talented individuals, without waiting for the development of a total national strategy. (*Education and World Affairs*, 1970). This is an extremely complex and potentially explosive issue in the circumstances of many African countries. Any ill-considered plan to repatriate outstanding nationals who had migrated may adversely affect the morale of those who stayed behind. It is indeed to the good of a nation to identify the ablest leaders in critical fields, and to provide the conditions enabling them to stay at home and contribute most fully to the development and progress of the country. African universities and countries should marshal enough courage to defend any such action taken to support highly skilled and productive individuals and provide them with selective incentives. Such action should be seen in the light of fundamental realities. Highly trained and skilled manpower constitute the very foundation for national development and sustained economic growth: by training such people and losing them through the brain drain, African countries suffer a double loss. Yet such loss is inevitable in view of the severe and unabating international competition for able, well-educated and highly-trained men and women. Bold steps are, therefore, necessary to break this vicious circle. A less attractive but more affordable package will not solve the problem.

It is thus clear that policies and programmes need to be developed in Africa's universities and other institutions of higher education that can help stem the flow of Africa's finest intellectual resources to overseas institutions, and also reduce the need for African academics and trainers to supplement their salaries with second jobs or outside business interests.

### The Culpability of the African Universities

As we have seen, immediately before and following independence, many African countries created or were assisted to create excellent facilities in their universities and research institutions which produced some outstanding achievements. However, maintaining that excellence has proved a major problem. We have drawn attention to some of the causes of decline. In some cases, excellence had been maintained by external financing and expatriate staff. In some of such cases, standards collapsed when external financing and staffing disappeared, and nationals failed to perform well without expatriate leadership. The inability of the university communities to prevent the massive deterioration of the universities cannot be blamed entirely on factors external to the institutions themselves. If the state collapses, it is inevitable that the university should also collapse. Many academics have been part of governments that prey on their people to the point of total collapse. African university people have not always stood up on the side of democracy, or of imposing limitations on the exercise of state power. There seems to have been inadequate attention, even on university campuses, to the need to maintain excellence in institutions so vital to national development. Many academics seemed to have given up the fight to maintain conditions necessary for excellence too readily. Many appear to have just looked on as the virus of deterioration set in and began to take its toll.

Moreover, many of the universities in Africa became victims of their own success. In responding to society's urgent demands, they enlarged their functions, especially with regard to teaching and production of high-level manpower, often at the expense of other tertiary institutions. Thus, in many countries, there is considerable (university) graduate unemployment and underemployment, while intermediate staff are still under-produced. Yet, in the process, the universities continue to be emptied of their substance as both their material and human resources are strained and drained.

While it is true that virtually all African countries are afflicted by a pervasive and damaging economic crisis, many African universities have failed to forcefully exert sufficient, incessant, and concerted efforts upon their governments as to the absolute necessity of the university enterprise in the task of national development and progress, and hence the need to accord appropriate priority to the universities. On the whole, the universities have generally failed to give adequate information about themselves to the general public. The absence of an effective commitment, by governments, to the universities should also be seen as the failure of the universities to generate and sustain such commitment.

## Doing More With Less

The problems facing African universities and other institutions of higher education are indeed so complex that they cannot be solved by any one-dimensional approach. (Assie-Lumumba, 1993). Therefore, while some are more basic than others, any efforts aiming at revitalizing these institutions must deal with a whole range of issues. A general recovery in the quality of teaching, learning and research in the universities, throughout the continent, needs a long-term perspective; but long-term requirements should not deter immediate action. (Coombe, 1991). "There is plenty of evidence that the morale of university communities is highly sensitive to well-conceived, constructive action in support of academic values, such as enabling academics to gain access to the tools of their trade, and the means of academic communication. Even major improvements in the physical environment of universities, equally vital for students and academic staff, can be made quite rapidly, given the provision of funds for repair and maintenance, and essential furniture and equipment, as some governments have recently discovered".

The fact that public funds do not flow freely enough to meet the planned or desired targets should not make African universities to simply throw up their arms in despair. On the contrary, they must take up the task of finding ways of pushing aside the obstacles in order to make room for academic innovation and creativeness, despite the constraints on resources. This might become the essential challenge for Africa's institutions of higher education in the years to come. As put forcefully by John Sizer, (*in* Morris and Sizer, 1982), in a different but relevant context, the major managerial challenge of the universities should be to maintain institutional vitality, creativity and responsiveness to changing needs when all the pressures may well be working in the opposite direction.

When resources are limited, the task is how best to transform even the shortages into meaningful educational and institutional services. Allocation of scarce resources demands a commitment to realism and a determination to face a hard future and make the best of it. Nevertheless, the university in Africa should continue to be propelled by the quest to manage not just for survival, but also for excellence. This could well mean possible contraction, adaptation and restructuring: for example, discontinuing some courses, closing of some departments and units, or reducing the numbers of certain categories of staff - essentially squeezing existing activities to create funds for what must continue.

Contraction is always difficult, particularly within successful institutions. (Sims *in* Morris and Sizer, 1982). Decisions on where it should be effected demand very careful consideration; and "[t]here are no magic solutions to the problem of which path should be followed unless there are conspicuously weak activities, whether measured by student demand and quality or by staff achievement". Nevertheless, contraction must be achieved as far as possible by general consent and the ways in which such consent is sought and secured, as well as the areas in which contraction is to be achieved, will vary greatly from one institution to another.

African universities need to develop strategies for long-term resource mobility as well as for short-term survival. As elsewhere, in the absence of well developed plans, there is a danger that resource-allocating authorities might take decisions which are not consistent with maintaining the longer-term healthiness of the institutions. African universities must, therefore, develop planning capacities "so as to determine their objectives, measure their success and allocate resources to their priorities".

(Blair, 1990).

Academic decisions having been made about the institutional shape of the university, the difficult problem of achieving a fair and appropriate distribution of financial resources must be faced. (Sims, 1982, *in* Morris and Sizer, 1982). If government grants are enough, budgeting allocations to faculties and departments would be based on the criteria on which financial resources were allocated to the higher education system by government, and the operating budget process would be devoid of serious conflicts. (Mbajiorgu, 1991). But underfunding is the grim reality African universities face and the environment within which resource allocation decisions have to be taken is volatile and sometimes time-constrained.

What kind of internal financial mechanisms in the allocation of funds should be instituted in the African universities so that no proper activity suffers gross inequitable treatment? Are there agreed norms to guide internal fund allocation? "Since resource allocation is the framework within which an institution tries to achieve its goals, the style and substance of resource allocation procedures play a key part in allowing an institution to be effective". (Fielden *in* Morris and Sizer, 1982). An unambiguous participatory system makes great sense. This "calls for critical inputs at various committee levels in which priorities and ideals are traded off, departmental needs compromised, and strong opinions mitigated". (Mbajiorgu, 1991).

The concept of unit of resource (or formula financing) needs re-examination as not all necessary university activities are student number-related. (Sims *in* Morris and Sizer, 1982). However, African universities may find it not unreasonable that the portion of the government subvention relating to staff emoluments should be computed on the basis of an overall staff:student ratio of, say, 1 : 10 with respect to teaching and research staff taken together, and an overall ratio of 3 : 10 in the case of administrative and other support staff. (Republic of Zambia, 1989). However, universities should be free to engage staff in excess of these guidelines, but in that case, the 'extra' posts cannot be expected to attract funding from the public purse.

As circumstances may dictate, African governments and their universities should establish an unambiguous pragmatic system of allocating funds to these institutions, if none already exists. Among the most common systems are a university grants committee (UGC), and a triennial or quinquennial review committee. (TRC or QRC). The advantage of the UGC system is that it provides a mechanism for forward planning and commitments. However, in recent years, universities have tended to replace the UGC intermediate planning system with the practice of negotiating annual funds in direct discussions with relevant government officials. The shift to such short-term arrangements reflects the fact that many countries have found it difficult, if not impossible, to honour longer-term recommendations for planned annual financial allocations to their universities. (ESAURP, 1987). "While the UGC system removes the uncertainty of erratic annual cash flows, thus enabling the university to make firm forward commitments, the annual review system introduces a measure of flexibility worthy of recognition. This is especially true in situations of high inflation, when long-term allocations of funds are rendered virtually meaningless as a result of the unpredictable purchasing power of the various national currency units". Nevertheless, in order to provide some stability in the planning environment, it is necessary to get government, whenever possible, to make some commitment in advance to the university's three-yearly or five-yearly plans.

It is important to note that the imposition of strict cash limits, in a sector such as higher education where 'product prices' cannot be increased and where salaries are determined by a process of 'free' collective bargaining, has resulted in a majority of universities substituting short-term survival strategies for coherent academic planning. (Sims, 1982, *in* Morris and Sizer, 1982). Therefore, new developments have had to take second place to redundancy policies, a state of planlessness in which neither the 'consevative community of scholars' nor the 'progressive protagonists of national need' have found much room for manoeuvre, let alone for comfort.

The keynote for institutional survival has been and will continue to be 'flexibility'. (Fielden, 1982, *in* Morris and Sizer, 1982). "Flexibility will be needed in several senses:

- In attitudes, expressed as an openness to new proposals, which may challenge conventional structures or approaches but which will aid the prosperity of the institution.

- In resource-allocation techniques and procedures since, as has already been shown, the environment within which resource decisions have to be taken is volatile and sometimes time-constrained.

- In structures and powers, with an acceptance of possible risk-taking by people to whom decision-making has been delegated. Formal structures may remain, but as endorsing bodies, holding individuals to account for their decisions".

**Financing of Higher Education**

The politics of higher education takes various forms. It centres largely on questions of access, equity and equality of educational opportunity, financing, and the influence of external forces. What policy options might there be which deserve serious consideration and can be resorted to in the circumstances?

The squeeze on resources is certainly a major challenge to the African governments and the institutions of higher education themselves. For many governments and institutions, the search for a coherent higher education policy has been an elusive one. However, financial inadequacies are forcing state officials and administrators to reflect, more fundamentally and determinedly than hitherto, on the goals of higher education and the priorities thereof, as well as the place of higher education in the entire educational system of the country. The financial cutbacks are exposing inefficiencies in higher education policies and flaws in institutional management which were previously masked by growth.

In 1988, the World Bank published a very important policy study on Education in Sub-Saharan Africa, following extensive consultation with African Ministers of Education, with African educational specialists, educationists in industrialized countries, the staffs of the World Bank itself, and other donor agencies. The World Bank Report recommended *adjustment* as the answer to austerity. Adjustment can take two main forms: (a) diversifying sources of finance or increasing the financing of higher education from sources other than public expenditure; and (b) unit cost containment or increasing the efficiency of the delivery systems. However, before embarking on such long-term adjustment, priority will need to be accorded to the *revitalization* of existing infrastructure to restore quality and to identify certain critical aspects for highly selective development. There is need for countries and their institutions of higher education to examine these possibilities. What is clear, however, is that the solution to the serious crisis of higher education in Africa cannot be achieved without some sacrifice. (Goma, 1989).

Governments and managements of higher education institutions in Africa must realize that planning with stable or contracting resources is not simply a variation of planning with the expectation of growth. The quantitative and qualitative gains achieved in higher education so far are likely to deteriorate further unless new planning methods, as well as new strategies, are developed which recognize changed circumstances and respond to them positively. In future, managers of higher education will need to learn to compete more effectively for resources against the claims of other types of public agencies and institutions.

It is unrealistic to imagine any immediate replacement of the state in the financing of higher education in Africa. (Assie-Lumumba, 1993). The financial squeeze has led to greater attention being given to the question of financial diversification as a strategy for financial stabilization. (Assie-Lumumba, *op. cit.*; Blair, 1992; Saint, 1992; World Bank, 1988, 1989). Of the various possibilities for financial diversification which exist, perhaps the most promising and yet most explosive is that of requiring contributions from beneficiaries and their families; and thereby shifting public resources from providing student welfare to providing education. As William S. Saint (*op. cit.*) indicates, as an alternative to the total collapse of the system, the practice of cost recovery through student fees is gaining acceptance, particularly when applied to specific services such as registration, library access, laboratory use and student activities. Sizeable shares of higher education budgets are consumed by providing students with free room and board at public expense. Anglophone governments spend 12 percent of tertiary education budgets on student services, whereas Francophone governments spend a staggering 55 percent. More effort can still be made to recover the costs of student housing and meals. However, where students are crowded into dormitory rooms, lack sanitary facilities, and subsist on poor quality food, the introduction of cost recovery may provoke strong reaction. Such changes need to be linked with initial investments to improve the quality of meals and accommodation so as to justify increased fees.

Similarly, where this is not already the case, tuition fees should be introduced, "although they should not be applied uniformly. The real payment capacity of students and their families must be analyzed. These fees ought to be symbolic for students from low-income families but quite high for a well-off minority". (Assie-Lumumba, 1993). It is also essential to create student loans schemes to ensure that, by providing needy ones with access to financial credit, qualified students are not kept out of higher education on financial grounds.

Other possibilities for increased income generation include contract research, consultancy services, continuing education programmes, business enterprise, facilities rental, and fund-raising through alumni associations. Among these, continuing education and the marketing of university facilities appear to hold the most immediate promise. (Saint, 1992). In this regard, commercial enterprises can be regarded as beneficiaries of higher education, and a tax levied on their profits. In such cases the revenue accruing should be devoted to research from which the companies can directly benefit, sometimes in lieu of establishing their own R&D (Research and Development) departments. "Consultancy services and business activities should be approached with caution and careful cost monitoring, as it is not clear that universities possess a comparative advantage in these areas". It is also important to bear in mind that income generation activities must not detract from the main mission of the higher education institutions. (Republic of Zambia,1989). Ideally, institutions should target those income-generating activities that relate to their mission and where they have expertise which they can sell.

**Dangerous Ambivalence**

It is agreed that higher education is of paramount importance for Africa's future. Even the World Bank (1988) admits that "Africa requires both highly trained people and top-quality research in order to be able to formulate the policies, plan the programmes, and implement the projects that are essential to economic growth and development. Preparing individuals for positions of responsibility - in government, in business, and in the professions - is a central role of the continent's universities; supporting these individuals in their work - with research, advice, and consultancy - is another equally important role". But how can the universities in Africa be expected to fulfill these roles when their development is being stifled? Many in Africa feel that the policies of the World Bank as applied in the past, or even now, do not favour the development of African universities. (Assie-Lumumba, 1993). The same attitude is portrayed by many in the donor community. Yet countries in the modern world are developed by elites, who are responsible for their scientific and technological progress. "The industrialized countries are aware of this and make higher education the engine of their development, which is based on a mastery of science and technology. Without higher education, Africa would be eternally dependent; participation in the creation of knowledge requires higher education ... The perception of the World Bank's message [and that of many in the donor community] is that others will take care of creating this knowledge for the Africans". (Assie-Lumumba, 1993). It cannot be over-emphasized that only Africans can really understand the problems confronting them, and that any real solution must be developed from within. External support helps; but what Africa needs most urgently is the right African capacities. If African countries lack the appropriate expertise, Africans will not be able to participate effectively, if at all, in major decisions that affect them. African universities and other institutions of higher education are the key to the development of the needed capacities. Therefore, any attempt to undermine the development and progress of African universities, through negative influence by outsiders, should be seen as dangerous and quite unacceptable.

There is a ground swell that African countries should accord high priority to primary or basic education. Accordingly, there is a hardening of attitudes against higher education. The 1990 Jomtien World Conference on Education for All is being distorted in some quarters in such a way as to undermine higher education. But the Jomtien World Declaration on Education for All does not devalue higher education. It states quite clearly that many kinds of expertise and skills will be needed to carry out various initiatives targeted on basic education. "Managerial and supervisory personnel, as well as planners, school architects, [teachers and] teacher educators, curriculum developers, researchers, analysts, etc., are important for any strategy to improve basic education". (Inter-Agency Commission, 1990). But for the African continent, as elsewhere, these resources must be developed, produced, and supplied by the universities and other institutions of higher education. It is, therefore, grossly misleading to suggest that the development and provision of higher education in Africa works against the continent's development and provision of primary/basic education.

Many technical agreements and donor funded programmes provide for the employment of so-called "experts" from the donor countries. The need for high-level manpower is recognized by these countries; and there are no qualms about the employment of their own nationals. But the production of such human resources locally, at African universities, seems to excite little enthusiasm and support; for, it is denied or grudgingly offered. Donor attitudes to technical assistance have to change. "Instead of being seen as an employment opportunity for a national in the donor country - as it is in many cases - technical assistance must become an opportunity for an African to pick up a skill, for African institutional infrastructure to be built, for Africans to do the job. This means that donors will have to give up some control: in the choice of a project - an African priority, not theirs. And in the implementing mechanisms - African, not externally-devised". (Jaycox, 1990). Furthermore, instead of earmarking funds for narrowly defined projects, donors should target their higher education assistance on longer-term institutional development. (Saint, 1992). In order that African capacities can be built and needed indigenous human resources developed, international financial organisations and the donor community should exert a more positive and effective influence towards African higher education and be unambiguously supportive of African universities and other institutions of higher education than has hitherto been the case.

## Access and Equity

Managing the social demand for access to higher education is perhaps the

single most difficult task faced by the tertiary sector in Africa today (Saint, 1992).
Burgeoning population growth, rapidly rising numbers of secondary graduates, and
persistent economic stagnation, combine to exert intense pressures on governments
to expand university access. The elite nature of university graduates, together with
the fact that university education is publicly subsidized, makes university access a
contentious political issue. (Klitgaard, 1991, *in* Saint, *op. cit.*).

The various interest groups involved, including students, families, teachers,
researchers, administrators, the state and governments, perceive and experience the
problems of higher education differently. (Assie-Lumumba, 1993). Thus, for rural
families in village communities from which only a handful of young people have been
able to continue their studies to university level, the problems pertaining to large
numbers appear remote, and do not even seem to make sense. Much more pressing
issues are the costs they must directly bear, the expansion of the system, so that a
larger number of their children can have the opportunity to attend university, and the
prospects of obtaining a scholarship and a job. Among students and teachers, the
subjects most often raised are the mismatch between student numbers and infrastructure
capacity, and the low internal and external efficiency of the system. States and
governments are more inclined to be concerned about financial issues and the control
and absorption of university graduates.

The solutions proposed, particularly by donors but also by some local leaders,
for dealing with the excessive numbers of university students tend to favor the drastic
shutting off of this flow. (Assie-Lumumba, 1993). A number of ways of doing this
have been suggested. One would involve the pure and simple elimination of automatic
admission to the university of those who have passed the secondary school-leaving
examination, where such admission is now the case as in Francophone African
countries. But "in searching for solutions for controlling student numbers, it is
important to bear in mind that the combined effect of the adoption of a system of
competitive entry into the university and payment of tuition fees in higher education
may be to create an unprecedentedly selective and elitist system". However, if access
depends on the payment of tuition fees that are beyond the reach of certain social
classes, there is a serious risk of the latter becoming under-represented.

It has been argued that even the impact of student fees on certain groups and
the admission of a small segment via competitive entry or some selection procedure
will not reduce enrollments to the point of creating a satisfactory match between
student numbers and university infrastructures. (Assie-Lumumba, 1993). "Any
measure to reduce enrollment simply by making it impossible for some of the students
finishing secondary education to get into the university is socially unacceptable in

terms equity and equality of opportunity, and would be politically infeasible. It is not hard to see that the socially underprivileged [especially those in the rural areas] would be disproportionately more affected. Those with economic and political power would not accept that their children could not go beyond the secondary level. Even if merit were made the main criterion, they would also want their less deserving children to have a chance to succeed, and success is the aim of the young in all social groups".

The *numerus clausus* system - "cut-off point", that is, controlling student numbers by limiting entry into the university - operates in many African countries. Realities dictate that other African countries cannot escape it indefinitely. However, it is imperative that efforts to control student flows to the universities must go hand in hand with the creation of a more differentiated higher education system which offers a wider range of satisfactory alternatives at the end of secondary education. (Assie-Lumumba, 1993; Saint, 1992). This will mitigate the risk of creating profound inequities and preparing the ground for social unrest. Efficient and equitable selection mechanisms will be necessary to allocate students within a differentiated higher education system. In other words, selection policies must be seen as fair if the result is to be accepted as legitimate. A key component of a satisfactory selection procedure should be some type of competitive entrance examination.

No discussion of access and equity would be complete without taking into account consideration of groups that have been traditionally discriminated against, whether deliberately or inadvertently. Women in general, and blacks in the South African situation, constitute two of the most notable such groups. As political systems work towards the democratisation of their societies, it becomes clear that inequities must be redressed at all levels, giving access to higher education as much as possible to all those who qualify for it, and ensuring that adequate facilities are provided at primary and secondary school levels so that no group starts off at a disadvantage. Further, because past discrimination has inflicted almost irreparable damage on these groups, the issue of affirmative action must be explored with a view to compensating them for the harm done and, as quickly as possible, bringing them to a level where they can compete with others on an equal footing. Affirmative action is, however, a two-edged sword and must be handled with extreme care so that discrimination against past oppressors does not become institutionalised. Affirmative action must be used only as a remedial tool for a short period until balance is re-established.

### Campus Politics

Most African universities have experienced some form of student unrest or disruption over the past several years. The causes of student unrest are very complex indeed. However, this phenomenon has ceased to be unusual and can be anticipated when certain developments take place, especially those which, in the opinion of students, affect them negatively. But there is a new worrying phenomenon creeping into the universities, in some of them at least. University campuses are becoming unionized, fragmented into rival unions - of students, workers, academic staff, and administrative and technical staff - that may be tempted to place the interest of their particular unions before the overall interest of the university. Thus, they sometimes pull in opposite directions, making incompatible demands that tear the university apart. This is, in part, a response to the distressing situation in the universities, and the effort of different groups to fight to protect their own interests as best they could. Perhaps the worst of this is the phenomenon of academic staff unrest and trade unionism which it has introduced, when academic staff refuse to teach and/or mark examination papers or provide records of the results of continuous assessment of students.

The causes of academic staff unrest could be complex. They relate largely to dissatisfaction with their remuneration and other conditions of service. They, sometimes, relate to disenchantment with the university administration and especially the Vice-Chancellor, President or Rector whose resignation or removal they demand. They could also relate to a power struggle within the university. Very rarely do they relate to poor or grossly inadequate teaching and/or research facilities or resources.

The effect of such (academic staff) unrest is, of course, the disruption of the normal functioning of the university. The dangers of this are many. The temptation to have the university closed by the authorities is only one of the possible consequences. The academic profession is bound to grow considerably less distinguishable from other enterprises, and reduce the perceived distance between the world of learning and the ordinary spheres of life. Academic people in the African universities will find it increasingly difficult to persuade the public that they are, as elsewhere, in some generic way, distinctive. But the more crucial point is that contemporary academics will find it increasingly difficult even to persuade themselves so. In the words of Walter P. Metzger (1975): "They have grown less certain not only of what it is that makes them different from other workers, but of whether differences, even if they could be found, would be necessary, proper, or worth preserving. The slings and arrows of an untaught public may inflict lighter injuries on this [academic] profession than does its own enfeebled sense of self".

Equally, movements to organise non-academic employees through external labour organizations and to use the traditional union devices, such as the strike and the picket line, confront the developing university in Africa with an unusual challenge.

How much should such movements be given free play in the university? And how much can they be thought to be contributing primarily to the fundamental purposes of the university? Some will say that these developments in the African academia are inevitable. Nevertheless, we need to consider to what extent the 'inevitable' is merely that which is not resisted with determination.

## Obstacles to Change in African Higher Education

As pointed out by the Right Reverend Alphonse-Marie Parent: universities generally have, as organisations, rather conservative habits of reaction. "They shelter many inventive and creative minds and many people capable of reflecting in a free and bold manner on all kinds of problems. But as soon as a really profound and unexpected change is suggested in the curriculum or in the pedagogical or administrative structure of a department or a faculty, the professors who see some improvement in this are few indeed". (Parent, 1966). It is thus not surprising that universities are among the most change-resistant institutions in the world. This has certainly been the experience with the African universities, even with their relatively short history.

To bring about important innovative and creative developments in the African universities will, therefore, not be easy. Such tasks demand courage. Some people will be inhibited to move forward by the past and the well-beaten path. Others, perhaps not fully appreciating the challenge and the opportunity proffered by proposed changes or possible new directions will use their immense influence at home and elsewhere to defeat or place serious impediments in the path of possible new developments. Still others will simply be fearful of the unknown.

There is no denying the fact that some valuable and, indeed, promising initiatives have taken place here and there. But, as expected, success has not been easy and usually not gone very far. (Goma, 1989). In some cases, the problem has been indifference; in others, it has been the stone wall of opposition to change. Change can make the well established authorities lose part of their power over areas of their knowledge and competence. Who then is to introduce changes that will be backed by recognised authority and stand a good chance of being accepted? Who is to implement the changes and face the possibility of redundancy and loss of job among some whose areas of expertise may no longer be required? These issues have to be confronted squarely. Doing more of the same thing is a dangerous escape from the challenge of promoting significant reform and change in African higher education.

At different times in the past, there has been some spirited resistance to radical reform and adaptation in the curriculum and pattern of university courses to suit African conditions. In the 1960s, some African intellectuals, especially those educated in Britain, resisted such changes which they confused with a lowering of standards. (Eric Ashby, 1966). They accordingly became suspicious of any attempt to diverge from the British pattern. They considered that any radical changes in the pattern of degree courses, or the introduction of unconventional subjects of study, was a sure way of disarming them intellectually. Similar attitudes have been demonstrated among those educated within the French pattern of higher education. In confronting the problems of the 1990s, it is important to ensure that such resistance to reform is dealt with firmly.

Chapter 8

## SPECIAL ISSUES

## I. ACADEMIC FREEDOM AND UNIVERSITY AUTONOMY

The twin concepts of academic freedom and university autonomy are among the most important issues concerning the existence, mission and role of the university throughout the world. Universities have always considered the ideas of freedom and autonomy to be indispensable values and have defended them as such. Autonomy protects the corporate rights of self-regulation which the state confers upon the university as an institution in the law setting it up. It's extent and definition, therefore, depends on the nature of the state, and may need to be negotiated from time to time between the academy and the state. Autonomy can, therefore, not connote independence of the state and is best understood in the spirit of partnership with the state. (Moja, 1995). However, with the technology and the bureaucracy available to most African governments at this time, it is believed that more efficiency will be achieved if there were more, not less, delegation of power by the state to expert corporations and groups of professionals. Academic freedom refers to the immunities which the university teacher as a professional needs to enjoy in order to function effectively. This is obviously related to, but goes beyond, the general rights of the citizen to freedom of thought and expression. These concepts have been discussed widely and the literature on them is extensive. In Africa, as elsewhere, the need for efficient management, accountability and periodic evaluation are also forcing their way to centre stage, especially in the face of strangulating stringency and declining resources. A major issue, then is the extent to which these pose threats to academic freedom and university autonomy.

### The Continuing Relevance

No one familiar with the operations of the university in the discharge of its mission and role in society can doubt the value of academic freedom and university autonomy. Briefly, academic freedom and university autonomy are essential to the advancement, transmission and application of knowledge. In practical terms, academic freedom and university autonomy relate to the protection of the university from day to day direction by government officials, specifically on:

1. the selection of students;
2. the appointment and removal of academic staff;
3. the determination of the content of university education and the control of degree standards;
4. the determination of size and rate of growth;
5. the establishment of the balance between teaching, research and advanced study, the selection of research projects, and freedom of publication; and
6. the allocation of recurrent income among the various categories of expenditure.

The challenge, especially for African universities modelled after the British universities, has been how to secure, defend and protect these freedoms. Universities in other parts of Africa have been influenced more by practices in continental Europe where the selection of students, the appointment of academic staff and the determination of curricula are taken out of the control of the universities. They are processed by university people, but with legal control vested in the National Ministry of Education. For example, candidates for academic appointments are evaluated by academic bodies, but the actual appointments are made in the name of the Minister of Education. He also approves the curricula, and he supervises the detailed operation of university budgets. Thus, in the European system, the emphasis is not on university autonomy as such, but on academic freedom. Government supervision is done without interfering with the academic freedom of the university teachers. Indeed, teachers in Francophone African universities, for a long time, enjoyed more than adequate protection because they inherited the immunities enjoyed by French teachers under what is known as the *university franchise*.

Academic freedom finds its principal justification in its functional significance with regard to the advancement of knowledge which demands that the processes of seeking objective truth should not be corrupted by ideologies and interests. (de Moor, 1993). "For such [advancement] cannot be fostered by hampering creative minds in their attempts to follow the path of discovery which they consider most promising". At the same time, however, "this definition does not imply that the advancement of knowledge, and therefore of academic freedom, requires that an academic should be completely free as to his choice of subjects to teach and research". It has its limitations: for example, as a principle, academic freedom is neither a licence for incompetence nor protection from quality control. (de Moor, *op. cit.*) Another limitation is to be found in ethical considerations. "Not every approach to scientific work is ethically acceptable: some experiments with human beings, for instance, may be forbidden".

For the university in Africa to play a meaningful role and discharge its responsibilities effectively, it must enjoy a high degree of institutional autonomy, in addition to the academic freedom of its academic staff. As part of its autonomy, it must have freedom to run its own affairs, without external interference; it must have the right to organize its internal affairs, to make decisions, and to establish its own academic programmes. (Kamba, 1993). However, because the financing of higher education has increased tremendously (and most African universities are financed entirely by the state), "the research undertaken in the universities and the pedagogical role of universities as well, have become increasingly dependent on political and economic decisions taken by governments, parliaments, and public and private authorities". (de Moor, 1993). What is the likely effect of this development on the management of universities?

Although academic freedom and university autonomy are considered essential to the advancement, transmission, and application of knowledge, "these concepts are often used to defend privileges which are not beneficial to the well-functioning of universities, either with regard to teaching or to research". (de Moor, 1993; See also Alexander, 1986, p. 466-7). We have shown above how expatriate staff used it to defend their privileges in the colonial universities and how in the `white' universities in South Africa, even the `open' English-speaking ones, it was invoked to defend the right to exclude the majority African population. Similarly, in a number of their actions against their governments and/or university authorities, students in many African universities claim that they are doing so in defence of academic freedom and university autonomy. (Goma, 1989). University autonomy can indeed also be the cover for corporatist attitudes, for abuses of privilege, such as the quasi-automatic granting of tenure, the practical effect of which is to weaken claims to autonomy and encourage those discriminated against to seek state intervention. (Mayor, 1993).

In many African universities academic values and university autonomy have been confused, and academics and their supporters in society have taken it for granted that the protection of academic freedom and institutional autonomy somehow guarantees the establishment and maintenance of high standards. (Austin, 1980). But of course that is by no means the case. "Indeed, the attempt to defend formal structures of university administration left over from the formative colonial years has absorbed a good deal of the critical energy that might more helpfully have gone into teaching and research". There has been an unfortunate tendency among African academics to belittle the place of efficient management. And yet the argument has been advanced that effectiveness and efficiency cannot be achieved without university autonomy.

Institutional autonomy is not and cannot be absolute. (Millett, 1984) It should be realized that no country in the world has a government which does not retain some control over its institutions of higher education, which are considered as public services. Nevertheless, it has been argued that government intrusion into the university can lead to the strangulation of the institution. The problem really is where to draw the line. As Derek C. Bok, a distinguished American scholar, has asked: "How much autonomy should universities have in carrying out their functions? Under what circumstances may the government intervene? And when the government acts, what methods of regulation should it employ to achieve its ends with minimum damage to the academic enterprise? Thus, our task is not merely to strike a proper balance between public needs and the private needs of the academy, but to decide how governments and universities can work in harmony so that higher education will make its greatest contribution to the welfare of society".

## Accountability

Autonomy is one side of the coin; accountability is the other. The accountability of the university, which is demanded, is ultimately no different from that of any other social actor: it must demonstrate the relevance of its role to the needs of society, and it must allow the effectiveness with which it performs that role to be subject to review. (Mayor, 1993) The proportion of national income that goes into university budgets is such that governments need to make universities accountable. Governments have to justify the size of the allocations to universities relative to allocations to other agencies competing for public funds. "They want to know how the money is spent, what the results of teaching are, that is, whether or not students are really well-educated when they graduate, and the results of research, that is, whether or not they can be put to good use by society and whether or not their quality stands up to international comparison.". (Andren and Johansson-Dahre, 1993).

The question is: how can the autonomy of the university be reconciled with government control of finance? Certainly, the price of the institutional autonomy of the university is "an impeccable level of efficiency, performance, and service to the community, and an administration which can demonstrate that this is so to the point where it is fully trusted by the community and the government it elects". (Baxter. 1968). Indeed, the state is answerable for public funds and has, therefore, a specific duty and responsibility to allot public funds in a manner which assures the efficiency of the educational system and an economical use of available resources. The danger to watch is that in the process, government finance officers may thereby be taking crucial decisions about the university; and, thus, public officials who may be ill-equipped to make educational decisions are moved into a position where they come to manage higher education without bearing any visible responsibility for the success or failure of the decisions they make. (Goma, 1989).

Equally unacceptable are situations where university governing councils, in exercise of powers granted them under the constitutions of their respective universities, without prior consultations, take decisions which commit governments to increased expenditures not already budgeted for. (Goma, 1989). Specifically, the question of the salaries and other conditions of service for university staff and of the fees to be paid by students, could lead to serious difficulties in this regard. "When university governing bodies cannot take final decisions on these matters because the money to implement them must be sought and secured from government, are they abdicating their responsibilities and duties or is the government usurping such responsibilities and duties?" (Goma, *op. cit.*).

Government provides funds to universities from a limited purse and cannot afford to allow the universities a free hand in the expenditure of funds. Accordingly, financial autonomy as desired by some universities becomes difficult to secure. Even so, it is recognized that some degree of financial autonomy is essential for the effective operation of the African universities. For example, universities should be allowed a fair measure of autonomy in deciding allocation of general university subventions among the departments and institutes. However, the key to university financial autonomy is to try to diversify sources of funding. Therefore, in the face of increasing inadequacy of government funding, and in order to increase university financial autonomy, it is imperative to consider alternative ways of funding university education in Africa: introducing student fees where these do not exist; student loans to assist those who cannot raise the fees through their own efforts; consultancies, *et cetera*. The question of student welfare costs and possible contribution by beneficiaries to their education is a touchy one and needs to be handled with great care and compassion.

The realities are that, irrespective of the university model adopted in Africa, governments use financial control to influence, and sometimes even to direct, their universities on the rate of growth both in terms of capital development and student intake; the staffing of universities and the remuneration payable to academic staff. (Goma, *op. cit*). Conditions attached to the supply of money may be considered as an erosion of the autonomy of universities. A contrary view is that these and other governmental interventions should be seen as other than the intrusion of hostile external authorities. More than financial accountability is involved. That resources be carefully and efficiently used is a minimum requirement to be met. State and society may equally demand that universities have high teaching standards, that they produce a sufficient number of graduates, and that they take the interests of society into account in their research. (de Moor, 1993). Even philanthropic donors rarely give money without attaching conditions which enable them to monitor how effectively the funds are being managed.

Quality control is no longer an unknown phenomenon in the academic world. Preferably, institutions should develop their own internal systems of quality control. (de Moor, 1993). "In this respect, autonomy is not a right to be demanded from the government, but a responsibility to be implemented on the initiative of universities". It should not be surprising that, unless the universities themselves introduce an effective quality control mechanism, others will be tempted to do it for them. (Mayor, 1993). What seems to be required, among other things, is a well-defined policy of staff development, including pedagogical training and continued refresher opportunities in the speciality of each staff member, linked to a genuine system of evaluation covering both teaching and research. Some African universities have made appreciable progress in this direction, but most still have a considerable way to go.

Autonomy, as it is conceived by many academics, often makes the university a kind of veto-organisation. (Zemsky, Barblan and Green, 1993). But a university cannot be a republic of sovereign faculties. It is, therefore, important that the internal organization of a university should be characterized by strong administration at the centre, and at the faculty and departmental levels. Only strongly administered, effective, and efficient universities can resist the inherent tendency of the state to interfere. (Zemsky, Barblan, and Green, *op. cit.*).

In dealing with questions of freedom and autonomy in the African university, the fundamental point to note is that research and teaching seem to suffer both when they are entirely autonomous and when they are rigidly supervised. (IAU, 1977). Academics as decision-makers need a partner to whom they are accountable. This partner may be a state bureaucracy, or their own university administration, or a foundation - any authority to which they must periodically demonstrate the scientific and social relevance of their activity and which in turn grants them the necessary autonomy and resources while mediating social demands. Therefore, if they are to be adequately accountable, African universities must seek to meet the expectations of their various stakeholders - the government, the civil society, the staff, and the students.

## Effectiveness and Efficiency

Although there is much talk of the need for greater effectiveness and efficiency in the management and performance of African universities, there is considerable lack of precision about what is meant and how efficiency might be assessed. Some people, "some of the time, may speak as if effectiveness is the same as efficiency; others as if it is measured in terms of excellence; and others again as if it is equivalent to equity. We have seen that all these considerations are relevant, and none uniquely so. In the end we have no alternative but exercise our judgement. If justice is to be done we need a sensitive pair of scales: we cannot read effectiveness [and efficiency] off a tape-measure". (Becher, 1971). The obvious is often difficult to see. But it has to be emphasized that effectiveness is a relative and not an absolute term. It is a value-laden concept. "To assert its possession is to praise, and to deny it is to condemn. Different people, attaching different weights to one tribute or another, may find themselves in disagreement, even where there is no question of fact in dispute between them".

There is a growing need to redefine the role of the African university so as to emphasize research, creativity and the generation of new knowledge. In this connection, the efficiency of universities is no longer to be measured by the number of graduates produced, but by their quality and capacity to produce the knowledge required to reduce the widespread dependence and marginalization of the African countries and continent. This development may, however, be frustrated by practices which tend to disregard the autonomy of universities, in the supposed quest for effectiveness and efficiency. Autonomy implies that the nation's most competent experts on the functions which the universities are established to perform are to be found in the universities and not in government ministries and they should be allowed to get on with their work . Yet, in many African countries, higher education is managed virtually in the ministry of national education rather than in the Vice-Chancellor's or Rector's office; the ministries lay down policies which university authorities are obliged to carry out in the face of hostile communities of students and restive assemblies of staff.

Several things need be done to improve the effectiveness and efficiency of the African university. These include possible structural reform; effecting collaboration in teaching and research; cutting down the present wasteful and time-consuming proliferation of staff committees, student committees, and staff-student committees; and requiring academic administrators to become more professional. Developments along these lines might at first be seen as encroaching on the autonomy of the university and its individual faculties. To achieve efficiency, the university needs mechanisms to promote contacts for example in research, between different faculties and departments.

## Periodic Evaluation

The matter of periodic evaluation in the university raises the obvious questions about what should be evaluated, how it should be evaluated, and who should do the evaluation. Such questions cannot be divorced from judgement about the mission of the university. Evaluation may be aimed at an overall appraisal about the institution, or it could be selectively targeted at the performance of the administration or the academic staff with respect to their teaching and/or research competence. However, if such evaluation is directed by external authorities, irrespective of whether it is conducted by outsiders or by university people or a combination of outsiders and university people selected and appointed by those external authorities, it will have infringed the autonomy of the institution concerned and the academic freedom of the staff involved. That is why the Acts of some universities provide for periodic reviews ordered by the Visitor or Chancellor as head of the university. Unfortunately, all too often, such visitations are diverted from true evaluation of the content and quality of education into details of campus politics.

In order that their institutional autonomy and the academic freedom of their staff are protected, African universities should on their own initiative institute periodic evaluation both of the performance of the institution and of the teaching and research of their staff. In doing so, they may involve outsiders in the task. But it is important that competence be judged by competent people and that the resulting judgement be immune from special interests and ideologies. (de Moor, 1993).

Innovations are frequently created on the initiative of individuals responding to new needs and new opportunities. (Sizer, 1982). Vice-Chancellors, Deans, and Directors of institutions of the university need to create an environment which motivates individuals and fosters, rather than frustrates, such initiatives. It is important that universities should recruit and support staff of high ability, but the performance of all staff should be reviewed regularly with a view to increasing their effectiveness. This involves establishing objective criteria for recruiting and promoting staff, and also ensuring that these are applied as fairly as humanly possible. It is in the firmness and fairness with which staff are evaluated for promotion that they could be motivated to pursue excellence in their research, teaching and publishing.

There is also need for an evaluation and appraisal of university programmes on a continuing basis so as to ensure their relevance and responsiveness to changing national development efforts and strategies. It would greatly facilitate such an exercise if the universities knew the fate and performance of their graduates. It would, therefore, be necessary to institute tracer projects.

Periodic evaluation, especially of the university's programmes, may save the institution from the pitfalls of decadence and immobility in a rapidly changing world. Continued academic investment in dubious programmes, under the cloak of academic freedom and institutional autonomy, can well invite interference from those outside seeking to ensure unquestionable relevance in the work of the university. It is unwise to simply take attacks on universities entirely at their face value. The dubious and "the perfectly real decadence which at times [afflict] universities [have] to be carefully distinguished from the complaints hurled by outside interests whose demands have been ignored". (Minogue, 1973).

## Handbook on Academic Freedom and University Autonomy

As we have tried to show, universities all over the world have found that they cannot function effectively without some degree of institutional autonomy and individual freedom within the academy. It is therefore important that university communities in Africa should ensure that they too enjoy these in their work. To enjoy and to defend these, it is necessary to understand their implications and limitations. Because of the prevalent confusion, with abuses and misinterpretations, of the concept of academic freedom and university autonomy, even on university campuses, it would be a good idea if the universities in Africa were each to produce a brief and concise handbook on these twin concepts, for distribution to their students, academic and non-academic staff, and administration and technical staff. The handbook should be made available to all new students and new staff. It should spell out the responsibilities of the various elements comprising the university community.

One of the issues that such a handbook might examine is the question of who should be the beneficiaries of academic freedom. One view is that academic freedom should be restricted to certain persons within the academic community, notably researchers and teachers. (Andren and Johansson-Dahre, 1993). Another view is that all members of the academic community, including the students and administrators, should have access, perhaps a more limited access, to academic freedom. Whatever the case, it is considered that the corporate autonomy of the university is a precondition for the exercise of academic freedom at the individual level. The confusion and some of the negative "mass" actions experienced in many African universities derive from lack of clarity on this question of the proper beneficiaries of an essential and universal concept.

There are far too many people who are presently exploiting, or abusing, the 'cloudiness' over academic freedom and university autonomy to further their own ends. Those who should advise the 'militants' do not seem to know what advice to give, since they themselves are ignorant or unsure about the real meaning of the concepts. In the absence of clear guidelines, the administration seems powerless to act and respond appropriately.

The integrity of the university is, among other things, buttressed by the integrity of its staff. It is, therefore, quite proper that the African university should concern itself with, and strive to uphold, the integrity of its academic staff. A *Code of Behaviour for Academic Staff* would be crucial in the achievement of this goal. Such a code should, however, ensure the protection of the academic freedom of the staff and the autonomy of the university.

## II. UNIVERSITY GOVERNANCE

In the light of the many daunting problems and challenges which African universities confront, several issues concerning university governance, the appointment and removal of the principal officers, orientation and efficiency of the university in managing with less in the face of the "winds of stringency" and declining resources, have surfaced with great force. What reforms are desirable and feasible in this area? The positions taken by a number of African governments indicate a desire to impose large-scale change on the universities and increase political and administrative supervision over their work, but such efforts have often done more harm than good.

"University governance can be defined as the mechanisms whereby an institution incorporates the participation of relevant interest groups in defining the scope and content of its work - including the capacity to mediate among these interests when they enter into conflict - and the means whereby it demonstrates accountability to those who support it through its mission mandate and the application of its resources in pursuit of these goals". (Saint, 1992). The governance of African universities, as is the case with other universities elsewhere in the world, is legally provided for in their Acts and Statutes. The characteristic features of the university institution are its relatively fragmented organizational structure, the diffusion of decision-making power among its many semi-autonomous units, and the substantial amount of authority and initiative vested in individual academics, especially the professoriate [and Deans], over important matters. (Sawyerr, 1992). "This dispersion of authority and decision-making power gives the university unusual flexibility and strength in its dealings with the outside world, and a capacity to absorb and diffuse outside pressure, changing as little as possible in the process".

William S. Saint (1992) has recently summarised university governance structures across Sub-Saharan Africa as follows. They are generally derived from the institutional models of higher education established by former colonial administrations, although they have often been modified in practice by national political philosophies and associated approaches to development administration. Within the anglophone countries, universities are normally quasi-statutory organizations created by an Act of the National Parliament. In most anglophone countries, the Head of State or Government also serves as Chancellor of the university. The Vice-Chancellor is the academic and administrative head of the institution. Responsibility for institutional policy decisions resides with a University Council whose membership is normally drawn from government, the university, and (less commonly) organizations from the private sector. Academic affairs are managed by the University Senate which possesses full responsibility for this. Teaching is organized through faculties, departments and specialized schools or institutes. In most cases, deans of faculties are elected, although heads of department tend to be appointed.

In the Lusophone countries, a more autonomous structure exists. Universities are incorporated as largely autonomous public institutions. University Councils are responsible for institutional policy-making, but their membership is drawn entirely from within the university. The Rector possesses considerable authority. Instead of a Senate, a Scientific Council manages academic affairs. Faculty deans and department heads are named by the Rector. Although funded by government, in practice these universities tend to be somewhat more independent than their sister Anglophone and Francophone institutions, although it is far from certain for how long this level of autonomy can be sustained.

Within Francophone Africa, universities are characterized by more centralized governance. Although accountable to the Minister of Education (or of Higher Education), the Rector controls daily financial and administrative matters directly. A university council, drawn from staff but containing no outside representation, sets academic policy. Deans and department heads are generally elected, and possess certain decentralized responsibilities such as admissions. The administrative model is strongly hierarchical and tends to be inflexible in the face of changing circumstances. A modified version of this exists in Yaounde where the Chancellor with the status of a junior Minister, administers the university on a full-time basis as Chief Executive, with the Vice-Chancellor, an academic, as his deputy.

It must be understood that governance is not an end in itself, but a means to serve educational purposes. (Martorana and Kuhns, 1975). The governance system, whatever its variety, is one in which power is shared by representatives of constituencies within the university and the outside community. There is an intimate relationship between governance and the implementation of academic programmes of a university. Effective and good governance can provide the stability necessary for the institutional development and progress of African universities. (Saint, 1992; Mwiria, 1992). "At present, conflictual relationships characterize the various groups within universities. Academic staff and students frequently disagree with university administration over living allowances, terms and conditions of service, and their perception that university administration promotes governmental rather than university interests. Effective mediation of these conflicts is important for at least two reasons. First, academic staff and central administration need to cooperate if institutional goals are to be achieved. Second, differences between students and administration often generate grave consequences for universities". Student unrest has frequently resulted in "damages to the university image as a source of inspiration and service ... massive destruction of university and public property; loss of life for both students and the public; increased costs in running universities due to stoppages of instruction; creeping de-professionalization of the academia; loss of public esteem and respect for the teaching staff..." (Issa M. Omari, 1991. "Student Unrest and Qualitative Improvements of Higher Education in Developing Countries", cited by Saint, 1992).

In many African countries, political forces and the economic crisis have seriously exposed the universities to pressures that push aside the traditional character and legal standing of the governance of African universities. There is a mistaken and, thus, unfortunate tendency to see university governance in terms, not of partnership, but of conflictual government-university relations. In the process, important issues are ignored and not given the attention they deserve. By thus perpetuating external and internal tensions, many of the existing mechanisms of governance prevent universities from fulfilling their potential major role in the progress of their countries. (Mwiria, 1992). "Changes in these mechanisms that will transform them from agents of destabilization to structures for stability are essential to the revitalization of higher education on the continent".

Conflicts between groups within universities need to be resolved before they get out of hand for several reasons. (Mwiria, 1992). "Academic staff members should not view the university administration as a buffer between themselves and government but more as persons playing a supporting role to their own. On their part university administrators should be seen to play such a supporting role as objectively as they can without appearing to be defenders of state as opposed to university interests. ... There are also compelling reasons for the urgent mediation of conflicts that arise between universities and the governments that support them. Universities need government for both financial support and for ensuring a climate supportive of institutional development. Equally important for universities is the need for them to win the cooperation and goodwill of governments in order to be assured the necessary level of institutional autonomy". This is what constitutes good governance.

In their conflict with outside forces, especially government, some universities have emerged institutionally stronger than before. They have survived because of the legal framework governing them. Where the legal framework has given the university institutional autonomy and where the proper procedures have been clearly spelt out, insisted on and followed, some universities have survived irresponsible charges and pressures from the outside. But if those in power have no respect for the law, as has happened, for example, in governments under military dictatorships, there have been problems of contending with external threats and violation of the integrity of the university.

Since a university is not a parliamentary body, and even less a place where total participation is possible, the existence of a strong executive authority is essential. (Meyerson and Graubard, 1975). Only where such authority exists is there any possibility that proposed innovations and progressive change will be debated, tested and, when appropriate, implemented. If the executive function is to be strong, but accountable, and not only to the governing council but to faculty and students as well, "there must be an organizational structure that encourages the flow of communication and provides opportunities for initiative and review. Some institutions may find senate, committee, and other existing structures adequate for consultation and participation; others may find new mechanisms more functional". The call for a strong executive authority is intended to ensure that leadership is exercised in a manner that gives weight to the opinions and values of the whole university community.

In conditions of change, which call for imagination and innovation, university management must provide imaginative, innovative, and adaptive leadership as well. (Rice, 1970). "And if university management is to be supported, the management of its sub-institutions must also provide imaginative, innovative, and adaptive leadership. A university cannot afford to let its management degenerate into an arid administrative function".

Whatever external bodies and individuals may have to do with the control and monitoring of universities in Africa, one thing must be made clear: that, for the sake of good governance, once university management has been appointed to carry out a task and has been given and accepted its terms of reference, it must be allowed to do the job - to formulate and implement policies that are in accordance with the statutes governing the institution.

## Appointment and Removal of Principal Officers

In terms of day-to-day operations of the university, the Vice-Chancellor, or Rector, or President is the topmost principal officer of the institution. The variety and burden of work that a modern university requires of its executive Head call for the appointment of a strong and able person. The present-day spectacle of so many Vice-Chancellors, or Rectors, or Presidents in serious trouble does not mean that they are all incompetent leaders, but that the tasks they are expected to perform are becoming virtually impossible. (Rice, 1970). Since these leaders need to relate to several constituencies, the universities should seek ways of facilitating their work, for example, by increasing the number of their deputies.

The question of the identification, selection, and appointment of the Vice-Chancellor, or Rector, or President of the University is a matter of serious debate in Africa. The common practice is that the executive head and other senior officers of the institution are appointed by the government. It is immaterial that the appointment is made in the name of the Chancellor or Visitor; if he is also the Head of Government, it is still seen as a government appointment. The Vice-Chancellor, or Rector, or President and his or her administration are, therefore, seen as acting to the dictates of government. In times of conflict, they are immediately labelled as "stooges" of the government. The situation is getting more and more complicated with the recent emphasis on the multi-party system of government in Africa. The head of the government which appoints the principal officers belongs to a particular political party and an ethnic group. Accordingly, the university leadership appointed by him are considered not only as government representatives but also as representatives and supporters of the ruling party or particular ethnic group. Multi-party politics has thus become another factor splitting the university into rival groups. The effects of this during hotly contested elections, or in the event of a change of ruling party, can be very destabilizing.

Government appointment of the university's chief executive is often a major cause of conflicts between university administrators and the academic and other staff, with the former being seen as more accountable to government than to the university. (Mwiria, 1992). "This is especially true of cases of disagreement between university staff and students on the one hand and government on the other. ... academics feel uncomfortable with vice-chancellors and their senior administrators who sometimes play a role very much similar to that of high school headmasters and often command academics and students into submission especially during university riots. University administrators have also tended to be more sympathetic with governments when the latter have failed to meet their financial obligations to universities and as such have been viewed as defenders of governments as opposed to university interests. This need by university administrators to conform to government wishes is not altogether unusual as they have, like most other employees, striven to be accountable to their employers".

However much they wish to be accountable to the university, many senior administrators feel insecure because their tenure depends on the government's goodwill.

The most effective university leaders are likely to be those who can find a formula for simultaneously serving both government and the university community. (Saint, 1992). Such a balance might best be achieved if the heads of Africa's universities were appointed through a process that ensures their acceptability to their constituencies. According to William S. Saint (Saint, *op. cit.*), the process for the governmental appointment might be improved through the use of a nomination system that takes into account the views of staff and students. The practice of Nigerian universities may provide an instructive model. When a Vice-Chancellor position falls vacant, it is sometimes publicly advertised. Council sets up a search party presided over by the Chairman of the Council. The screening of applicants or potential candidates is done by a joint Council and Senate Committee which draws up a short list of possible candidates. "This list is forwarded to the University Council which reduces it to three or four. Council then forwards this list, ranked in order of preference, to the head of state for a decision. Although the first name on the list is usually chosen, selection of one of the other candidates is not likely to produce much dissent since the list was produced by the university community. In a like fashion, Council and Senate could play equally prominent roles in the selection of other key administrators such as deputy Vice-Chancellors, [Registrars,] and deans of students".

Malawi is a notable exception to the practice of governmental appointment of university heads. (Saint, 1992). There, the Vice-Chancellor is selected by the University Council. This practice is also followed by the University of Witwatersrand in South Africa.

One cannot be categorical that, in the context of Africa, the emerging practice of advertising the post of the university chief executive will significantly change the prevailing uneasiness about appointment by the government, when those drawing up the short lists and those taking the final decision on the appointment are themselves deemed to be "government persons". Nor is it clear that governments will accept direct election by the university community or the three electoral colleges once adopted in Khartoum. It is still necessary, therefore, that within each university or national system, methods of appointment of the chief executive be worked out such that the resulting candidate is acceptable to his/her various constituencies, and is enabled to serve both government and the university community. The staff, students and government will need to have inputs into working out such new procedures.

There is another aspect of the problem with regard to the appointment of the university's chief executive. In many African universities, the Acts and Statutes are not clear on the criteria for appointment. There are no guidelines. Sometimes, ethnic balancing has been noticed, especially in countries with several universities. But African academics must accept some blame for this: they have been critical of government appointment without working out acceptable objective criteria. And whenever vacancies occur, their own unseemly rush and competition for the office makes it easy for governments wishing to ignore laid down procedures.

The post of chief executive is crucial for the development and progress of the African university. To be able to exercise the level of authority and personal leadership called for, the candidate should be a person of academic distinction. The requirements indicated by Akilagpa Sawyerr, a former Vice-Chancellor of the University of Ghana, are most pertinent: "For the Vice-Chancellor whose only claim to leadership in the university is his official position will soon find himself reduced either to virtual impotence or to futile authoritarianism. An effective Vice-Chancellor must, therefore, be a considerable scholar, preferably with experience of university-based research and teaching, and a reputation within his field of scholarship. This puts him in a position to be able to command the respect of a scholarly, merit-conscious community, and act as its pre-eminent representative to the outside world". (Sawyerr, 1991).

Just as in the case of appointment, the removal of the executive head and other senior officers of the university has been and is naturally a matter of great concern in Africa. In most cases, it has been done by government executive action. It can be sudden and with no explanation given. Often it is political, in that a totally independent Vice-Chancellor is an unwelcome entity to those who wish to manipulate the affairs of the university. Equally, a critical Vice-Chancellor, or Rector, or President creates problems for the government, especially a military or corrupt one, because he could shake the government to its knees. Similarly, the executive head of a university which, as an institution, or in which a significant portion of the academic staff or students, is perceived to be opposed to the party or government in power, can face instant removal. Equally, one who refuses to submit to demands by government or particular ministers however unreasonable or unfair the demands are, could face removal. Ethnic factors have also played havoc. The removal of the Vice-Chancellor, or Rector, or President may also be instigated by students and staff of the institution who do not like the particular person possibly for spurious reasons.

These actions can have destabilizing effects on the university and could set the clock back. Frequent changes of the head has been a major factor of instability in many an African university. It divides the university community and heightens the sense of insecurity in his successor and incumbents in other universities. If the affected person was outstanding and progressive, the standing of the institution may be in serious jeopardy. And where the replacement is mediocre, the standards and objectivity of the university may not be maintained, and when they fall, recovery is usually difficult. It is, therefore, imperative that mechanisms be established to ensure careful selection and, once appointed, to guarantee security of tenure for the chief executive of the African university.

## III. GENDER PERSPECTIVES

The aspiration of women for emancipation and access to higher education began with a small group of women, mostly daughters of professors. They were the first to be emancipated and it was then extended to the rest of society. Although some women studied secretly in institutions of higher education, the first university in Europe to open its doors to women was the University of Zurich (1840). The post-elementary education of women in Britain was given a boost by the initiative of some professors at King's College, London, which grew out of their interest in the Governesses Benevolent Institution, and culminated in the establishment of the Queen's College for Women in Harley Street, in 1848. This was closely followed by the Ladies College in Bedford Square in 1849. While the Queen's College has continued to educate women at the sub-professional level, the Bedford College began to take the degrees of the University of London when they were made open to women in 1878. It was incorporated into the University by Royal Charter in 1909. (Grimal, 1974, vol iv, pp. 214; Kaye, 1972). After a long and obstinate campaign, the University of Cambridge began to admit women in 1865. Oxford did not immediately follow suit, but many women excelled at their studies and other institutions were thus obliged to progressively admit them. Even then, certain disciplines remained closed to them, notably medicine. With time, even the resistance from the Association of Physicians was overcome.

These examples show that the struggle for the emancipation of women, by both women themselves and men sympathetic to their cause, is long and indeed far from over. Women in Africa did not have to struggle for the right to enter universities as they benefited from the fruits of the struggle of their European and American sisters. They, however, still have to struggle on many other fronts which are no less important if they are to achieve equity of access. For example, the National University of Zaire was established in 1954, but it was not until 1962 that the first woman was admitted, even though there was no law barring their admission.

The proportion of girls in primary schools South of the Sahara, whatever the overall numbers of students, is very low. This proportion becomes progressively less the higher one climbs the educational ladder. The enrolment of girls in scientific and technological disciplines is particularly low. The findings of a study commissioned by UNESCO (1974) and another by Rose Eholié (1993) are that the enrolment of girls in primary schools in Côte d'Ivoire was approximately 18.3% in 1946; 36.3% in 1970; 38% in 1972 and 40% of overall student figures in 1992. The figures show steady progression over the years, but the studies further found that there were major disparities from region to region.

At secondary school level, the percentage of girls in the first four years (forms 1 to 4) was 21% in 1970 and rose to 30% in 1992. At the upper or 'A' levels in 1970, however, these percentage dropped considerably, and such disparity between figures at the lower and upper levels remained noticeable up to 1992 in spite of net increases in enrolments. Thus, in 1970-1971, at the National University of Côte d'Ivoire, women constituted only 6.75%. Figures on virtually all other African universities, with the exception of the universities in Botswana, Lesotho and Swaziland, and South Africa indicate similar tendencies. The situation in the case of these countries can be explained by specific local historical circumstances. In order to redress the balance in Africa as a whole, a major and consistent effort must be made at primary and secondary school levels to identify and eliminate the bottle-necks that keep women from gaining admission to universities. (Assié-Lumumba, 1993; Eholié 1993).

When the United Nations (UN) instituted the International Decade for Women in 1975, it was in recognition of the fact that women, who represent slightly more than 50% of the earth's population did not have a fair share of the available resources and opportunities:

Women, a majority of the world's population received only a small share of developmental opportunities. They are often excluded from education or from the better jobs, from political systems or from adequate health care. (UNDP, 1993).

When, in 1985, women convened in Nairobi, Kenya, to review the terrain covered in those ten years and to formulate forward-looking strategies for further action, it became clear that there was opposition to gender parity embedded in the very cultural, social, legal and educational institutions that should have been promoting it. Because the majority of these institutions were managed by males, and society, so far, functioned to their advantage, they understandably did not sense any urgent need for change. Indeed, many did not see the need for any change at all. The question now is whether African universities, as bastions of knowledge, guardians of society's future, and indispensable tools for development would spearhead the needed change in order to promote a more equitable society that would ensure the well-being of all its members?

The Association of African Universities, recognising that the time was now ripe to pro-actively address the issue of gender equity, commissioned a paper to be presented during the AAU's 8th General Conference and 25th Anniversary Celebration in January 1993, in Accra, Ghana. Katherine Namuddu, Senior Scientist with the Rockefeller Foundation, presented a well-researched paper entitled *Gender Perspectives in the Transformation of Africa: Challenges to the African University as a Model to Society*. In the debate that followed, it became clear that the majority of the leaders of African universities, most of them male, were not even aware that gender parity was an issue. This may be understandable in the light of the many other problems that plague universities in Africa, as this study makes explicit elsewhere, including governance and financing. Thus, gender parity has not, until recently, been perceived as a major issue. Indeed, it may further be assumed that the women themselves were so involved in Africa's struggles for independence, post-independence rehabilitation, economic recovery and sheer survival that they had not turned their attention to their own plight.

The statistics on the participation of women in education in Africa have been available as far back as the early 50's in ILO and UNESCO publications, and in studies by individuals. As noted above, the overall numbers have been increasing over the years, and it can be expected that by the year 2000 girls can have the same access to primary and secondary level education that boys have. But the more intractable problem is that a much larger proportion of girls than boys drop out. The reasons for this are multiple but revolve around the woman's multiple roles as home keeper, wife and mother.

The figures show that, currently, the percentage of women in tertiary level institutions in sub-Saharan Africa at only 25 percent of total enrolment, is much lower than at secondary level and this latter is, in turn, lower than at primary level. Researchers have given various interpretations of this data, but there is agreement on the fact that further urgent work needs to be done if African women are to have access to, and complete their studies in, the various institutions of learning. Enough data has now been accumulated for researchers to be able to assert that a problem does, indeed, exist. African universities can only ignore it at their own risk. Data also exists to show that women are not proportionately represented either in the student or professorial bodies of African universities. A recent study indicates that women represent 20%, on average, of students in African universities. In 1986, Margaret Peil implied in her study that less than 3% of the professoriate was female. Eight years later, there has been very little change.

What can the universities do to remedy this situation? First, there is need for the sensitization of the university community at all levels; for, only when this community recognises that a problem does, indeed, exist, can there be hope for a solution. Further, the community must be made aware that the empowerment of women would contribute to all areas of development to the benefit of the entire society:

> Educating girls quite possibly yields a higher rate of return than any other investment available in the developing world.... The social improvements brought about by educating women are more than sufficient to cover its costs. Given that education also yields higher wages, it seems reasonable to conclude that the return on getting more girls into schools is in excess of 20 percent, and probably much greater". (Summers 1992, cit. Namuddu, 1993).

The "return" referred to here should be seen as the return to society as a whole. Because of the multiple roles that women play, their education has a multiplier effect: "When you educate a man, you educate an individual. When you educate a woman, you educate a whole nation". This argument alone should be enough to convince any doubting Thomases: the education of women will determine the pace of the development process on the continent.

The universities can also set up units to promote the maintenance of gender balance at all levels of the university's administration and academic structure. It may initially be difficult to convince the principally male university community of the necessity for this but there can be no possible moral or ethical justification for maintaining one of Africa's (and, indeed, the world's) majority in perpetual servitude:

> Gender specificity is an established fact. Consequently males cannot be viewed as being representative of the whole society ... it follows then that any activity such as social and economic transformation that involves the whole society should of necessity have a gender balance in participation at all levels.

And, finally, the universities can encourage teaching and research on gender-related issues. Traditionally, such research has been initiated and undertaken by female scholars, usually of the militant type, thus condemning it to a kind of intellectual ghetto. Scholars of both sexes and experienced researchers should now be encouraged to turn their attention to this crucial area, much as they did to Africa's democratisation process. For without the empowerment of women, without their unhindered participation in all decision-making processes, the word "democracy" will remain void of any real substance in Africa.

## IV. CHANGING PERCEPTIONS OF THE MISSION

Current rules of management dictate that an organization or institution will function more effectively if it takes time to define its mission, that is to say, long-term objectives. This should then be accompanied by strategic planning which sets out more specific goals for the short and medium term range, with periodic evaluation of how far it has achieved its goals in the pursuit of its mission. Hitherto, there was not the same insistence on definition of mission. The assumption was that the mission was obvious and non-controversial. Discussion was therefore focused on role, that is, the manner of pursuing the mission, the part of the wider mission which is highlighted for immediate action, the immediate goals and objectives in the short or medium term.

In the mid-19th century, in the transition from the slave trade to the imposition of colonial rule, those who were asking for an African University saw the mission of the university as the mental liberation of the African from the shackles that slavery and religious dogma had imposed. Hence they wanted a secular university, emphasizing African and classical studies, science and technology. What they got were Fourah Bay College and Fort Hare. In the colonial period, they saw the mission of the university as the renaissance of Africa, emancipation from colonial rule and the establishment of African nations able to take their place in the 'comity' of civilised nations of the world. In the period of decolonisation, they saw the university as part of the effort to bring the nation into being, having the same mission as the nation, that is mental, economic, and political de-colonisation. After independence, the university people found that they were no longer the ones defining the mission: the state did and universities took their cue from that to define their role. It was the state that crystallized the mission as Development.

There were antecedents to Development - Civilisation, Europeanization, Westernization, Modernization. A major problem with Development as a definition of mission, or role, or goal was not that it was too wide, but that neither the state nor the university was in control of the specification at any given time. At different times, the emphasis was on strong national government and centralized planning to build necessary infrastructure; rural development and population control, stressing provision of basic human needs; income re-distribution and equality of access; structural adjustment and multi-partyism; human resources and capacity building, stressing sustainable development. These shifts of emphasis produced different impacts on the perception of the mission and the role of the university. As Sawadogo (1994 pp 8-9) has observed, one reason for the crisis in higher education has been:

> the almost mythical proportion of a Sisyphus-type pursuit of ever changing definitions of concepts ... Indeed 'development', the pursuit of which African universities have been engaged in since their creation, has been an elusive concept generally defined with little input from Africans and very little consideration of internal resources, socio-economic realities and needs ... This pursuit of definitions (often-times fads) is that since countries don't have much control over the frequency and timing of these new prescriptions, they end up squandering resources, reorienting their training goals to focus on prescriptions that most likely will be changed before they have met them.

The reference to Sisyphus is apt - the mythical Greek god who was sentenced perpetually to roll a heavy burden uphill and, before he reaches the top, it rolls down and he has to begin all over again.

The pursuit of development is certainly an uphill task, but it is not the weight so much as the lack of clarity at any given time that constitutes the burden for the universities. The colonial university colleges had emphasized "international standards." In the reforms of the early 1970s, this was rebuked as elitism, creating an Ivory Tower in the midst of rural poverty, ignorance and disease. Rural development and population control dictated direct involvement of universities in extension work, community service, and adult literacy programmes. With emphasis on income redistribution and equality of access, student enrolments mounted and the number of universities were multiplied. With the economic recession and structural adjustment, resources were diverted from higher education, and educational standards declined to the point of collapse. Private universities began to be advocated and new prescriptions for human resource development and capacity building are still coming in. Fortunately this highlights the importance of higher education as the key to development, and could lend crucial support to the pressure from within for a re-invigoration of the universities.

One casualty of the state takeover of the control of the universities has been the capacity for independent thinking. The state in destroying the elitist Ivory Tower and trying to make the university a parastatal at the market place has further exposed both itself and the university to the shifting emphasis and current fads of donors and officials of the World Bank. It is indicative of the loss of autonomy that African universities have had remarkably little of substantial weight to say about national goals and mission of the university, to lead rather than to merely react to prescriptions from abroad. Even now, it appears that there are people who, probably reacting from American attitudes, believe that African "universities are still very elitist in their admission requirements, because university training in all of Francophone Africa is exclusively reserved to students who have succeeded in the baccalaureate exam., (Sawadogo, 1994, p 4) whereas the managers of African universities blame the uncontrollable rise of student enrolments on the open admission of all who have the baccalaureate. It is legitimate for donors and the government of the day to communicate policies demanding certain activities from the universities. University autonomy indicates that the universities themselves should be allowed the critical thinking to evaluate such demands and, at least, to formulate the priority with which the demands could be met. But the state has generally preferred compliance to critical thinking on university campuses.

What is required in the 1990s, in the move towards human resource development and capacity building, is that the universities themselves be challenged to redefine their missions. Such definitions should no longer be based on the assumption that the mission of the university is co-equal with that of the state. The functions of the university must be limited. Their area of specialization is higher education. African countries have a right to expect them, through research, teaching, and community service to acquire and transmit the knowledge and skills necessary to turn Africa around. The mission remains the same: "the pursuit of learning and acquisition of a liberal education as are appropriate for a university of the highest standing" as the

Act of the older universities used to say. The emphasis now must be put on:

- *quality*; the pursuit of excellence as the trade mark of the university; that
  is to say the teachers, students and administrators must aim at the highest
  level they are capable of; they must not be afraid of the elitism of merit;

- *creativity*; in research, training, thinking, problem-solving; an aspect of
  quality that goes beyond the established routine, to get at the solution that
  truly works;

- *relevance*; measured not by how much the teacher and the student share in
  the life of the village, but how much their ideas, the knowledge and skills
  that they produce, can transform the life of the village.

To the extent that the university communities are themselves involved in the
re-definition, they should be convinced of the value and importance of their mission
and be prepared to defend it. While in no way advocating a re-establishment of the
Ivory Tower, one must deprecate the ease with which many university people confuse
being part of the society with blending their values and standards with those of the
wider society or, rather, with those of the ruling elite. You cannot defend values if
there are no frontiers drawn. You need power to defend values, but this will not
come from trying to rival politicians at their job or becoming their surrogates. Power
will come from using the knowledge, skills and achievements of the universities to
help empower people, to demand accountability from governments, and insist on
setting limits to the exercise of power by politicians. These issues will be explored
further, in greater detail, in the following chapter.

# PART III: TOWARDS THE TWENTY-FIRST CENTURY

Chapter 9

## THE MISSION OF THE UNIVERSITY REVIEWED

**Introduction**

The university is one of the great world institutions that has taken root widely in modern Africa; and the three universal missions of the university - the acquisition, the transmission, and the application of knowledge - are accepted as crucial in the development and progress of the continent. Thus, in addressing the role of higher education in Africa over the following two decades, the 1962 Tananarive Conference on the *Development of Higher Education in Africa*, "proposed an idealistic and ambitious mission. Universities were viewed as key instruments for national development. They were expected to produce the skilled human resources necessary to manage newly independent countries, to generate developmentally relevant research, and to provide community service. Universities were asked to contribute to African unity, and to serve as cultural centers for their nations". (UNESCO, 1963; Saint, 1992). These goals were subsequently refined and re-stated at the 1972 Accra Workshop on *"Creating the African University: Emerging Issues of the 1970s"*, (Yesufu, 1973), which sought a new working definition of university, to emphasize its commitment to knowledge, not just for its own sake, but for the sake of ameliorating the conditions of the common man and woman in Africa. The African university of the 1970s was expected not merely to wear a different cloak, but also to be differently motivated. It must move away from the traditions of western universities, and evolve a different approach to its task. The truly African university must be one that draws its inspiration from its environment; not a transplanted tree, but one growing from a seed that is planted and nurtured in the African soil.

When African countries achieved independence, their leaders were confronted with gigantic problems of national development. Among these was the acute shortage of high-level manpower. Such shortage and the corresponding dependence upon expatriates made it essential that, if independence was to have visible meaning, this dependency be removed as rapidly as possible. In this connection, there can be no doubt that African universities have contributed immensely to the production of the much needed indigenous manpower for the administration and the professions critical for national development. (Court, 1974; Saint, 1992). However, after three decades or so, the great expectations that the African universities would contribute much more significantly to the overall rapid development and progress of independent Africa have been blunted by several realities as indicated in earlier chapters, and so remain unfulfilled. (Goma, 1991).

Today, the African continent remains largely undeveloped. There is, therefore, a certain amount of disappointment and attendant disenchantment with the universities in Africa for their inability to have had more significant impact on the continent. On the other hand, it seems clear that the mass of Africa's people do not as yet understand what the university is all about. They do not look up to it to provide answers to the questions that bother them: how to quickly improve the quality of their lives; how to provide moral guidance and promote a sense of values in present-day circumstances; how to engender respect for the indigenous values of African societies; how to stem the ever rising crime rate and violence against persons everywhere; how to achieve the objective of "doing unto others as one would have them do unto him"; how best to secure and maintain national unity and peace; and so on. (Ajayi *in* Yesufu, 1973; Goma, 1987a). And when they look up to the university with regard to these problems, "they rarely, if at all, get the answers that they can understand or find relevant to their predicament". (Ajayi, *op. cit.*).

While legacies from the pre-independence era still shape the structure and substance of African universities in important ways (Saint, 1992), criticisms that the founders of the universities of Africa did not immediately adapt to local conditions are useless and unprofitable. (Mayor, 1991). It must be admitted that the first of these universities "were not founded in a ferment of new ideas, nor influenced by a dynamic thrust of controversial propositions on new universities in new societies. The claim cannot be advanced that the first generation of planners and advisers were men of radical views, or pressed by innovative ideas, appropriate to the momentous fact that empires had come to an end, and that emancipation was launching millions of men [and women] into the most revolutionary period of their history. Those who went forth to man the universities, once they had been planned, came with too little wealth of objective scholarship dealing with the history, ethnology, or the economics of the land which they came to serve, too little range in analysis and debate to give fresh content and substance to the'institutions which they were to build" (de Kiewiet, 1971). However, because the compulsion to provide the rapid training of individuals to man the burgeoning economic and administrative institutions of the new nations was viewed as essentially the furnishing of qualifications with which these individuals could `legitimately' replace the incumbent expatriates, it did not seem to require much change in the inherited and imported pattern and role of the African university. (Court, 1974). "This definition of the role in turn tended to lock the universities into a desire to preserve inherited `international' academic standards and qualifications along with the recognized means of their achievement".

Moreover, it is perhaps not sufficiently appreciated that both the new independent nations of Africa and many of the African universities have shared the same period of existence, development, and progress. (Goma, 1991). The implications of such contemporaneity especially with respect to fundamental questions of the impact of one on the other and *vice-versa*, in the overall quest for the transformation of Africa, have not yet been fully understood. Many of the universities, particularly in the early years of many African countries as free independent nations, were themselves as new as the nations they were expected to serve and, therefore, did not have sufficient experience and maturity to participate effectively in the endeavours to transform these countries and their societies as rapidly as was desired. Similarly, the newness and inexperience of the countries also had some significant influence on the universities themselves. The enthusiasm with which these countries embraced the 'received' universities could only encourage those concerned that they were on the right tract.

Nevertheless, it has been argued cogently, that "Africa's universities currently stand in crisis at a pivotal point in their development. The mandates given to them at independence now require reassessment as a result of changes in the world, in Africa, and in the universities themselves". (Saint, 1992). Thus, the debate on the mission and proper role of the African universities continues unabated. The validity of the universal missions of teaching, research and public service remains unquestioned. But, in the words of James A. Perkins: "[Teaching], research, and public service - in what proportions? The advancement or application of knowledge - in what measure?" (Perkins, 1976, *in* Thompson and Fogel 1976).

## The African University in a Changing World

As Africa approaches the close of the twentieth century and stands on the threshold of the next millennium, the environment in which the continent's universities must operate has changed greatly, and is changing rapidly; and, therefore, the future has become increasingly unpredictable. Among the most momentous and historic developments are the end of the East-West conflict and, thus, of the Cold War; the collapse of communism and the disintegration of the Soviet Union and Eastern Europe; the coincidence of the 'democracy epidemic', ethnicity and nationality upheavals; the spectacular advances in science and technology; and the increasing scale of the widespread devastation of African economies.

The end of the East-West ideological divide and the collapse of communism have not only unleashed powerful forces in favour of market economies and political pluralism but engineered the marginalization of Africa both economically and politically in the world. The emergence of global markets has created a competitive world economic system characterized by rapid knowledge generation and technological innovation. This has unleashed on Africa the package of compulsory retrenchment generated by structural adjustment programmes, privatization, and economic liberalization, leading to reduced demand for high-level manpower in the public service and the corresponding increased demand in the private sector of the national economies; the increasing problem of unemployment and underemployment of university graduates going hand in hand with a severe shortage of high-level manpower in critical science and technology-based areas, which is compounded by the troublesome phenomenon of the brain drain. At the same time, Africa's high population growth rates and increased access to education, have boosted the social demand for higher education, leading to rising university enrolments, making many of the continent's universities to become large complex institutions operating under severe financial constraints. (Mudenge, 1993; Saint, 1992; Thiam, 1991).

These developments have far-reaching implications for Africa and its institutions of higher education, especially the universities. Both structural adjustment and technical change have an impact on the level, type and spatial location of occupations available to higher education graduates: adjustment programmes bring about shifts in the sectoral allocation of jobs, while technological innovations influence the evolution of employment structures and job contents, with related changes in the skills required and training needed. (Salmi, 1991). Thus, "the structural adjustment programs currently being implemented by most African countries appear likely, over time, to influence labor market demand for university graduates. Liberal arts preparation for public service is expected to give way to science, engineering and business management training needed to support private sector development and respond to growing opportunities for self-employment. University curricula will have to shift accordingly". (Saint, *op. cit.*). Furthermore, "the accelerating pace of scientific advancement has produced a range of new developments - from agricultural bio-technology to synthetic materials to computerized information systems - that have combined to undercut the earlier comparative advantage of many African economies, often heavily dependent on natural resource exploitation and the export of raw materials. Economic advantage is now increasingly based on technology-reliant management efficiency and on national human resource capacities to manage these increasingly complex systems. The rapid pace of technological change means that economic rewards are most likely to accrue to production systems which possess flexibility and adaptability".

When considering or contemplating reforms in higher education, it is often not sufficiently emphasized that, as countries develop, the needs for talent become more diverse, students have increasingly different aspirations, and academic programmes and institutions become more specialized to take care of these specialized needs. (James A. Perkins, *in* Thompson and Fogel,1976). There is, therefore a case for considering whether to develop new universities, and new forms of higher education, to respond specifically to new issues of concern as they emerge. For example, the revolution in information and communication technologies offers tremendous opportunities for exploiting distance learning to meet the increasing demand for higher education in Africa. What needs to be considered is the cost-effectiveness of either creating autonomous `Open' universities devoted to Distance Learning, or expanding facilities for Distance Learning in existing partly residential institutions. (Rumble, 1992). Similarly there have been suggestions for separate Women universities as one approach to reducing the gender imbalance. Another suggestion concerns the emergence of Universities of the Faith, distinct from seminaries and theological institutes for training religious leaders, as a way of reducing imbalance or mobilizing support of particular religious communities for university development. Any possible advantages of such special universities need to be considered along with the obvious dangers.

In spite of the tremendous changes that are taking place, the African continent remains mired in a state of pervasive underdevelopment. For the vast majority of Africa's ordinary people, with the preponderant proportion of them living in rural areas, the problem of development is one of everyday life. It continues to manifest itself with pressing practicality as poverty, hunger, disease and early death, ignorance, unemployment, lack of decent and adequate housing, and the experience of losing values that used to give meaning to life. Nevertheless, the people entertain and, through false promise, are made to entertain a hope for better things to come. The problem here, in the words of Peter L. Berger, "is not in the making of policy or the plausibility of theories, but in coping, from day to day, with suffering and dilemmas caused by the often bewilderingly rapid change in the social [economic and political] environment". (Berger, 1974)  Then there are problems of millions of African men, women and children who suffer the anguish of homelessness, having fled their homes and/or countries because of liberation wars, ethnic conflicts, natural disasters, persecution, *et cetera*; problems of national integration and the preservation of cultural diversity; the institution and consolidation of democracy; and the protection of the environment.

In the light of all this, the mission and role of the African university as envisaged at the 1962 Tananarive Conference,  and refined and re-stated at the 1972 Accra Workshop remain valid;  but their interpretation and realization must now take into account the practical needs  generated by the fundamentally new and future  realities. This calls for greater creativity, innovativeness and resourcefulness than has been demonstrated hitherto.  The national authorities in charge of higher education and the African universities themselves, in re-examining the missions and roles of these institutions, should be addressing such questions as:

- How can the universities, in these circumstances, evolve and contribute to the necessary socio-economic change?

- How can higher education and its research contribute to and  play a more active role in the elimination of poverty, hunger, disease, ignorance, over-production  of "useless" university graduates, scientific and technological marginality, and the enfeeblement of the power of knowledge?

- What type of qualifications and personality should result from studies at higher education institutions; in other words, what kind of graduate does Africa want in order to face up to the new and continuing challenges of the continent?

These questions can be summed up as follows - what should be the mission and role of the African university in the context of Africa's needs as it approaches the end of this century and enters the 21st century?  This must also be seen as part and parcel of a world-wide process of the re-thinking and reform of higher education in order to face the new needs of society which are plural and diverse.  (UNESCO, 1993).

The changing environment thus calls for profound reforms of institutional structures and study programmes as well as of the means and methods of teaching, training and learning.  But this does not rest the debate on the mission and role of the

African university. There are still serious "prevailing uncertainties surrounding the concept of a university mission - the form it can profitably take, how to secure it, how it should be owned by all concerned and, thereby, inspire sound management and have the best chance of being successfully accomplished". (UNESCO, 1992). The practice of many African universities of simply defining their mission in terms of the three functions of teaching, research and public service is inadequate for the future. There is great need for these universities to go beyond mere pronouncements about their *mission*: they should set themselves certain fundamental and unambiguous goals to be targeted for accomplishment within a realistic and specified time-frame consonant with their capacities and capabilities; and to determine the strategies for their achievement. This requires clear vision of the mission and of the action that has to be undertaken; and it must be approached with the conviction, determination and singleness of purpose with which (i) missionaries went out of Europe in the nineteenth century with a *mission* to follow "the clearly defined path of duty at any and all hazards, convinced that it was necessary for them to go"; and (ii) an entire industry in the United States had a *mission* to put man on the moon within ten years, clearly articulated, and forcefully and suitably presented to those who had to carry it out. (UNESCO, *op. cit.*). Equally, when Wilhelm von Humboldt and his associates conceived and founded the University of Berlin as an agent of change in 1809, the *mission* of the new university was "*to take intellectual and scientific leadership away from the French and give it to the Germans*". The result of this was world-wide leadership in scholarship and research for Germany.

There are, however, several challenges to be addressed, if the African universities are to avoid failure in such an endeavour. Whatever the ultimate phrasing of the future *mission* of these institutions, and whatever the structures established for carrying it out, an important key to success of the entire enterprise is that it should have gained the widest possible acceptance not only in the university but also in government circles and among moulders of public opinion within the community. It is imperative that there should emerge a compelling sense of a *mission* to be accomplished, fortified by the creation of a coherent corporate culture within the university, as well as an innovative, entrepreneurial, effective and efficient management. (UNESCO, *op. cit.*).

Although the fundamental activities of universities are universally of a long-term nature, the realities of the African continent are such that it is not sufficient to reflect on what Africa's universities might do in an ideal situation. In the face of demands which far exceed their capacities, these universities would have to be highly selective and consider very carefully what they could expect to achieve, say, by the end of the first decade of the twenty-first century, which would be crucial, given the means actually at their disposal. There are several deserving critical areas. However, it is important for the universities to strike a balance between what is essential and possible and what is desirable and possible but not essential. Moreover, setting targets for accomplishment within a specified time-frame demands the existence of a strategic plan. Such a strategic plan can and should serve to give direction and purpose to the university's efforts.

Among the top priorities for the consideration and possible action by the universities of Africa is the task of overcoming one of Africa's intractable problems, evident in the sheer multiplicity of things - from infrastructure to high-level decision-making - which work below par because of widespread incapacity and incapability to respond to the imperatives of sustainable hard work, efficiency, timely action in doing the right things, and sound management. (UNESCO, 1992). This task should seek to accomplish the following target(s):

> (a)  to maximize, within the specified time-frame (i.e., by the end of the first decade of the twenty-first century), a measurable flow of managerial effectiveness and efficiency into the public and private sectors through university alumni;  or

> (b)  to establish, within the specified period, African universities in the vanguard of a crusade to replace poor management by an observably sound, innovative, entrepreneurial, honest, effective and efficient management seen to compare favourably with what obtains in the economies of the newly-industrializing countries of South-East Asia;  or

> (c)  to bring, within the specified time-frame, managerial as well as scientific and technological skills - and their application - within the grasp of the majority of university alumni.

In addition to the production of the requisite graduates, African universities should also provide continuing education specifically targeted at realizing this particular task.

It is, moreover, imperative that the African universities should, through their own performance, become shining examples of excellent work. Creativity, innovation, commitment, and determination should enthuse these universities in their functions of teaching, research and public service as well as in the management and administration of the institutions themselves. When society sees that the universities have succeeded in eliminating the 'virus' of working below par, even under the difficulties now strangulating them, these qualities are most likely to take root outside the academy as worthwhile and essential professional values. In order that they can make really effective contribution in this direction, African universities must themselves, therefore, first set their own house in good order and demonstrate that a progressive work ethic is possible to attain. Theory and mere preaching will not produce the desired results.

## The 'Developmental University'

African universities and scholars have contributed new thinking regarding the role of higher education by introducing the concept of the 'developmental university'. (Yesufu, 1973; Court, 1974; Saint, 1992). In a world in which the standard and quality of life in any country depend more and more upon the power of knowledge, and socio-economic development is becoming more and more knowledge-intensive and is relying increasingly on professional and managerial specialists with advanced training, the role of higher education becomes a crucial element for any development programme. (Goma, 1991; UNESCO, 1993). The university is a key player in providing the nation with the power of knowledge. It is, therefore, quite proper to expect that the university in Africa would be involved in tackling some of the substantive development problems that the countries of the African continent face. Accordingly, the imperatives of national development and progress should determine the place and the scale of support for institutions of higher education.

The questions that immediately arise are: (i) What constitutes the development of a nation? (ii) What are the factors or conditions that affect such development? (iii) In what way can a university most effectively influence these factors or conditions and thereby contribute to national development? The needs which are subsumed under the concept of national development in Africa, as elsewhere in the developing world, are so complex - with social, cultural, economic, and political dimensions - that they are not easily specified with much assurance; they can change quickly and abruptly; and they are unlimited, while the available resources are not. (Goma, 1984; Wandira, 1977). They are not merely domestic since National development also embraces the need to win and hold the respect of other nations.

As has been said repeatedly, if the university in Africa is to make significant contributions to national development, it must proceed from informed criteria. It must engage itself in a continuous search for the real problems confronting the development of African countries. It must thus contribute to understanding the nature of the challenge of development and to lead in helping to define the national, regional and continental response. (Court, 1974). In seeking to pursue the right policies, the African university "needs to undertake the necessary research to identify the necessary goals, seeking the means that can most effectively be pursued given local conditions, local materials and limited funds". (Ajayi, 1989). It must accept increasing responsibility for moving ideas along the road to action, to develop the knowledge needed, and to apply such knowledge towards achieving national development objectives. The research work of its academic staff and postgraduate students could meaningfully be directed towards this goal, without endangering the much treasured autonomy of the university and the academic freedom of its members. Indeed, something has been accomplished already along these lines.

However, so far, only an insignificant number of African universities have demonstrated the ability and willingness to make the study and alleviation of underdevelopment a central and organising concern. (Court, 1974) Indeed, the observations by Colin Leys more than two decades ago remain valid today: "There are relatively few issues among all those raised during the debate - on the developmental role of universities in the developing countries - of the 1960s which appear to have been resolved. There are comparatively few areas of university life and practice where one can say that a particular way of doing things, or even an accepted set of guiding principles, has been generally established as right or best from the point of view of making the maximum contribution to development". (Leys, 1971). As one reviews the prevailing situation, one is bound to ask the question: "How much did all that discussion, all that protracted debate really matter? If these issues were important in determining the effectiveness of the universities' contribution to development, how can we justify the failure to resolve them? If they did not matter, then the debate itself must somehow have missed the point. What explanation can we find for this?"

Furthermore, there does not appear to have been any comprehensive assessment by any African university of how it can best contribute - for example, through research, consultancy or other forms of public service in which many African universities have been engaged - to national development apart from steady growth in programmes and in the number of graduates produced. Even those in the university who are qualified to deal with this topic seem not to have been called on to map out the area within which the university can contribute most effectively to national development. It is regrettable that the demand for policy-oriented research, especially in the social sciences, has often not been communicated with sufficient clarity or insistence to elicit a constructive response. (Court, 1974) This in turn has been due to the fact that many of the policy makers in a position to make demands for research and information are not sufficiently familiar with the nature of research activity to know what kinds of requests they could justifiably make on the university.

It would seem, therefore, that the preoccupation with the training of manpower equipped purely with university degrees has, in major ways, put limits on the creative responsiveness of the university to other developmental problems. (Leys, 1971; Court, 1974) These limitations need to be addressed with vigour in the future. Specifically, African universities must contribute to the development of a culture of continuing and life-long education.

## Enhancing Profile

It has been said that the basic reason why poor countries remain poor is unquestionably because they lack knowledge, and the ability to utilize available knowledge effectively. The global divide in the coming decades is being rapidly transformed from an income gap between the rich and poor into an information or knowledge gap between the haves and have-nots of know-how. (Kwapong, 1992) Indeed, the most serious handicap facing most African countries today, in their development efforts, is deficient knowledge and the shortage - sometimes extreme shortage - of really competent high-level trained manpower. Thus, a "single concept cuts across all the items on Africa's strategic development agenda: the imperative of building local African capacities. Whether in agriculture, industry, [health], education or natural resource management, Africa lacks the necessary skills and well-managed public and private institutions for long-term sustainable growth". (McNamara, 1990). The various changes in emphasis in African development strategies during the past three decades or so, "have all lacked one ingredient: they did not incorporate, as a central feature, the building of indigenous African skills, knowledge and institutions. Capacity building has been the missing link". (Jaycox, 1990).

The universities of Africa cannot escape the responsibility of responding, in a new and creative way, to the serious challenges of capacity building and human resource development in Africa which is now being accorded such high profile. They must do more - and differently - than hitherto to meet the professional, management, and leadership requirements necessary for the development efforts of their countries. They must strive to be key contributors to national capacity-building processes: in that case,

> they will have to demonstrate continuing relevance in a rapidly changing world. Their teaching and research will be called upon to support the efforts of the continent's emerging private sector, including non-governmental development

organizations and business enterprise. To this end, course content may need to give greater emphasis to the development of critical thinking and problem-solving capacities, and to impart specific management and administrative skills. At the same time, greater flexibility in academic programs may be needed to incorporate interdisciplinary approaches and accommodate part-time or continuing studies." (Saint, 1992).

Thinking on development has certainly shifted repeatedly during the past thirty to forty years; and since most of the thinking has been external, African countries have been merely forced to shift with each new policies imposed on them. As Robert J. Berg has said: "First came the infrastructure builders to provide the backbone of economies. ... Then in the 1970s came basic human needs to connect people and development. The next major challenge for the development community is how best to engage in development in the context of the seriously deteriorating environment." (Berg, 1989). This latest shift has given birth to the current bandwagon - "sustainable development", coupled with "good governance" - onto which the development community has jumped. But African thinking on African development has been marginal and that is why African countries have found themselves easily influenced by the outside world, and often coerced into programmes not really their own. The African universities have stood by watching it all. Even where these universities have created applied research units, especially in the social sciences, there has tended to be an overly uncritical acceptance of approaches engineered overseas. There has not been sufficient recognition of the fact that some of the social sciences which flowered dramatically in these research units was a new type of intellectual technology derived from an industrial context and particular model of development not consonant with the actual realities of a developing continent and, therefore, an embryonic science yet to be tried under the African conditions. (Court, 1974).

It is not surprising that there is a growing dissatisfaction among social scientists with the way people think about the developing world. (Randall, 1992). Thus, some recent publications expose "a sense of deep disquiet about the theoretical frameworks that have dominated our studies and the concepts, methods and values they imply" which have produced misleading definitions of `development'. The universities of Africa must engage in serious re-thinking of the concept of development. They should not countenance the values placed on certain pre-conceived notions of outsiders as to what development in Africa should be. They should be guided by the imperative of greater respect for indigenous or `traditional' society and undertake a re-evaluation of what it is that is being `developed'. It should be emphasized that the pressure to get the universities to be more relevant to development is not making much fruit because they fail to take enough account of the elements of the surrounding and permeating culture, and unless they learn how to do this, African societies will appear impervious to change and development will remain elusive. (Court, 1974).

There can be no doubt as to the need for the African university to remain committed to its developmental role in the future. But in order to fulfil this role more adequately than hitherto, the first responsibility of the university is to educate itself to be development conscious and development oriented. (Ajayi, 1979). Contrary to usual assumptions, the level of this consciousness in the average African university throughout the continent is often very low. A very large proportion of the academic staff of these universities have been trained, especially at the postgraduate level, in Europe and North America; and many of them "have had few opportunities to formulate concrete policies for development.. Most of the discussions that go on about the goals and indicators of development and the role of universities, involve senior officials like Vice-Chancellors and Deans", and do not usually include most of the university staff. Even those in the Social Sciences whose disciplines embrace studies in the theories of development, do not usually relate this to the broad goals of the university or even to the roles of particular faculties or departments". (Ajayi, *op. cit.*). It is imperative that in future, the universities of Africa should adopt conscious strategies to formulate policies to achieve greater and more widespread development orientation among their staff and students than has been the case so far. Development consciousness on campus "could be achieved by way of public lectures, seminars, and symposia to generate the necessary awareness among the university community as a whole. Such awareness could then gradually become the major theme and motive force of regular university classes, whatever the discipline concerned". (Ajayi, *op. cit.*). Furthermore, in order that they can contribute more substantially to the debate on development and to achieving greater and more widespread development orientation on campus, African universities should create, where they do not already exist, viable Centres or Institutes of Development Studies. It appears that institutes for African studies have, on their own, proved inadequate for this task.

## Deteriorating Quality and Accelerating Demand

The picture painted by Esi Sutherland-Addy (1993) of the universities in Ghana sums up a widespread depressing reality in Africa: most of Africa's universities are indeed "a mere shadow of their earlier glory: drained of teaching staff; lacking in equipment and teaching materials; housed in degenerated infrastructure; surrounded by an air of demoralization and incipient decay. They are, at the same time, besieged with a growing demand for high quality service and public accountability". African universities have failed to maintain themselves as centres of excellence. It cannot be overstated that under conditions of poor teaching and learning resources, many faculty members who were previously competent and enthusiastic become incompetent and indifferent through frustration and disillusionment. (Goma, 1989). The available staff become under-utilized and the students under-educated. There may emerge a creeping sense of futility among both groups. Able staff and able students are thus denied the opportunity to contribute to the vitality, usefulness and growth of their university.

Nevertheless, the demand for opportunities for higher education in Africa is increasing at a rate with which existing institutions cannot cope. At the same time, as can be expected, there are serious misgivings about the quality of the higher education and services being offered and rendered by these institutions now. But the influx of students continues unabated. There can be no doubt that the influx of more students than a university has been designed for can only lead to overcrowding, poor teaching, impoverished research, frustrated, embittered students and academic staff, and unsatisfactory service to the community.

The coincidence of deteriorating quality and accelerating demand is not only a most serious threat to higher education in Africa; it also raises some fundamental questions which should be addressed as Africa looks to the future. (Goma, 1989). What is the reason for the accelerating demand for higher education in an environment of declining quality? Is it a case of mediocrity attracting mediocrity - the mediocre products of the declining school systems feeling attracted to the deteriorating institutions of higher education; - i.e. more a function of "push" than of "pull"? On the other hand, perhaps, out of ignorance of the real state of higher education, even good students are "pulled" and challenged by the illusion that they would get a good education For such students, disillusionment and frustration can be expected. Equally, good academic staff will be disappointed if they have to be saddled with poor quality students gaining access to higher education institutions.

The universities are themselves somewhat to blame for contributing to the deteriorating quality they now suffer from. In attempting to respond to the demand for a rapid increase in student numbers, they have succumbed to the temptation to admit students of low calibre, recruit academic staff of mediocre ability to cope with the increasing teaching load, and resort to improvisation of the physical facilities. The university cannot thrive under such circumstances; its proper development and the fulfilment of its mission and role   will correspondingly be seriously undermined.

There is of course the issue of democratization and access to education as a fundamental human right, advocated sometimes out of conviction, sometimes out of political expediency, and sometimes as part of the package imposed from abroad. Nevertheless, the priority of the university must be first and foremost to ensure that it gives credible education . Universities must not shirk the responsibility of doing that which ensures that the education they give is good, relevant, and in furtherance of their mission.

Whatever the real motivation for the accelerating demand for higher education in the circumstances of deteriorating quality, there is an imperative need to control the influx of students into the universities. Admittedly, for many African countries, the urgent need for indigenous university trained manpower to meet the requirements of national development is a root cause of this demand. But, it has to be appreciated that if the training of the graduates is poor in quality and substance, their contribution to society will be inferior and a stumbling-block to real national development and progress.

Apart from meeting manpower needs, African countries should also look to their universities for greater productivity in other ways: to find new uses for their raw materials such as cocoa, coffee, cassava, etc. and thereby reduce the exploitation they now suffer under the prevailing international economic order; to create new products and services; and to develop new technologies responsive to Africa's changing needs. But much as the universities might wish to respond positively and properly to such demands and challenges, they will fail to do so under conditions of declining quality in their performance. There is, therefore, urgent need to halt the process of institutional decay and reverse the trend towards recovery.

Then there is the problem posed by the gifted and uniquely talented students. (Goma, 1989). Should, and, indeed, can anything be done about providing special opportunities for such students, and, trying to identify and select them? Will this be considered as defeating the tenets of democratization of higher education? Surely, equality of educational opportunity must mean more than the opportunity to develop mediocre competence in the area of someone else's strength. Equality of educational opportunity must mean being provided with the necessary tools to develop one's own special talents to the point of excellence. It is, therefore, contended that work with the gifted and uniquely talented students, the probable geniuses, must be one of the major tasks for African universities and other institutions of higher education. What can the universities do to prevent the possible intellectual destruction of such students, in the circumstances of declining quality? Africa, and indeed the world, needs such people. The university can be expected to provide the best facilities it could for a wide range of students. In countries where there are only one or two universities, there seems little they could do specifically for the really gifted students, except perhaps to send them abroad, if necessary. In any case, universities cannot easily know who is a genius. May be, the development of centres of excellence in countries with a multiplicity of universities might perhaps cater for the gifted and uniquely talented students.

**The Quest for Excellence and Relevance**

African universities have been criticised for aspiring to reach standards of academic achievement which will ensure that they have to be reckoned with in the world. (Goma, 1991). It would, however, seem that these attacks have been prompted by a gross misconception of what the quest for excellence and prestige is really all about. It arises not so much from a sense of competition with overseas universities as from an appreciation of what could best serve the interests of African countries. It needs to be said again and again that the universality of the university institution does not imply a universal gold standard of excellence. But any university that ceases to be committed to the pursuit of excellence and enthronement of merit in the variety of tasks it has to perform soon loses its value and its worth as a university. The university cannot function effectively if it does not submit to the imperative of excellence. Making fundamental breakthroughs demands it; real progress demands it; the advancement of science and of knowledge demands it. For African universities, however, excellence must be dictated primarily by African aspirations, and by the quest for the ability to deal effectively with African problems.

This point needs elaboration. The call for the pursuit of excellence and the invigoration of the universities and of the culture of science and technology must not be mistaken for a return to modernization as a model of development, with import substitution industries that obtain all their raw material from abroad, and with technologies that only the foreign partners have mastered. It is African societies with their traditional structures and rural populations that need to be developed. We must begin by responding to their needs and solving their particular problems. We must begin by developing their agricultural practices, crafts and industries, so as to provide employment and multiply production. But in trying to solve these problems, we must pursue excellence and creativity. We must not ignore the most relevant technologies and the most fruitful strategies. We require excellence in the science and technology needed to multiply production, find new industrial uses for our primary products, new solutions drawing on traditional herbal knowledge to confront our health problems, always seeking to offer solutions to the problems of the people at cost within their means.

To meet the demands of excellence is no easy task anywhere. As the African experience has shown, to declare a quest for excellence and relevance is one thing; to realise it is quite another. Even when appropriate academic/study programmes, structures and institutions have been established, achievement of basic goals may still elude the university and the nation it seeks to serve. The university must have adequate resources, human and material, to do its work; but quantity, particularly in the case of human resources, is not enough: what is needed is high quality. Equally important is that the material resources, in the case of books and other literature and laboratory equipment, *et cetera*, must be appropriate.

African universities must produce and deliver high quality goods. Their graduates must be people whose competence and performance can contribute significantly to the renaissance of African countries. As Ade. Ajayi has said, we need "to restore our confidence in our ourselves, to enable us to plan with a sense of purpose and direction, and to make our choices for the future deliberately and responsibly instead of merely drifting in the face of massive choices open before us". (1979). Surely the universities must set their goals with such standards in mind.

But these things will not be realised if the African universities succumb to the 'virus' of mediocrity. It can be said that mediocrity can only attract, sustain and be sustained by the mediocre. The consequences of declining quality may not be felt for many years — until graduates reach decision-making levels of responsibility in public and private institutions. (Saint, 1992). The prestige and acceptability of a university's graduates depend on satisfying national as well as external notions of good university education, however vaguely expressed. (Wandira, 1977). Often, the brightest of a university's graduates may wish to go to other universities in search of higher degrees or specialised forms of training, such as may be organised under staff development programmes. They could be rejected if the standing of their university is unacceptable. "A university which does not enjoy international acceptance of its standards, prejudices the academic future of its most promising graduates". (Wandira, *op. cit.*). African countries and governments have, therefore, a heavy responsibility *not* to countenance or support the existence of mediocre universities in their midst. Mediocrity in higher education must be consciously fought and defeated wherever it surfaces. In this connection, it is important to realise that the 'quality slope' is steep and slippery: while the downward slide is easy and fast, the upward climb to recovery is extremely difficult and slow. (Goma, 1989).

The reputation of a university, which determines its capacity to attract and hold good faculty and good students, and maintain high standards, depends ultimately on the quality of its outputs - graduates, postgraduates, professional practitioners, and research findings and publications. (Rice, 1970). The university must provide opportunities that permit highly creative faculty members to produce their best work. "Without such opportunities, the most creative will not join the institution, or, if they join, they will not stay. When they go, they will take others with them. Without the very good, the institution is not likely even to retain the good".

For these and other reasons, it is agreed that establishing or re-establishing a culture of quality is one of the most important undertakings that the African university must now assume. (Saint, 1992). "The norms and values that prevail in the university environment will shape the expectations and behavior that students will take to their professional careers. Where students observe that their elders ignore professional commitments and compromise on standards, they will learn to do so. The result will be a weakening of the nation's capacity to manage its own [social], economic and political affairs".

The demand for increased relevance in higher education must go hand in hand with the demand for enhanced quality. (UNESCO, 1993). Quality is not a novel concern in African universities; but it has become crucial in the current policy debate concerning the development and reform of higher education. Quality should permeate all university functions and activities: "quality of teaching, training and research - which reside in the quality of its staff and of its programmes and resources; quality of learning - as a corollary of teaching and research, but also implying quality of students; quality of governance and management - which has a determining impact on the teaching, learning and research environment".

Chapter 10

# NEW EXPECTATIONS AND RE-ORIENTATIONS

## Introduction

The end of the apartheid system in South Africa, the drafting of a new constitution, and the emergence of a Government of national unity involving the majority African populations for the first time, provides an opportunity for social transformation and renewal in which higher education obviously has a major role. The educational system hitherto based on the provision of separate and clearly unequal facilities for whites and blacks is to be transformed to a more democratic and integrated system. There is consensus that this has to begin with the improvement of the quality of elementary and secondary education available to non-Europeans while absorbing non-Europeans into existing universities through programmes of affirmative action without undermining the quality of the universities as centres of academic excellence providing effective training. The universities have to cooperate with other institutions of higher education in order to energise the whole educational system into meeting the new challenges.

Thus the universities of South Africa are facing problems of social and political transformation similar to the ones faced in the rest of Africa in the 1960s. Yet, to a large extent it may be said that the independence that most African countries had in the 1960s was not any more effective than the 1910 independence of the Union of South Africa in meeting the aspirations of the masses of African people for growth and development. The crisis of the universities that we have been discussing, the challenges facing them, and the need for reform, re-orientation and reinvigoration, are not very different north of the Limpopo as to the south of it. If anything, the `white' universities of South Africa have survived better than the best of the universities north of the Limpopo and are available as reservoirs of knowledge and technical skills necessary for the processes of social transformation.

## The Content of Education and Degree System

The content of the education offered and the structure of the degrees largely determine the kind of graduates produced by a university. In the period of decolonization, it was anticipated that many of the graduates of African universities would be called upon to advise on high-level policy and to take decisions on a wide range of matters not necessarily related to their field of academic specialisation. Accordingly, it seemed logical that the degree system of these universities should aim to combine the development of a capacity for critical judgement as its supreme object with a sufficient breadth of exposure to different fields of knowledge and academic disciplines, to give their graduates the flexibility and breadth of vision necessary for the performance of varied roles within the respective nations. Regrettably, many African universities failed to rise to this challenge and stuck to irrelevant inherited models.

Three decades after independence, the question being asked is whether the standard academic programmes and the original structures should continue. Can they prepare young Africans for the tasks of promoting rapidly accelerating development involving revolutionary changes in the social, economic and political structures, and ways of life and attitudes, which these countries require? In most African countries, the civil service is now largely indigenized, and the training of public administrators can no longer be a priority. An emerging problem of graduate unemployment and under-employment, and inadequate performance on the job, indicates that the current university education may be getting out of tune with today's job market in Africa. The question arises then: what kind of university graduates does the Africa of today and immediate tomorrow need?

No one disputes the fact that knowledge is not only expanding rapidly, but is characterized by important revision of categories into which it is divided and by the constant alteration of relationships between them. At the same time, modern life is made up of complex situations which demand the use of knowledge learnt from various disciplines, combined in a coherent and dynamic way. The knowledge explosion has resulted in a considerable increase in the number of study programmes which are offered or could be offered by higher education institutions, especially the universities. (UNESCO, 1993). A characteristic element of this explosion is the interdependence and inter-connection of various disciplines. In the light of this, there is a general consensus on the need for enhancing the inter-disciplinary and pluri-disciplinary content of studies.

In order to respond to the challenge of knowledge explosion in the circumstances of Africa, African universities must strive to adapt their study programmes to meet the imperative of inter-disciplinary research and teaching. Initiatives aimed at the renewal of teaching and learning must, therefore, involve the introduction of creative and innovative interdisciplinary courses and the adoption of appropriate flexible structures which would allow the involvement of specialists from diverse sectors in the teaching of particular university study programmes, and the search for solutions to particular problems.

This raises several questions which need to be addressed by the African universities: for example, should there not be a reconsideration of such fundamental issues as the relationship between university education in the Humanities, Social Sciences and Technology? Should these continue to be distinct, as they have been traditionally, or do the future needs of the African countries demand that they be integrated in some new way? There are other related questions: what should be the proper relationship between university study, or other forms of higher education, and involvement in productive work? Is the idea of full-time academic work and professional study valid for the present or for the future, or should participation as a worker in various sectors of the national economy be regarded as a necessary part of university training? Is it possible to evolve course structures, curriculum content, and programme instruction, in such a way as actually to bring the African university student into continuous contact with his environment, which, for the majority, is mainly rural? (Goma, 1989).

An improperly oriented social science could lead to forms of alienation that might retard economic development and social transformation. (Keita, 1989). The economic theories taught and researched in Western society are geared to the perpetuation of Western economic control and influence in those areas of the world open to Western economic penetration. Currently the student of economics in most African universities is unduly exposed to theories of economic decision making more appropriate to the economic life of the technologically advanced Western nations.

> The student is led to believe that the ends of economic decision-making are nothing more than the short term maximization of profits and utility. He is taught that only the market economy is capable of generating the supply and demands of goods and services, that labour is a factor of production, that the international economic system operates best under the principle of comparative advantage, and that the currencies of the Western nations are the only real ["strong"] currencies". (Keita, *op. cit.*).

The weakness and danger of this kind of education for Africa are exemplified by the intellectual paralysis of the  products of many current economics curricula in the African universities. Their fellow Western-trained economic advisers and decision-makers in contemporary Africa, seem equally powerless to deal with the situation in which African nations control neither the prices of the raw materials they produce, nor the prices of the manufactured goods they import from the industrialized West. The content of the discipline of economics and other social sciences must be changed creatively, but drastically, with inputs from the African experience. For example, such a common phenomenon as the domination of distributive trade in many parts of Africa by market women who compete effectively with the supermarkets should certainly be analysed and included in what students of economics are taught. Similarly, political science should be addressing the issue of political instability which is so prevalent on the continent.

Given the great practical need for technological development at the moment, it would seem that instruction in the natural sciences should be geared especially towards practical applications and problem solving. But serious account must be taken of the reality of rapid knowledge generation and technological innovation, so that the science graduates of African universities and their countries are not saddled with the burden of scientific and technological obsolescence.

## The Imperative of Science and Technology in Development

As the twentieth century draws to a close and the next becomes imminent, Africa is confronted with a monumental challenge to its survival and long-term development. At the base of this challenge is Africa's ability to participate in and benefit from the emerging sciences and technological revolution. (Hassan, M.H.A., 1993). Science and technology are unquestionably powerful tools for the accelerated development and progress of nations in the modern world. A notable example is the capacity of modern electronic technology for creating, processing, storing and distributing information. Indeed, throughout the world, development is becoming increasingly dominated by the new forces of modern science and technology. This has been underscored by Thomas R. Odhiambo of Kenya in these words: "The world of today is knowledge-intensive and technology-dominated. Mere possession of capital, or mere heritage of natural resources are not preconditions for national development". Accordingly, future developments in the economic, social, cultural, and environmental fields will be more and more technologically-based. The widespread scientific and technological underdevelopment found in Africa today is, thus, a major handicap which will be a crippling disability in the future if not redressed. (Goma, 1991).

Indeed, there is now world-wide recognition among those concerned with the African economic crisis that the rapidly deteriorating socio-economic conditions in the continent are closely linked to the failure to develop and sustain indigenous scientific and technological capacity. The two declarations adopted by the African Heads of State and Government, the Lagos Plan of Action (1980) and the African Priority Programme for Economic Recovery (1986), both call for sustainable development based on self-reliance in science and technology applications. (Hassan, 1993). However, although the importance of science, technology and research is acknowledged by governments, political realities have indicated that higher priority should be accorded to other needs, such as broad-based elementary education, and support of a large bureaucracy and law-enforcement agencies, servicing of foreign debts, high energy costs, etc. (ICIPE, 1988). The consequence of all this has been a deterioration of scientific and research infrastructure and the attendant failure to create an effective African science and technology capacity. Many of the African countries have slipped further behind in the scientific and technological sphere, to the extent that in many fields they possess neither the facilities nor the qualified staff essential to their development.

Already some African countries have become casualties of advances especially in the materials science field; which has produced synthetic alternatives to their main exports while a new spectrum of scientific and technological knowledge continues to unfold with great speed outside the African continent. (World Bank, 1988). Africa, therefore, faces the prospect of being de-linked from the dynamics of science and technology and, thereby, that of the crisis of continued scientific and technological marginality. The literature is replete with calls for the countries of Africa to strive determinedly to become active and significant contributors to scientific and technological advancement; to refuse to be mere recipients of or mere spectators to, the rapidly emerging sciences and technologies; and struggle to promote a culture of science-inspired creativity and technology innovation linked to the entrepreneurial enterprise. But how can the African continent move beyond rhetoric? There is a challenge here for the universities of Africa within the time-frame of 'before the end of the first decade of the twenty-first century'. And it is this: what will they contribute, to the quest of African countries to transform the present generation which has neglected to develop a science culture to one that is infused with science and technology, so that it can fit into the twenty-first century which will be dominated by science and technology, but still ensure that the culture remains grounded in the essence of African tradition of human compassion? They should take on this challenge as a major component of their mission.

In the decade of independence, a major effort was made in a number of these African universities to establish some fine scientific institutions/departments of international standing. These institutions attracted some of the best young brains in the continent and produced some of Africa's most outstanding scientists. (ICIPE, 1988; Hassan, 1993). A few exceptions still do so. Unfortunately, maintaining the scientific infrastructure in the African universities became a low priority at the advent of the economic crisis in the mid seventies. The consequences of this are that the quality of university graduates in Mathematics, Science and Engineering in many African countries has fallen sharply, and many highly qualified African scientists, engineers and technologists have left the home universities and/or the continent in search for better jobs and research opportunities abroad.

If African universities and scientific institutions are to attract young talents into a scientific career, their laboratories and libraries must be provided with adequate and up-to-date facilities, (Hassan, *M.H.A., op. cit.*). Resources should be shifted to science, engineering and other related science-based fields, as a matter of a deliberate policy. Moreover, the budgets of science departments or institutions must be protected from capricious government cuts.

Scientific institution building is a long-term endeavour that requires clear vision and a specific agenda. It should, therefore, be appreciated that it will take some dedicated, continuing effort over at a least one generation to have built up the necessary human capacity and the scientific and technological infrastructure for effective science-led development in Africa. (Odhiambo,1993).

Because of the essential role of highly qualified and talented men and women in science and technology in national development endeavours, a recent World Bank (1989) report calls on African governments to commit themselves to training a cadre of world-class scientists and technologists if they are to avoid economic and social catastrophe on an unprecedented scale in the next century. The task of producing such cadres will have to be undertaken largely by the African universities. To meet this challenge demands that some radical measures be taken. These include: according top priority to the revitalization of the degenerated infrastructure in the natural sciences, engineering and other science-based fields, at the expense of other disciplines and sectors of the university; increasing substantially the investment in scientific training, research and development at the university, more than has been attempted hitherto; the commitment of both the government and the university itself to provide sustained support for the scientific units or departments especially those in which excellence and relevance are fostered; and reversing the prevailing lopsidedness in university enrolments, so that a greater proportion of students would be pursuing the natural sciences, engineering and other science-based disciplines, not the humanities and social sciences, using the quota system and the government scholarship or bursary policy that deliberately favours the scientific disciplines to achieve this objective.

The universities should also seriously consider the possibilities of novel orientations in their teaching and research in the natural sciences, so that they can have practical relevance to the African situation. (Keita, 1989). Thus, in the field of chemistry, for example, instruction and research should be undertaken with an eye to its possible utilization in the low cost manufacture of items such as dyes, soaps and fabrics. The abundant sunlight available in local environments should serve as an impetus for the formulation of instruction geared towards the exploitation of solar energy. In the biological sciences, easily implementable principles of genetic engineering and bio-technology, which can be instrumental in raising agricultural production, reversing land degradation and conserving bio-diversity in the ecologically fragile zones of the African continent, should feature distinctly in the curricula.

The argument here is essentially this: because the new forces of modern science and technology offer immense possibilities for solving many of the complicated problems which are currently impeding economic and social development in Africa, African countries must strive to master modern science and technology and apply them to their own development requirements. (Hassan, M.H.A., 1993). But this will not be achieved if African universities remain pedestrian in their approaches to human resource and scientific talent development endeavours. It should, however, be added that, building up such indigenous capabilities is not enough; they will disappear unless the African social and political environments are prepared to utilize their talent. The scientific and technological empowerment of Africa is only the start, and this is undoubtedly a major part of the mission of the African universities.

## Steadfast Deployment at the Knowledge Frontier

To advance the frontiers of knowledge is among the principal universal missions of the university in the modern world. What African universities contribute to the development and progress of the African continent become part of the world reservoir of knowledge, for the benefit of mankind as a whole. It is of course no longer true that there is a common heritage that provides open access to the world's stock of knowledge. Knowledge is power, and national governments now control the flow of knowledge. There is, thus, a market in knowledge. Although knowledge is the only commodity you can sell and still possess, you do not trade at the market unless you have something to trade with.

All the best universities the world over claim that the advancement of knowledge is their pride and job. Indeed, the prestige of being identified as a centre of research and scholarship is a legitimate part of the aspirations of universities throughout Africa. (Goma, 1989). However, the genuine cultivation and advancement of knowledge, at a serious level, takes place at only what is a rapidly diminishing small number of these universities; and the overall research performance of African universities as a whole has so far been clearly deficient. As a consequence, the research output and the resultant generation of new knowledge has lagged far behind the training accomplishments of the African universities. (Saint, 1992). In short, African universities have made little progress in fulfilling their mandate to generate applied and policy-relevant knowledge as inputs to national development processes or contributions to the world's stock of knowledge.

It is regrettable that, for various reasons, a vast number of Africa's institutions of higher learning have been forced to retreat from the 'Knowledge Frontier'. There can be no doubt, however, that the lack or inadequacy of proper funding of research has been the basic reason. Many African governments generally do not encourage the serious pursuit of research at their universities, or recognize superior performance in this area. Instead, the pseudo-research produced by quick consultancies is often a financially more attractive option. (Saint, 1992). By not committing themselves to building national research capabilities and capacities through supportive policies for research, and the sustained funding and use of local technical expertise, African governments inhibit the quality and output of the research in their universities. On the other hand, the African universities themselves have not always accorded research sufficient priority.

There can be no dispute as to the great and continuing need for the steadfast deployment of African universities at the 'Knowledge Frontier'. This underscores the need to accord the revitalization of research a very high priority at these institutions. Since research funds and staff will always be at a premium, it is the duty of each university to ensure that both of these commodities are used at maximum efficiency. But, as in the case of its teaching function, the university faces a dilemma with regard to what sort of research it should encourage its staff to pursue. If the university attempts to enforce rigid control over staff research, it seriously threatens academic freedom. (ESAURP, 1987). Moreover, excellence may not be encouraged if the skills and interests of current staff are not matched to the research that is undertaken. Furthermore, the choice of research topics should usually grow out of the interpretation by individual scholars of the needs of the university and/or of the country. Such choice and the definition of research problems in the 'developmental university' obviously express definite conceptions of the nature of the country's development, (Colin Leys, 1971) and/or the direction in which the university is moving. It is important to make these conceptions explicit, and that the universities, that is to say the people who will do the research, decide which to adopt. There are several dangers to be avoided. One is that, if care is not taken, research may serve only the narrow professional interests of the researcher, and no other important social purpose at all.

The poor countries of Africa can only afford to support a limited amount of research at their universities, and yet there are vast areas of immediate concern to the society which remain unexplored - from the field of tropical diseases to the oral history of ethnic groups, from rural agriculture to the creation of employment in the textile industry, from the improvement of local brickmaking to rural and regional planning (ESAURP, 1987). These areas provide scope for research which can reach heights of academic excellence while still being immediately relevant to the developmental needs of the society.

In the quest to fulfil their research mission, many African universities end up with a plethora of research projects that advance neither the cause of knowledge, nor the worth of the university, or the real development of their nation. They undertake too many isolated, often inconsequential, research projects at the instance of individual members of staff. By frittering away effort and resources in this way, the development and progress, and indeed the usefulness, of the university can be seriously hampered.

In these circumstances, it is necessary for the university to indicate areas of research it favours and encourages; and, if quality is to be preserved or attained, a policy of concentration is better than one of dispersal. (Goma, 1989). It is better to do fewer things well than more things badly. In other words, it is imperative for the university to identify fields of research where it can expect to excel and to concentrate effort and resources there. Accordingly, the university should create a University Central Research Fund, if one does not already exist, and it might be necessary to have some clearly stated guidelines which it should apply when making grants for research projects from the Fund. Such guidelines should include the following:

(1) The proposed research project should clearly be relevant and geared to the needs of the country itself or in the wider context of Africa. [In this connection, the standard practice should be that of insisting on a rational demonstration of its bearing on the development problem.] OR The proposed research project should have potential or demonstrable academic worth, so that it can contribute positively to the standing of the university as a seat of scholarship.

(2) For the sake of continuity, the proposed research project should be invested in the university rather than in an individual or individuals. It should, thus, be clearly relevant to active research already being pursued, or to the principal interests of

the subject area to which the applicant is appointed.

(3) The proposed research project should be subjected to the demand that the research should be fundamental - in the specific sense of not taking as given things which it is possible to question.

It would be important for the university to publish both the research guidelines and statements of research priorities, specifying broad areas of concern rather than narrow research topics, and perhaps to tie allocation of local research funds to these priorities. (ESAURP, 1987). Those not wishing to abide by these guidelines should not be prevented from carrying out research, if they secure financial and technical support from elsewhere and such support covers the reasonable costs of using university facilities for their research work.

The principle of the indivisibility of teaching and research should remain valid for the African universities even under the prevailing difficult circumstances and in the future. The 'pure *versus* applied research' debate is a futile endeavour in the realities of Africa. The experience of the Kenya-based International Centre of Insect Physiology and Ecology has amply demonstrated how pure research can have direct relevance for applied research in areas crucial for the development and progress of the African continent and other tropical areas. Nevertheless, it is by undertaking research and consultancy services relevant to the needs of the society, that African universities can be seen to be responding to the developmental needs of their nations. This in turn should contribute to the creation of a culture of relevance that could positively influence the attitude of students towards their areas of specialization. But this should not dismiss the importance of those who may be or may wish to be engaged in cutting-edge research considered worthwhile by the university.

The need for the urgent reinforcement of the research function of African universities cannot be over-emphasized. Because of the costs involved, many countries, experiencing serious economic difficulties have tended to resort to cuts in funding research in the universities, despite the fact that they are sometimes the main, and in many African countries the only, places where any significant research takes place. Short-term considerations and the pressure of budgetary constraints can lead to serious long-term consequences for higher education institutions. (UNESCO, 1993 - May 1993). It should be said that research, although costly, is wise investment:

> research departments in higher education institutions, although costly, are nevertheless a crucial resource in the context of the present-day global and

dynamic economy based on knowledge, innovation and the almost constant state of technological change. One way to make the general public, the governmental bodies and the economic organisations better aware of the role of research in higher education is to demonstrate, through convincing results, the quality, value and relevance of research.

A multi-faceted strategy seems required. While greater public discussion of the important relationship between research capacity and national development is needed (Saint, 1992), it is equally imperative that such discussion also takes place within the university community itself. In many of the universities of Africa, as is the case in some other parts of the world, the notion of research is surrounded by shibboleth. Much activity labelled 'research' is simply high-level busy-work which furthers neither knowledge nor its transmission or application, but only the publication lists of the individuals concerned for the purpose of seeking promotion. (Goma, 1989). The many and varied obstacles currently impeding the prosecution of sufficient quality research in many African universities need to be addressed urgently. Due to the growing numbers of students enrolled, the professors and their colleagues find themselves involved more and more in undergraduate teaching and, thus, find it increasingly difficult to get on with research. For organizational and financial reasons, they may also be denied sabbatical leave, or even attendance at international seminars; they may, thus, be out of touch with current developments and progress in their fields. For these and other reasons, a number of African universities currently suffer from lack of strong and able academic leadership in the various departments, faculties and research units. Departmental headships, faculty deanships, and research unit directorships sometimes fall on the shoulders of relatively young and inexperienced academics. This could lead to impoverishment and lack of solid achievement in the field of research. The importance of strong academic leadership should not be underrated by any university of consequence.

Perhaps the biggest obstacle is financial deprivation. Budgetary allocations for research in African universities are generally small and, in some cases, non-existent. (AAU, 1991; Saint, 1992). Annual allocations received by the majority of the universities range from 0.0% to 3.8%. If these universities are to keep up with their mandate of conducting research relevant to their societies and environment, a substantially much higher percentage allocation to this function is imperative (AAU, *op. cit.*). A UNESCO/AAU Seminar on the Management of African Universities, held in Dakar, Senegal, in November 1992, recommended that at least 5.0% should be allocated to research as a separate and earmarked grant; and that, of this, at least

65.0% should be reserved for actual research costs other than personal emoluments. It should be pointed out that this does not necessarily mean that governments alone should contribute to this level of allocation for research. The private sector that can use the results of the research as well as external agencies could participate in this activity. (AAU, *op. cit.*).

The financial squeeze and the attendant foreign exchange crisis has hit hard at the research requiring the purchase and acquisition of equipment and materials from overseas. Moreover, scientific equipment deteriorates rapidly and becomes obsolete when replacement of parts or components is delayed. The financial constraints have also produced gross inadequacies in library facilities, so that the pursuit of learning and the advancement of knowledge, even in the relatively inexpensive fields of the humanities and social sciences, has similarly suffered. The AAU's *Report of a Study on Cost Effectiveness and Efficiency in African Universities* recommends that African universities must devote at least 5% of their funds to the libraries and at least 60% of this should be reserved for the purchase of books and journals. (AAU, 1991). However, in order to ensure that libraries do in fact receive and utilize the funds allocated to them, such funds should be provided as separate or earmarked grants, and no diversion should be permitted. Furthermore, in the light of the proliferation of electronic data bases and networks, and when the conversion of many international bibliographic and research abstract services are changing over to micrographic and CD-ROM technology, the libraries of African universities should desist from continuing to expand on the previous pattern. They must take on the new technologies and exploit the informatics revolution as fully as necessary. In view of the strangulating financial stringency, this calls for careful policy formulation.

Steadfast deployment at the 'Knowledge Frontier' is impossible with an army of academic men and women who see their vocation as simply pushing a little further along a well-trodden path which requires little more than diligence, and good resources. African universities seeking to secure a bridgehead at this frontier must build up critical mass of active researchers and scholars, in the words of Edward Shils (1962), "whose interests complement each other and whose standards of work are sufficiently high to reinforce each other's attachment to those standards and to keep each other on their intellectual toes". To secure, in real and concrete terms, such an essential population of talented, highly motivated, inter-acting academic community demands greater efforts by the African universities.

## Postgraduate Education and Training

In recent years, there has been a proliferation of postgraduate programmes which cannot be sustained at standards required to ensure professional competence because of declining budget allocations, and staff retention difficulties. (Saint, 1992). Indeed, an AAU review of postgraduate training and research within ten West African universities records a severe decline in postgraduate programmes. (Nwa and Houenou, 1990, *in* Saint, *op. cit.*). There is full agreement that the institutional deterioration has been severe throughout much of the African continent, and that even universities with well-established research cultures and postgraduate programmes are holding on only with difficulty. (Coombe, 1991). However, university people do not readily concede that this grave crisis spells the end of research and postgraduate education and training in African universities.

Apart from financial stringency, there are several other reasons for the prevailing dismal state of postgraduate education and training in Africa. They include the fact that governments, industry, and private business in Africa do not seem interested in   postgraduate studies or the graduates they produce; and that African universities themselves are uncertain as to what is the best way to organize the management of such studies.  A number of African universities do not yet offer postgraduate studies due to the fact that a sufficiently qualified and stable professoriate has not yet been produced, while the material infrastructure to bring about this kind or level of training is also lacking.  In some others, the demand for postgraduate studies is increasing; but the facilities and opportunities are rather limited, and few of the academic staff dealing with postgraduate studies have had previous experience with the supervision of such advanced studies.

The management of postgraduate studies so that they are not only protected but also promoted requires careful handling.  Would a separate postgraduate faculty with the more experienced teaching staff wholly committed to higher degree teaching offer the best option?  This is dismissed by some authorities as totally out of the question, not only because of the cost, but also because in principle the most senior academics should also contribute to undergraduate teaching.  But a separate postgraduate faculty facilitates the provision of multi-disciplinary Masters programmes more than the regular faculties.  However the success of a Postgraduate School as an autonomous administrative entity depends on the level of funding it can attract.  Many universities have settled for the provision of postgraduate education and training, together with undergraduate studies, within the same regular departments and faculties. (Coombe, 1991).

There are many people who refuse to accept the possibility of postgraduate education and training being offered by institutions other than universities. Accordingly, the broadening of the capacity development base to involve independent research institutes and similar centres of excellence in postgraduate education is a relatively novel idea in Africa which has not been embraced without some doubt and contention. There is need in Africa to break out of the traditional mould, and accept the notion of Graduate Schools in specialised areas attached to advanced centres of solid research. The African Regional Postgraduate Programme in Insect Science (ARPPIS) at the International Centre of Insect Physiology and Ecology (ICIPE) in Nairobi and Mbita Point Field Station, Kenya has shown the way. (ICIPE, 1989).

The main features of the ICIPE experiment are the establishment of a postgraduate education and training programme within ICIPE, with all thesis research supervision led by ICIPE's senior research staff who have academic inclinations and experience, whereas the coursework is undertaken under a mixed teaching group of ICIPE senior staff and visiting faculty members drawn from a consortium of African universities. Already, this educational experiment, ARPPIS, has been in existence for over eight years with 10-15 students at Master's Degree level being admitted each year for the 3-year Ph.D. programme. Successful candidates take their doctorate degree from one of the 15 ARPPIS participating universities. The students officially register with their relevant home university participating in the programme. The programme has been an outstanding success, with all 40 or so graduated Ph.D. holders still in Africa working in an atmosphere of belonging and high morale. (Tsuma, 1993). As there is a compelling need to move urgently to develop a critical mass of first-class specialists in insect science and pest management, ICIPE is considering uplifting the ICIPE postgraduate education programme into a fully-fledged degree-awarding Graduate School, separate from ICIPE in academic matters, but operating under the overall umbrella of the ICIPE. It will not be a university; but the Graduate School, which will concentrate entirely on the formation of Ph.D.-level graduates, will continue to be a member of the ARPPIS network. (ICIPE, 1989; Tsuma, *op. cit.*).

This ARPPIS and Graduate School model of continent-wide educational training and high-level research and development (R&D) has proved successful in the case of insect science. It is especially attractive because of the element of linking the African university system with a relevant advanced centre of research in a field critical to Africa's development. This innovation should be extended to other equally important fields such as tropical health, tropical agro-industry, engineering and technology, *et cetera*. (Tsuma, 1993).

Under current difficult economic conditions, regional cooperation in postgraduate education and training offers an attractive, cost-effective option for expanding the numbers of specialized professional and academic staff on the continent under acceptable conditions of academic quality. (Saint, 1992). Since not all countries can afford to support good postgraduate studies in all disciplines, innovative forms of regional cooperation and institutional linkage will become increasingly necessary, indeed unavoidable.

The justification for an increase in the range and volume of postgraduate study lies not only in the manpower needs of the African countries but also in the many-faceted role which postgraduate study plays in a university. For example, postgraduate studies provide opportunities for the research interests of the academic staff and for professional collaboration with mature students which enable both the student and the teacher to bring new knowledge and insights to teaching. Postgraduate work also provides a corps of junior staff useful for teaching, demonstration and other academic tasks, thereby helping to free the time of senior staff for more demanding duties. In the circumstances of many African universities, postgraduate studies should also play a positive role in staff development programmes. Thus, postgraduate studies are critical for national capacity building because they select and produce highly skilled professionals, including the academic staff of universities; they are key determinants of the quality of undergraduate education; and, it is at this level that research skills are acquired and new knowledge is produced. (Saint, 1992).

The problem of the level of financial support available to postgraduate students will need to be addressed. This is a matter which universities and other institutions involved have to take up with the potential sponsors, the actual or prospective employers, including the universities and/or respective institutions. Since postgraduate studies are almost all vocationally specific, the cost to the sponsor can justifiably be linked to benefits. (Coombe, 1991). The financing of the mobility of students and academic staff within Africa, in order to benefit from the existence of regional centres of excellence, also presents a practical problem which deserves special study, taking into account the variety of currency areas and free trade arrangements in place. There are clear advantages in limiting the hard currency requirements of postgraduate student exchange, but where these are unavoidable, donor assistance would be helpful (Coombe, 1991).

**The Imperative of Regional Co-operation**

There are over one hundred and thirty universities in Africa. It is clear, however, that some of these universities may not have adequate resources to support certain areas of their academic and research programmes. Although many of them have maintained strong linkages with their former metropolitan universities, a good number of African universities with many years of experience offer potential opportunities for cooperation and collaboration in teaching and research. (AAU, 1991). There could be effective sharing of facilities in special areas of university education and research. This could take various forms. There could be a cluster of disciplines which a particular university could offer to others. Well equipped departments should not be closed for lack of students locally, as has happened in certain cases; but should be filled with students from elsewhere in Africa.

Indeed, the indications are that the way ahead for the development of research and postgraduate capacity in African universities is through selective concentration of resources within the university system, and the achievement of collaborative links among African universities, and between African universities and research institutes. (Coombe, 1991). This is an area where AAU's role is vital and critical. Providing effective leadership to facilitate meaningful regional inter-university cooperation among African universities may help to ease the resources constraints and to build a viable educational enterprise in Africa capable of meeting the challenges ahead. (AAU, 1991).

The AAU Report on Cost Effectiveness and Efficiency calls upon the leadership of African universities to explore the possibility of greater regional cooperation and linkages in the implementation of their academic programmes. It also recommends that the concept of regional graduate schools with international faculty drawn from individual university departments, be adopted for major disciplines; and that the AAU should facilitate this.

It can be said that, while it is imperative for each African university to aspire towards excellence, none of them can ever hope to attain such excellence in every field. A crucial challenge facing African universities is, therefore, how to achieve collective self-reliance buttressed by excellence in those disciplines, areas of research and new knowledge both of immediate and long-term concern to the development and progress of the African continent. The answer lies in the increased role of inter-university cooperation, through which the marginalization of certain institutions can be avoided and academic excellence can be made more readily available through a "division of tasks" among some African universities which transcend national barriers. (UNESCO, 1993). An interlocking system of international centres of excellence can certainly provide a much needed important boost to higher education in Africa. (Coombe, 1991).

There is no doubt that developing a network of centres of excellence would enable African universities to share their scarce resources in the development of local research capacity. (ESAURP, 1987). A number of such centres of excellence already exist such as ICIPE in Nairobi, Kenya, the International Institute of Tropical Agriculture (IITA) in Ibadan, Nigeria, the International Livestock Centre for Africa (ILCA), in Addis Ababa, Ethiopia, the Tropical Disease Research Centre in Ndola, Zambia, the Regional Health Training Centre at the University of Zimbabwe, Harare, and the East African School of Librarianship at Makerere University in Kampala, Uganda. But there is urgent need to create more, and especially networks of research and training centres of excellence in various fields of frontier science and technology and other areas of knowledge which are most likely to have strong impact upon the economic and social development and progress of the African continent.

Modern technological advances render the creation and functioning of centres of excellence in Africa, as elsewhere, particularly promising. They allow the expansion of the concept of academic mobility so as to include not only the traditional mobility of students, teachers and researchers, but also a sort of mobility in reverse, i.e., placing the shared potential of several institutions the best teachers, the most complete data bases, the newest experiments, etc. at the disposal of students, teachers and researchers of institutions situated in far-away places. (UNESCO, 1993). The UNESCO Chairs Programme involves the creation, in partnership with universities and other appropriate bodies, of professorships enabling mainly visiting scholars to provide the core expertise for the development of centres of excellence in key disciplines and fields related to sustainable development and other main problems of the world. African countries and their universities should seek to take full advantage of this programme.

The AAU Report on Graduate Education and R&D in African Universities, which came out in May 1990, proposes the identification and selection of certain departments as centres for postgraduate training in particular disciplines. While the earlier World Bank Policy Study of Education in Sub-Saharan Africa (1988) agrees with this, it warns that: "Determining which institutions will participate in postgraduate programs of excellence will not be easy - for African governments or for their international partners. Questions of international and regional comparative advantage must be squarely faced, since resources will never be sufficient for every country in Africa or even for the continent as a whole to develop capacity at the highest level in all fields and sub-fields. Ultimately, decisions must be made discipline-by-discipline and in the light of regional requirements".

A meeting of deans of graduate education from ten selected universities from the West and Central Africa Region, held at Ibadan in May 1990 to deliberate on the AAU Report on Graduate Education cited above, agreed that: "Considering the present difficult economic situation which limits the financial resources available to the continent, it is recommended that every effort should be made to identify institutions that are known to be good in certain disciplines and strengthen them in those disciplines". (cited by J.S. Djangmah, 1991 - ICIPE Bellagio Report) In other words, the chosen faculties, departments and institutes will need strengthening in order to equip themselves for their expanded roles. (Coombe, 1991).

Despite the very wide agreement that inter-university collaboration is the only rational path to follow, the policy of rationalizing research and postgraduate capacity within African regions is not working fast enough. Unfortunately, the success of the policy must face the danger of being compromised at the implementation stage by national governments or university authorities putting their own ambitions above regional solidarity. (Coombe, 1991). Moreover, postgraduate student mobility relies upon the consent of the students concerned, which cannot be taken for granted. It is not unreasonable to suppose, indeed expect, that no student will willingly take up a postgraduate place in a strange country whose political stability and economic conditions are rated worse than they are at home, or when the portends are that completion of the programme there, in good time if at all, is not guaranteed.

**Redressing the Gender Balance.**

As the African University moves towards the 21ˢᵗ Century and as the world struggles to topple the last fortresses of dictatorship, discrimination and exploitation, efforts must be made to ensure that women, who constitute over 50% of the world's population, become equal partners for development with their male counterparts.

The University must offer an environment in which women can effectively function. There is need to take into account women's reproductive role and offer facilities that can allow women with children to function effectively. The academic institution must find ways of accommodating a woman who, for example, delivers a baby at examination time. Further, concepts such as the open university which are women-friendly must be fully explored and publicised so that women can take advantage of them to study while still nurturing their families. Regulations that limit the age of admission to university, and of access to certain scholarships, should be reviewed as they most likely, perhaps inadvertently, discriminate against women who often have to interrupt their studies to start a family. Further, women should be encouraged to resume or continue their studies and careers so that they cease to regard their motherhood role as punishment. This, in fact, seems to have happened in the North where population growth has dropped to zero or below zero and governments are taking drastic measures to persuade women to continue giving birth to children. Africa is, of course, for now facing the reverse problem of overpopulation but all measures undertaken should, of necessity, predict future tendencies.

Because of the historical, social, sexual and economic interaction of men and women, the university must struggle to find the delicate balance between over-protecting and refusing to nurture female students. Ways must be found to encourage particularly women students who qualify but cannot go to institutions of higher learning. This can be done through earmarking scholarships specifically for women, establishing Trusts and Endowment Funds for them, and perhaps exploring other ways of making it possible for disadvantaged women students to work part-time, although this latter measure could equally apply to male students.

The gravitation of women towards the so-called "softer options" has been interpreted by some as an indication of the intellectual inferiority of women. Recent research however indicates that, given equal opportunities, women will perform at least as well as men in most disciplines and better than men in some. This has been manifested particularly in girls-only schools where the staff are essentially female and thus constitute role models to be emulated. If the up-coming generations of women are to be freed from the burden of exploitation and discriminations, older women must organise themselves and become their "mentors".

It is of utmost importance that women who aspire to academic careers in universities be encouraged by being compensated on the principle of equal pay for equal work. Some universities do not pay married women housing allowance on the assumption that they will be "housed" by their husbands, while some men take advantage of their wives' better housing arrangements but are still paid housing allowance. While the principle of one house for one family can be defended, it must be applied to men no less than to women.

Because most university committees are composed of men who constitute over 90% of the teaching staff, it must be ensured that criteria for promotion are so clearly elaborated that women applicants are not penalised especially when they do not conform to the gentle, soft-spoken, submissive image that the society at large has of women. Adequate arrangements must be made for maternity leave without prejudice to the woman's career progression.

Further, both men and women must examine their language in the classroom, in meetings and in private interactions to ensure that sexist implications and derogatory jokes are eliminated. It is only in this way that strong, intelligent women can feel safe in their interactions with men at all levels and abandon the counter-aggression that, for the younger ones, seems to characterise the so-called "feminist" movement. They must struggle to ensure that the media project a balanced image of women. They must ensure that all laws and Acts are devoid of discriminatory clauses. The African University of the 21$^{st}$ Century must struggle to become a place where the pursuit of knowledge is indeed freely and equally available to all citizens, irrespective of age, sex, religion and race.

## Chapter 11

## THE OUTREACH

### Marginalization of the African University

One result of the economic crisis confronting the African continent is a growing marginalization of African universities from the intellectual and informational mainstreams that shape development possibilities in the rest of the world. (Saint, 1992). But there is an even more fundamental concern: the university in Africa is a grossly marginalized entity in the sense that its resources are not fully utilized. Government has no clear-cut policies on how best to use the products and resources of the university. In the overwhelming majority of African countries, university administrators and other authorities are excluded by design from policy formulation. Many governments rarely take the university into consideration or involve it in the national manpower development plans of the country. In any case, there is often really no manpower planning as such: so the university goes on producing people without knowing what they will be doing after graduation. The marginalization of the African university can also be seen by the uncaring attitude of some governments: at a time when a university is afflicted by acute staff losses, and is unable to replace them, the governments still go ahead to take away more badly needed staff into government service by executive action.

The university is thus not a priority to most African governments and communities. It would appear that, contrary to what obtains in the industrialized countries, governments do not have sufficient confidence in their universities to rely on their expertise. Some governments fail to see the link between the university and the government, perhaps due to lack of understanding about the role and true nature of universities. Some governments are openly hostile to their own universities. There is clearly urgent need to generate the necessary understanding and also to create a culture of tolerance, so that governments can be more favourably disposed to their universities.

But the universities in Africa must also share responsibility for their marginalization and for some of the hostility towards them. As a participant in a recent round-table discussion for the AAU Study of the African Experience with Higher Education at one university put it bluntly:

But do we who are in the universities understand what our role is? We should ask ourselves this question. I don't think that we do always. If attacked by government, we are not able to take our stand and state what we are about. We don't sell ourselves enough. We don't have confidence in ourselves. Our research is not known locally because we prefer, or there is some compulsion, to publish it in so-called international journals - which are not available to the local communities both inside and outside academia. We thus get known outside but not locally. That is why our governments use foreigners and not us on things which we ourselves can do quite satisfactorily.

Lack of information about African universities and their academics contributes significantly to the marginalization now suffered by these institutions in their own countries and abroad. A lot needs to be done by the African universities and their academics so that they can become central and not as marginalized as they are today. The universities and the academics must, therefore, disseminate the necessary information to sell themselves to their governments and societies.

They need to do more than they have done hitherto to make people see their usefulness beyond the production of increasing numbers of graduates. There is need to create an environment whereby the university could be accepted fully and unambiguously by the government and the community. Presently, as remarked by a participant in another Roundtable at another African university, "we are not regarded as leaders by the community". The "we" and "they" syndrome must be fought and eliminated. It is imperative to make the universities in Africa seen to be really part and parcel of the societies in which they exist.

The end of the East-West conflict and, thus, of the Cold War and of the nuclear threat to the existence of mankind; the subsequent developments in what was the Soviet Union and Eastern Europe - including the special case of Yugoslavia; and the economic potential of the newly industrialized countries of the South - in South East Asia and Latin America, have combined to worsen the marginalization and abandonment of Africa. Africa is absent everywhere it matters. It is not on the agenda of the major world fora when the most powerful nations meet. Its voice is inaudible. The emergent New World Order, which is still being defined, may be more dangerous for Africa and other developing parts of the world. Africa should make a spirited effort to have a say in the creation of this New World Order, and the universities in Africa should treat this matter as deserving their serious concern and action to help the continent in its plight, by creating think-tanks on the problem.

But Africa will have to accept that it has contributed to its own marginalization and abandonment. One of the problems is that African countries have not successfully organized themselves to utilize their enormous resources and products to their own advantage. There is urgent need for them to take action - not merely talk - to strengthen regional and continental co-operation.

As participants at the first Roundtable cited above in connection with the AAU Study on the African Experience with Higher Education said, it is possible to take advantage of marginalization in order to build up self-reliance:

> The marginalization of Africa and of its institutions is inevitable as long as we Africans do not respect ourselves. You can, therefore, have self-marginalization. If Africa takes a self-pitying attitude, we are in trouble. Africa must, therefore, look inward and use our resources; forget about technology. Continuing to plead with outside powers will lead us nowhere. It is unfortunate that we were not marginalized much earlier. We should now be standing on our own feet. Marginalization is healthy for Africa. Marginalization should accordingly not be looked at negatively. It should help us with development independence. We should involve our universities in some of the industries to enable them to grow and tackle some of our problems. The universities should intervene at some proper point and level.

The marginalization of African universities at home also contributes to the overall marginalization of the African continent in the world. The African governments and their universities must together endeavour to tackle this aspect of the problem. The modern world takes serious note of those countries and institutions which make significant contributions to the world pool of knowledge. Each of the universities in Africa should, therefore, strive to develop some area in which it can excel, and which would attract anyone in the world interested in that particular field. Reducing the marginalization of universities in Africa will help to overcome the marginalization of the African continent in the world.

**University-Productive Sector Linkages**

Among the most serious problems of the African continent is the low level of industrial development in almost all the African countries. The most successful newly industrialized countries of the South are those which have been able to form a strong alliance between science, technology and industry. Universities are central to such alliance. Yet, few of the universities in Africa have taken the initiative to actively establish linkages with the productive sector. (IDRC, 1991; Hassan, 1993). And even in those few African countries where these linkages have been established, they are weak, poorly financed and largely ineffective. Thus, very few universities in the African continent, for example, conduct research and training programmes pertinent to the industrial needs of their countries.

There are several benefits accruing from the interaction between universities and industry. Among these are that it (i) enhances the reputation of the university; (ii) provides opportunities for staff and researchers to participate directly in economic development which should improve their social recognition; (iii) makes the curricula of university courses more relevant to the needs of society, and provides feedback on how well the university laboratory involved is performing; and (iv) benefits the industrial firms and the industrial sector, and, in the course of time, as industries develop, will benefit the universities financially; and (v) the complementary resources drawn from industry should enhance the financial autonomy of the relevant laboratories and thus encourage initiatives for further creativity. (Brunat and Reverdy, 1989; IDRC, 1991). Developing strong and complex links and partnerships with industry and other sectors of economic life facilitates the utilization of scientific and technological advances by the productive sectors, and is also vital for the future development of higher education on the continent.

Shortage of hard currency to import products, spare parts, *et cetera,* and international competitiveness, are encouraging industry to look to the universities for innovative ideas, improvement of production processes, quality control of goods, and the development of resources appropriate to the needs of industry. (IDRC, 1991). However, there are problems to overcome to facilitate university-productive sector (UPS) linkages. These arise largely because of the multi-disciplinary nature of UPS activities, the attitude of the universities, the lack of autonomy of UPS centres, and the inability of the African industrialists to clearly define their problems, through in-house research, and finance the research, among others. (IDRC, 1991).

As the IDRC (1991) review of the situation in Africa points out, the activities undertaken in industry are multi-disciplinary in nature. They do not easily fall into separate water-tight compartments. Unfortunately, many African universities lack multi-disciplinary departments which can be relied on to play leading roles in UPS linkage activities. Industries are calling for a multi-disciplinary approach to the solution of their problems. But most university departments lack the ability or the experience of work with other departments. This basic problem makes it difficult for UPS linkages to operate effectively, especially since African industrialists and entrepreneurs are unable to clearly define their problems in the first instance. (J. Aminu, 1987, *in*

IDRC, 1991). Hence the tendency of some industrialists to prefer to import the latest technology without taking the trouble to find out what is available or could be made available locally.

That there is a growing need to link some activities of the African universities to the productive sector cannot be in doubt. The real problem is whether, in view of the multiplicity of constraints, and the unfavourable environment within which both the universities and industry operate, the universities in Africa can develop effective linkages with the productive sector. To be able to do so calls for preparedness and willingness to adopt innovative and pragmatic approaches in the operations of both the university and industry.

African governments should support the establishment of universities interdisciplinary research and training centres in areas of science and technology most relevant to the development of local industry. (Hassan, M.H.A., 1993). In particular, greater importance should be given to the development of strong linkages between engineering institutions, small-scale industries and the agricultural sector with the principal aim of producing simple and modern tools and equipment required by farmers to increase their productivity and efficiency. Institutions of higher education also need to venture into non-traditional fields, such as entrepreneurship development, management for production, productivity and change; exploration, evaluation and extraction of mineral resources; the building up of capability to produce equipment, parts, implements and tools, as well as a wide range of areas in engineering and technology education which are as yet unexplored in African institutions of higher learning. (ECA, 1989; Ajayi, 1994). They would also have to modify their teaching practices so that as many opportunities as possible are provided to students to learn by doing.

As the universities in Africa establish UPS linkages, there is need for them to develop or improve their skills in marketing both their research services and any exploitable discoveries they make. The example may be cited of some universities with an exhibition gallery at the most open part of the university, such as the foyer of the University Library, showing the University's contribution in major breakthroughs in research, industrial or agricultural production, health, properties of local materials, etc. It is also important to realise that the contact between industry and universities relies on a relationship of trust, induced by the potential of the university and its track record in helping to produce commercially successful products. (Brunat and Reverdy, 1989).

**The Quest for Identity**

> *Instead of the cross, the Albatross*
> *About my neck was hung.*

The stranglehold of inherited traditions in African universities, which can be likened to the fate of the Ancient Mariner in Samuel Taylor Coleridge's poem, has frustrated efforts to make these institutions really proud of being African and doing things African. That the universities in Africa should seek to be more African than they are is no longer a matter of debate. The real challenge is to concretize this by doing things African with greater resolve and creativity. Too many African scholars are sticking to the traditional pattern of gaining recognition; for example, by preferring to publish in overseas journals. They seem to consider that departure from such pattern means being less scholarly. There is urgent need to break out of this stranglehold. African universities and academics should not feel apologetic about being African and being pre-occupied with things African as unambiguously deserving of intellectual endeavour at the highest level.

In dealing with this matter, there is no attempt to press for the construction of a single new model of African university development. It is argued that phrases like 'the African university' are wide off the mark if they give the impression of a single unified model. (Coombe, 1991). Diversity reigns in the African university community, as in African economies and political patterns. What is needed is that, despite the multiplicity of models of university systems, the universities in Africa should not only be relevant to the continent's situation, they should also be truly African and strive to make a specific African contribution to the world of scholarship, research, and knowledge, inspired by the African insight, historical experience and challenges.

Regrettably, African universities have not taken up certain important African issues with the necessary determination, aggressiveness and continuity. How many African scholars have cared, for instance, to study and understand the successes of African market women to which we referred above? Or that in agriculture, some traditional methods seem to have been more successful than several of the environmentally unfriendly modern methods? Or the fact that traditional medicines are coming into vogue even in the industrialized countries? What remains of African traditional society is an extremely important source of material for the intellectual endeavour of African universities. There are several areas in the African environment which should generate inspiration for creative intellectual exploration. But such creativity should be really profound. Not enough African philosophy, African psychology, African traditional medicine, African traditional agriculture, *et cetera*, are on the agenda of African universities, and so, are marginalized in these institutions and by African academics. Though this may be an indication of the current decline of research in Africa, it is largely the foreign or non-African scholars, scientists and others from or in overseas universities and research institutions who appear at the moment to show more interest in researching in African topics than the Africans themselves. This situation must be corrected. African universities and African scholars therein should be identified with leading roles in doing things African. This should be part of the *mission* of the African university to be accomplished by the end of the first decade of the twenty-first century.

A significant measure of the attention of African universities to things African can be gauged from the level of interest in African languages which are the key to understanding African patterns of thought, collective wisdom, historical traditions, and religious ideas. For each African community, its most distinct contribution is its language. The study of African languages is thus a vast field for intellectual endeavour. Most of the languages are known only to linguists. Many are yet to have a written form. Very few are used for writing, or for teaching even at elementary school level. The study of African languages in African universities is thus at only a preliminary level. Each university should select at least a few African languages to be studied along with their literatures and philosophies. Bodies of traditional African poems, proverbs, religious chants and other set texts should be translated and made available for study. The suggestion that the time has come when no undergraduate should take a degree in an African university in the Humanities without a course in an African language, literature or philosophy, or in the sciences without some attention to the science base of traditional societies, deserves attention.

The Social Sciences in African universities are presently not sufficiently detached from Western, especially American, jargon and influence. They have not really taken root in the African universities or been significantly inspired by the fundamental circumstances of African societies. They are, thus, not getting to grips with the real social and economic problems - the questions of unstable marriages and families; collective responsibility of kinship groups for the defence of moral values and shared responsibility for the avoidance of shame; voting patterns and the choosing of leaders through elections; the rapid and widespread rise of crime; and the growing drugs problem. There is need to look into these issues not just as an academic exercise, but for practical purposes also.

What should be the role of the Social Sciences in recreating African society? There is need to understand and preserve those things that made it possible to achieve and maintain a complex balance in African societies. The questions of the individual's human rights versus the rights of the group need to be addressed in the African context. On the ideological plane, the once hopeful vision of African socialism appears to have been largely discredited. (Saint, 1992). "The intellectual vacuum left is being filled by a dual doctrine of economic liberalism and political pluralism. These new orientations have yet to be tested, assessed and adapted in an African context". As Ahmed Hassanali has commented: "Unfortunately, at a time dominated by a single global ideology following the collapse of totalitarian communism, and accustomed as we are in viewing options in watertight colours rather than in variegated shades, by our willy-nilly embrace of the free-market ideology in totality, Africa may have started a process of shedding off its richly caring socio-cultural heritage which may transform its citizens into individualised replica of dominant factions of industrialized societies" (Hassanali, 1993). Here is a challenging field to African universities and African academics. There is great need for African inputs into the debate on development, and alternatives to modernization which obviously has not worked for Africa.

It is argued that the majority of Africa's decision makers in the area of economics and finance, although trained in modern techniques, have been unable to formulate relevant theories of economic growth and development. (Keita, 1989). A plausible reason is that the modern African social scientist is so imbued with western paradigms of analysis that his views on economic development and social transformation tend to coincide with those of the so-called Western 'expert'. But the West's views on African economic development are formulated principally to establish and support Western rather than African interests. African universities need to ensure that in their training of social scientists African interests are paramount and protected. Furthermore, Institutes of African or Strategic Studies should increasingly engage themselves in research geared towards not only the interpretation of the political, economic and military strategies of Western powers, as some of them do, but also to the formulation of counter strategies advantageous to the African world.

African philosophers have doggedly followed the paths originally blazed by Western philosophers. This excessive fidelity to Western modes of approaching the philosophical enterprise cannot but lead to a betrayal. (Irung , 1988). There seems to be a continuing debate as to whether there is an identifiable distinctiveness in African thought to justify a culturally specific label. Is there such a thing as African philosophy? This question has been the central focus of discussion among African philosophers during the past two decades or so. (Van Hook, 1993). Yet, anyone even superficially acquainted with Western philosophy is familiar with talk about British or American, French or German, or more broadly, Anglo-American and

Continental philosophy. Similarly, reference to Asian philosophy has become increasingly common in the West. So what is the problem with "African philosophy"? It may be that its existence is doubted because of the assumption that philosophy needs to come in written form; but it is difficult to escape the conclusion that the debate concerning the existence and nature of African philosophy reflects a Western colonial bias that Africans are not rational, or not rational enough, to have produced a body of thought worthy of being labelled African philosophy. Herein lies a monumental challenge for African universities and African philosophers.

An African philosophy department which is concerned only with Western philosophy, cannot contribute effectively, or indeed appropriately, to the debate concerning the existence and nature of African philosophy. The orientation of the department and the choice of scholars are, therefore, important. Some African scholars have expressed concern that an African philosophy which develops idiosyncratically apart from established philosophical tradition will be marginalized, but the predominant concern should be about the relevance of traditional thought to African philosophy and the fear of Western dominance. (Van Hook, 1993).

The peoples of Africa are afflicted by the ravages of underdevelopment and outraged by the indignities of unmitigated dependence on others even in matters of inspiration or policy on development. It is important to emphasize the links between philosophy and social action. In the review of Western philosophy in his *Consciencism*, Kwame Nkrumah sought to illustrate the thesis that philosophy, however academic, is always trying, explicitly or implicitly, to say something about society. According to Bertrand Russell:

> a man's philosophy has practical importance, and a prevalent
> philosophy may have an intimate connection with the happiness
> or misery of large sections of mankind.

African universities can, therefore, not afford to ignore the importance of philosophy which some people used to refer to as one of the "useless disciplines". Without doubt, the realization of effective and responsible government, the achievement of accelerated economic development, and the accomplishment of social and cultural renaissance can all be jeopardised by the cobwebs of irrationality, judgements based on crooked thinking, half-truths and unproved assertions, and the absence of a progressive national ethos. (Goma, 1987b). The nations of Africa need to re-appraise old African philosophies to consolidate their identities. More than that, they need constantly to reflect and, on a continuing basis, provide a rational framework for the prevalent concepts of development and social change.

As one authority has commented: African herbal medicines dispensed for centuries by traditional doctors are being studied, codified, and gradually received into the pharmacopoeia of modern practitioners. If only because of its relative inexpensiveness and ready availability, it delivers health care to more people in Africa than Western medicine. African herbal and other treatment are believed, for example, to control diabetes and rheumatoid arthritis more effectively than their Western equivalents. Traditional methods of orthopaedic surgery are also recognized as often more effective more rapidly than the normal western practice. African traditional mental health practice employed "free association" before Freud did, and also group therapy, long before it became fashionable in Europe. And yet some modern African doctors, trained in African Medical Schools of African universities, have nothing but scorn for African traditional medicine.

The developing world is increasingly offering solutions to many global problems. The developing world, including the African continent, is now becoming recognized as a vast repository of genetic resources vital to global medical research. The Natural Products Branch of the US government's National Cancer Institute is actively searching the developing world for materials that could combat a host of human cancers; and it receives roots, leaves and other plant and animal specimens from the oceans and tropical forests of more than 25 countries in Africa, Asia and Latin America. (Cherie Hart, 1991). While work has been going on for years on the African pharmacopoeia, much more should have been accomplished by now. Traditional medicine is an area where Africa and its universities and research institutes could have taken the lead and could still do so.

## The Continuing Need for an African Intellectual Community

According to Edward Shils (1962), an intellectual community is not a community in the same way as a town or a tribe constitutes a community bound together through loyalties which arise from the sharing of a common territory or from an awareness of the ties of blood and a common past.

> The intellectual community draws its cohesion and its discipline from the attachments which grow from a common intellectual culture, from the acceptance of certain common problems, and from the devotion to a common set of standards of intellectual performance. It is created through sharing certain intellectual traditions which hand on the concepts and categories by which reality is approached through interchange of ideas and observations, through the study of a common body of literature.

Thus, for example, the community of physicists or mathematicians accepts new members when they have shown, by their achievement in their studies and their subsequent practice, that they accept the standard of scientific and rational judgement shared by the established members of the community. The intellectual community can be local, national, and international.

We are rather far from the idealistic world of 1961 and the euphoria of the Decade of Independence when Edward Shils spoke at a Seminar on Inter-University Cooperation at Fourah Bay College, Sierra Leone. No one then doubted the necessity for an intellectual community, and the published Proceedings of the Seminar were in fact entitled *The West African Intellectual Community*. It is necessary to recall that initially, the drive towards independence had its roots in an intellectual movement grounded in Pan-Africanism. All the initial leaders of the movement saw themselves as intellectuals - Azikiwe, Awolowo, Nkrumah, Kenyatta, Nyerere, Kaunda, Senghor, Edwardo Mondlane, Agostinho Neto, etc. They followed after Edward Blyden, James Johnson, Casely-Hayford. They asked for a university before they demanded independence because they saw the universities as the instruments for making independence real, adding to the "political kingdom" all the other things that the politicians promised the masses. The intellectual community was to be the guardian of quality in the universities and the reservoir of ideas for those in government.

Today, the need for an African intellectual community is not universally shared. There are those who regard it as a lingering hangover of colonial elitism which has no place in the drive towards greater democratization, perhaps even as an attempt to re-establish the Ivory Tower after the autocrats had bulldozed it to the ground. On the other hand, there are those who believe that the crisis in higher education has come about not merely because of underfunding and the control by politicians who have little understanding of what the universities are about, but also because many of those within the academy who should be defending it against the onslaught of its enemies are less than clear about the values necessary for the success of the academy.

The intellectual life and the culture of the academy are interchangeable expressions, but intellectuals are not a monopoly of the academy. There are many intellectuals - writers, philosophers, serious journalists and others - who are outside the academy, and there are many in the universities who do not share the ideals of the intellectual life. Intellectuals are defined, not by membership of the academy, but by attitudes of the mind. Davidson Nicol in 1966 defined the intellectual as "an educated person who has an awareness of world currents of opinion and moral thought and respects them; one who holds carefully thought-out beliefs with integrity; one who is engaged in work which calls for an exercise of reasoning power, taking as his springboard a heritage of learning and experience of different civilizations. He need not have attended a university, although in fact most intellectuals have received some formal education beyond adolescence." (Nicol, 1967). The emphasis on awareness of world currents of opinion was characteristic of the period. It will be more to the point if we combine his "moral thought" and "integrity" with Edward Shils' "intellectual culture, devotion to the culture of excellence, open mindedness, questioning the orthodox in the belief that there must be a better way which captures more of the elusive quality of truth".

The reinvigoration of our universities demands the cultivation of an intellectual community with a Code of Behaviour intended to foster the kind of atmosphere in which scholarly endeavour can flourish. Such a code will operate on the basis of individual commitment rather than community enforcement. It will guide the behaviour of the intellectual in government. At the national level, the intellectual community becomes an unorganized group committed to certain patters of public life, characterized by professional ethics, culture of excellence, integrity, concern for the people, accountability. At the continental level, they become heirs to the ideals of Pan-Africanism, and the desire to see an end to the long history of the African as the perpetual underdog, always an object for philanthropy than for appreciation or admiration.

## Leadership for the African University of the Future

The leadership of African universities has undergone tremendous change since the inception of these institutions in the colonial period. At the beginning the leadership was largely in expatriate hands, and it cannot be claimed that the criteria for their appointment were universal or always clear. It is understandable that, in the ferment of African nationalism, some of them were considered to be colonialist, even racist, in their actions and postures. It should also be said that some of them were men of great stature and who made significant contribution to the building and development of particular African universities, and the tradition of higher education in Africa as a whole.

The leadership of African universities at the level of Vice-Chancellor, Rector, or President has of course been largely indigenised. (Peil, 1986). But the turnover of Vice-Chancellors in some universities has been high. Political interference is the important factor contributing to frequent change. While this may be understandable in the rapidly changing circumstances in Africa, it hinders the long-term development of the university because a vital leader is not around long enough to see plans through (Peil, *op. cit.*). Leadership turnover has also been high at the faculty and departmental levels, with the consequence that teaching and research programmes have suffered, as newcomers institute reforms and then disappear just as the results are beginning to emerge. Frequent change of leadership obviously does not make for the strong leadership necessary to initiate and sustain the kind of reform that could reinvigorate the universities of Africa.

Some of the serious problems and upheavals experienced by a number of African universities have been blamed on weak, incompetent, and shortsighted leadership. Students and staff easily exploit such leadership to their own advantage, but with consequent weakening of the institution. Gross government interference, control and overbearing intrusion contribute to the weakening of the leadership of the university, however good and progressive that leadership may be, making its position untenable. The real victim in all this in the end is the nation, which is denied effective and positive contribution of the affected institutions to national development and progress. Africa's universities, as elsewhere, need to have strong, yet compassionate, leadership in order to cope with the multitude of problems and challenges they are likely to face.

Persons who are called upon to lead the African university of the future toward greater effectiveness in meeting its mission and role will, in the words of S. V. Martorana and Eileen Kuhns (1975), have to "cope with change that is ubiquitous, penetrating and inescapable". Change in existing universities is necessary not only to meet the needs of society but to ensure institutional survival as well. The demands and pressures on the African university of the future are bound to be complex and far-reaching, such as the need to undertake new types of training and research and public service which may far exceed the ambitions of the university. In other words, the leadership of the university will have to respond to and guide new academic developments, new types of students and staff, new technologies and changing demands from labour markets. In these circumstances, professional management expertise, as well as academic ability and innate leadership qualities will be in heavy demand. It calls for leadership of enterprise, courage and creativity. It is unfortunately true that the initiative for change seldom arises from democratic processes. In the words of Rice (1970).

> Innovation and change occur when creative men and women exercise leadership. Sometimes they are followed by the majority and change is easy; sometimes they are followed by a minority, or by none at all, and then change occurs only if they are prepared to fight for what they believe in and are able to win.

# APPENDIX I

## HANDBOOK ON
## ACADEMIC FREEDOM AND UNIVERSITY AUTONOMY

### Introduction

The African experience with higher education has demonstrated the need for proper and deeper understanding, especially by university communities themselves, of the essentials and limitations of the twin concepts of **Academic Freedom** and **University Autonomy**. Such understanding should be helpful in fighting against the dangers to and violations of these concepts, in the context of the realities of Africa.

Academic freedom and university autonomy are clearly not the same thing, even though they are often discussed as if they were both synonymous and inseparable. Academic freedom relates to academics, that is to individuals, whereas university autonomy relates to the university as an institution, a corporate body.

This Handbook provides a brief outline of the essentials and limitations of academic freedom and university autonomy for the benefit of the university community. A brief bibliography is provided in the Handbook for those who may wish to learn more about the subject.

### Academic Freedom

Academic freedom can be defined briefly as the freedom of members of the academic community, individually and/or collectively, in the pursuit, development, and transmission of knowledge. In the pursuit of knowledge, academics may not be hindered from following the approach which they think is most fruitful with regard to scientific or scholarly discovery. They must be free to communicate what they consider to be scientifically or intellectually valid insights. With regard to the teaching function, the university teacher should be free to teach according to his/her conscience and convictions. In short, academic freedom is the academic's *right to freedom of thought and expression*. The researcher has a right to choose his/her research topic and method, to search for the truth without restriction, and to publish the results independently of the will of all kinds of public authorities. The teacher has the right to plan and to organize teaching programmes within given frameworks, and to lecture on topics which he/she considers essential. Accordingly, the principal vehicles of academic freedom are research, teaching, study, discussion, documentation and dissemination through lecturing, writing, and production.

Academic freedom is typically an individual right to which an academic may appeal, even against the authorities of his/her own institution and against his/her colleagues. But academic freedom is *always linked to responsibility*. The individual researcher and teacher is responsible to the academic and scientific community which compares and evaluates methods and results, thus serving as a correcting factor within university life and work.

The question of who the beneficiaries of academic freedom are is a controversial one. There are two main viewpoints: the first is that academic freedom should be restricted to certain persons within the academic community, preferably researchers and teachers; and that other actors within this sector, students and administrators, should have more limited access to academic freedom. The second, and less common, view is that academic freedom belongs to the *entire* members of the academic community, covering *all* those persons teaching, doing research, studying and working at the university. The constitutions of many countries guarantee the freedom of thought and expression to all citizens, and this covers university students and administrators, no less than university teachers. But academic freedom should be more, and relates specifically to the needs of the teacher and researcher for additional guarantees because of their vocation, their commitment to pursue knowledge and the truth.

## University Autonomy

University autonomy can be defined as the freedom and independence of a university, as an institution, to make its own internal decisions, whatever its decision-making processes are, with regard to academic affairs, faculty and student affairs, business affairs, and external relations. Therefore, university autonomy can be taken to mean self-government by a university.

There is a wide measure of agreement about the ingredients which matter most. To be autonomous a university must be free to select its students and (whatever the formalities of appointment may be) its staff and to determine the conditions under which they remain in the university. An autonomous university must be free to set its own standards and to decide to whom to award its degrees, even if, as in many African countries and elsewhere in the world, universities voluntarily set limits to their own freedom by the appointment of external examiners. An autonomous university must be free to design its own curriculum, although it may in practice have to do so within certain constraints, such as the requirements of professional bodies which recognize the degree as a right to practise, and the financial sanctions which may be imposed from outside to prevent a university creating, for example, a medical school. In those countries where degrees, or the licence to practise a profession, are regulated by law, the university should participate effectively in the formulation of the relevant curricula and the setting of academic standards. An autonomous university should have the final decisions as to the research programmes carried on within its walls. Finally, an autonomous university, having received its income from the state or private sources, must be free to decide how to allocate it among the different categories of expenditure.

There is a further condition of autonomy without which these ingredients are ineffective. In a university where non-academics participate in its self-government, and where they are in fact in a majority on the governing Council, it is essential that the non-academics should identify themselves with the university, and not consider themselves only as representatives of interests external to the university. It is essential, too, that all academic decisions should be delegated to the academics themselves. Without this internal coherence and internal balance of power, a university may be free of intervention from outside, and yet have its autonomy betrayed from within.

University autonomy does not imply that the institution should be encapsulated in a kind of insularity. True autonomy supposes openness within the university as well as between it and society. Related to this is the point that, because the trend nowadays is towards regional, national, and international partnerships, isolation cannot anywhere be considered or entertained as a way of defending university autonomy.

While academic freedom is an individual right, autonomy is an institutional right which is shared between the institution as a whole and its constituent units. In other words, university autonomy should not be understood as autonomy simply for the institution itself, but also, within certain limits, shared by all the principal parts of the university - its faculties, institutes, departments, and even teaching and research groups.

**Relationship between Academic Freedom and University Autonomy**

There is constant confusion not only about what the expressions academic freedom and university autonomy really mean but also how they are related to each other. It is a commonplace of history that an autonomous university can deny academic freedom to some of its members (as Oxford did in the early nineteenth century), and a university which is not autonomous can safeguard academic freedom (as Prussian universities did in Humboldt's time). Thus, it is possible to have academic freedom without university autonomy, and *vice-versa*. Within some university systems, such as in Britain, the emphasis may be on university autonomy, while in others, as in continental Europe, the emphasis is on the academic freedom of individual teachers.

Nevertheless, academic freedom and university autonomy impinge on each other at many points and the two concepts tend to be mutually supporting. Both should be encouraged if each is to flourish. They both depend in the last resort on a public opinion which understands what universities are for and is prepared to respect them. But whereas academic freedom is an internationally recognized and unambiguous privilege of academics, the question as to what constitutes autonomy in universities is anything but unambiguous, and the patterns of autonomy which satisfy academics in different countries are very diverse.

It can, therefore, be said that the existence of institutional autonomy in no way guarantees academic freedom. It may be a necessary but not a sufficient condition. Academic freedom is needed at least as much to protect individual academics from other academics as from politicians, the clergy, the press, and members of the public. Academic institutions, whether autonomous or not, are quite capable of being oppressive with regard to their individual staff members. If institutions are truly autonomous, it may be much more difficult for a threatened individual to gain effective redress or appeal against the judgements of such institutions.

### Limitations of Academic Freedom and University Autonomy

Any freedom has its limitations and the beneficiaries have special responsibilities. Academic freedom and university autonomy are, therefore, not feasible without some limitations. Pragmatism dictates certain limitations which academics and their universities must accept and put up with in practice.

Universities everywhere have created mechanisms for determining and/or regulating curricula and teaching programmes (e.g., faculty boards, departmental committees, heads of departments, etc.) as well as research policies and priorities (e.g., research committees and units), in the light of national needs and financial realities. In many universities, it is not unusual that the assignment of teaching duties is in the hands of a faculty board or that of a departmental committee or head. At the research level, the university, a research council or an industry may offer an academic a grant to do research in a specific field. Thus, it cannot be argued that the principle of academic freedom requires that an academic should be completely free as to his/

her choice of subjects to teach and research to undertake, irrespective of considerations deriving from these mechanisms and circumstances.

Academic freedom has other valid limitations. As a principle, it is neither a licence for incompetence nor protection from quality control. However, there must be guarantees that competence will be judged by competent people and that the resulting judgement will be immune from special interests and ideologies. Another limitation is to be found in ethical considerations. Not every approach to scientific or scholarly work is ethically acceptable: some experiments with human beings, for instance, may be forbidden. In applied science, the purposes of specific scientific interventions may be ethically unacceptable. In such cases, the limitations will be specified in legislation to which academics, like all other citizens, must conform.

Academic freedom cannot of course exceed the liberties allowed by the law of the land. So a country which does not permit freedom of speech and publication to its ordinary citizens cannot grant academic freedom to its universities. In such countries academic freedom is in eclipse and accordingly universities cannot flourish.

If academic freedom becomes a part of the culture of a society, the focus will not be on its limitations but on the underlying principle. A university must have a liberal, tolerant climate in which people feel free to express their opinions, argue and disagree, when necessary, without fear of victimization. In many societies, academic freedom has this broader meaning, covering not just the teachers and researchers but the whole university community, thus making the university a centre of critical, innovative thinking, not only in specific fields and disciplines, but in social, cultural, and political areas as well.

Taken simply, autonomy means the power to govern without outside controls. The truth, though it is often blurred by rhetoric, is that in the context of modern society, no university makes or can make a claim to complete autonomy. It derives its legal existence from an act of some external authority, usually the State: and its instrument of incorporation prescribes in some detail what it may do and what it may not do — for example, in relation to its property or in dealing with other institutions, or even with its own members. These requirements, however, merely define the framework within which its more intimate and formative decisions need to be taken. Even in relation to these decisions, it is not to be expected that the university can be free from external scrutiny and judgement. It might be so only if the university possessed resources, wholly within its own control, and sufficient for the maintenance of all its undertakings.

The fact is that no country in the world has a government which does not retain some control over its universities. In continental Europe, in particular, the various governments are responsible for the total national effort in higher education, including determining the ways in which universities are expected to serve society. With the possible exception of private ones, universities are public services. In the continent of Europe again, most of the universities are branches of the civil service, though their autonomy may be protected (as in Germany) by the provisions written in the constitutions of the states. The question, therefore, is not whether governments should have some control over universities, but rather, how much control and in what manner it should be exercised.

Autonomy is one side of the coin; accountability is the other. While autonomy, as stated above, means the power to govern without outside controls, accountability means the requirement to demonstrate responsible action. It has been argued, in theory, that a university may be both autonomous and accountable. In practice, one senses that, usually, the more accountability is required, the less autonomy exists. The ideal to aim at seems clearly to be a balance of both conditions. Too much autonomy might lead to unresponsiveness to society, on the part of universities, while too much demand for accountability might destroy the necessary academic and institutional ethos. Nevertheless, it is inconceivable that any university today will refuse to account to the government for the use of public funds made available to it, present an accurate budget, and integrate its plans with the broad university development scheme outlined by the country concerned. Such a university would be challenging its solidarity with society and with the government as representative of the state. To continue to set aside for it a share of the public funds would then seem hardly justified.

Limitations of academic freedom and university autonomy occur throughout the world, even in the industrialized countries. There can, therefore, be no doubt that while autonomy is a privileged status which society offers to universities, its practical enforcement may be limited by various factors, which have to be closely defined and analysed in each country. The same is true of academic freedom.

## Infringement of Academic Freedom and University Autonomy

If it is accepted that academic freedom and university autonomy are necessary, we must try to preserve them. Doing so will depend on waking up to the dangers that face them. The main dangers to academic freedom and university autonomy emanate from governments and are to a large extent a factor of the extent to which a democratic system exists and operates in a country. Historical experience demonstrates that the more undemocratic a system of government, the higher the degree of intolerance of other points of view, and the more likely is the suppression of academic freedom and infringement of university autonomy. It is, however, important to note that interference is not limited to governments; it may emanate from other bodies, public, private, social or religious. Society as a whole may threaten academia by putting demands on it that it cannot legitimately meet.

At the same time, not all of the dangers come from outside. For example, university autonomy may be jeopardized from within when organized political activity on the part of the student body, or by some members of the staff, antagonizes the government and encourages it to impose restrictions on the university. Danger may also come through betrayal from within when members of Council, or other authorities of the university, among other things, usurp functions delegated by legislation or by convention to the academic body.

Also from within the university arises the danger that particular faculties, departments or institutes - especially in the field of research - may initiate discussions and reach decisions in consultation with governments or other outside bodies before the university as a corporation has had the opportunity to express an opinion or to relate these discussions to its general policy.

More insidious, perhaps, but equally dangerous to the concept of university autonomy is the tendency of some universities to look inward rather than to be continuously conscious of the needs of the community. To fulfil their functions in the service of the community, universities need the freedom to choose their own mode of establishing, on a continuous basis, a critical awareness of the real needs of the communities they serve - which may not always be those that the community urges upon them so clamorously at a given moment of time.

It is also worth noting that excessive claims by the student body and/or by members of staff may jeopardize the autonomy of the university itself, even when they do not provoke undesirable reactions from the government and the community.

Experience has shown that whereas there are continuous threats to academic freedom, what have afflicted many African universities more are the outrageous and blatant violations of their autonomy. The overall situation seems to be that there has recently been a noticeable decline of academic freedom in the sense of direct threats, personal harassment, and physical attacks on academics in some African countries, and a serious escalation of more frequent and more brutal violations of university autonomy.

There are several lessons. One is that even though the autonomy of the university is on paper well established, this is no guarantee of self-government. The most enlightened university constitution is quite useless as a defence of autonomy when it can be altered by the stroke of the pen, as has happened under dictatorial regimes. In many cases, the lay members of the university council, not regarding themselves as part and parcel of a self-governing community, allow their commitment to other causes override their loyalty to the university; and fail to shelter the university from political pressures.

## Safeguards of Academic Freedom and University Autonomy

The only true safeguards of academic freedom and university autonomy are two:

(i) a coherent body of opinion among the academic community, appreciating the value of academic freedom and university autonomy to the point of being prepared to be united in its defence; and

(ii) a sufficient degree of enlightenment among the public to respect and support this opinion and put pressure on the government to accept it.

Academic freedom rests ultimately on opinion, and on that particular opinion called respect or esteem. There may be many institutional safeguards, but none is significant if there is not a substantial body of opinion which tolerates or supports academic freedom and university autonomy because it respects intellectual work and those who do it. Therefore, disregarding the bellicose pleasure in combat which plays some part, but a small one, the true sustenance of the defence of academic freedom is a conviction of the inherent dignity of intellectual effort and of the intrinsic value of the truth arrived at by science and scholarship.

One of the major factors which affects the position of academic freedom and the status of the academic profession in society is the indifference of the academic profession itself to its corporate freedom. Only if their own freedom or that of their immediate colleagues is infringed, would most scientists or scholars bestir themselves, or even pay attention to issues of academic freedom and university autonomy, and then they would do so in a narrow perspective. The sensitivity of the academic profession to the problems of academic freedom and university autonomy in most countries, even the freest, is not very great. But the price of academic freedom and university autonomy - like that of liberty - is eternal vigilance both as to the pressures from without and to indifference within.

The academic profession, like the legal and medical professions, must have some degree of autonomy guaranteed by the state in order to fulfil its purposes in the state. However, African universities would be unwise to ask for a blank cheque of academic freedom and institutional autonomy any more than the state legal or medical services do. The fewer principles they insist upon, the more united they are likely to be in defending them, and the more uncompromising they can afford to be about them. No occasion should be lost in explaining them to the public, not querulously - as tends to happen in a crisis - but coolly and patiently. Extremes of freedom and autonomy at any level of application may result in inefficient management and teaching and even anarchy - conditions which are the contrary of what are required for well functioning universities.

The best defense of freedom and autonomy in the area of research is for the universities themselves to develop strong research work and policies. Equally important is the thesis that, if universities as corporate bodies are to be allowed to run their own affairs, they must run them well: and, as internal bickering cannot be kept quiet, they must also attempt to consume their own smoke at their campuses.

Although universities insist on the greatest possible freedom from outside interference with their teaching, research, and educational policies, they must refrain, in order to merit such protection, from taking official stands or exerting collective pressure on behalf of their own political objectives. However, if they abandon official neutrality and begin to press for specific social and ideological goals, the custodians of power over the universities may not exercise such restraint let alone continue to provide financial support. Accordingly, the universities must stay clear of political partisanship, and leave such matters to the proper forums (in which, of course, their members may be as vocal as they wish). As long as the state concedes the ordinary liberties of democratic organization, the universities must, therefore, refrain from corporate political action in non-educational matters.

### The case for Academic Freedom and University Autonomy

The universities' claims to academic freedom and university autonomy, for their scholars and themselves, respectively, cannot be defended simply as traditions, for being such does not make them sacred. If traditions cease to be consistent with the needs of the times, there is no merit in retaining them for their own sake. Society, which to a large extent has created the universities and which supports them, must in turn be served adequately by them. Therefore, it is only if academic freedom and university autonomy are consistent with the premise that society is better served because of them that they deserve to be preserved.

Academic freedom is part of the general freedom of liberal democratic societies; but it is also something special. A case has to be made for it even in the most enlightened countries. There is nothing self-evident about the right to teach whom, what, when and how one wants. The proof that academic freedom is a desirable end is empirical. The best universities - those that pursue and spread their learning most effectively - seem to be those that govern themselves. It is true that such freedom can be justified on other grounds. A democratic society must try to limit governmental regulation and control; the more its institutions are free and independent, the more effective is democracy itself, and the more true freedom remains to its citizens. A state that tries to cherish such free institutions will usually put the universities high on the list: for universities are, or ought to be, not only a main home of knowledge and wisdom, but also the intellectual conscience of the nation. Nevertheless the practical case for academic freedom and university autonomy is that free universities are better than servile universities, and hence they serve the public interest.

Universities have always considered the twin principles of academic freedom and university autonomy to be indispensable values and have defended them as such. But the case for these principles in the context of the African continent needs to be continuously properly and widely understood and accepted.

The basic case for them is that academic freedom and university autonomy are universally necessary preconditions for universities to be able to fulfil their proper functions. Indeed, if a society accepts/holds the view that academic freedom contributes to the quality and proper functioning of universities, then it must permit them a certain degree of autonomy to protect them from undue pressures from the outside. Like a hospital, a university is a professional organization. Characteristic of such an organization is the fact that its principal functions, in this case teaching and research, are the tasks of highly trained professionals who are the best experts to decide what ought to be taught, what research is most promising, and how both should be undertaken. Thus, the principal influence on these primary functions comes from the professionals, whatever the formal decision-making structure may be. If a society wants teaching and research functions to be undertaken properly, then it acts wisely in leaving the decisions regarding these activities to the university professionals themselves.

As already indicated above, academic freedom applies to both research and teaching. Freedom in research is fundamental to the advancement of truth. Academic freedom in its teaching aspect is fundamental for the protection of the rights of the teacher in teaching and of the student to freedom in learning.

In its provision of highly trained and highly skilled manpower, the university must provide graduates who are creative, who are capable of generating ideas. This task can only be achieved in an environment which allows free, independent, objective and scientific inquiry, free from unnecessary outside interference. Without the products of free thinking and creative minds, the seeds of creativity cannot germinate. Therefore, academic freedom is not a right which is granted to the teacher solely for his/her own benefit but also that of the taught; because without it the student is deprived of sound education. Such education involves not only learning truth, without let or hindrance, but learning the very process of examining issues and arriving at the truth. Sound education thus requires both demonstration of these skills by the teacher, and practice in the process of truth-finding and judgement-making by the student.

Academic freedom finds its principal justification in its functional significance with regard to the advancement of knowledge which demands that the processes of objective truth seeking should not be corrupted by ideologies and interests. For such advancement cannot be fostered by hampering creative minds in their attempts to follow the path of discovery which they consider most promising. Scholarship cannot flourish in an atmosphere of suspicion and distrust. Teachers must always remain free to enquire, to study and to evaluate, to gain new maturity and understanding. To forbid the student to learn where and what he will, or the teacher to teach whom and how he will, is to put a curb on the hazardous adventure of thinking, and a nation where thinking is rationed simply cannot survive in today's world.

In a democracy academic freedom not only serves the needs of society but is essential to it. In other words, academic freedom is a necessity for the survival of a free society; for as yet man/woman has found no other way of establishing truth than by permitting ideas to compete with one another in the conviction that through such competition better ideas will ultimately drive out those of less worth. Freedom of thought and freedom of expression, freedom to teach, to study, and to learn as one's conscience dictates, were never more important than today, when we live in a rather conformity-oriented world. In a democratic society, moreover, the terms 'freedom of thought' and 'freedom of expression' have become synonymous with the idea of university education. Education, in any real sense, could only be a sham if it were otherwise. Knowledge and the truth which emerges from it are the primary concerns of institutions of higher learning. Their work can only be done properly in an atmosphere conducive to the full and free scope of thought and action. Nor is it in the exclusive interests of the academic community that such freedom be allowed: society will be the beneficiary of the progress which academic freedom promotes. Society as a whole, therefore, must assume the responsibility for maintaining a constant vigil to see that such freedom is preserved.

Whatever their varied patterns of earlier history, the universities' claim to autonomy and that of the scholar to academic freedom should not be regarded as an assertion of an inherent right to any peculiar status or privilege. The claim is not for exemption from social responsibility or from public accountability or from the duty to explain their policies and to have due regard to informed public judgement. It is simply that they are likely to fulfil their proper functions and high service most adequately when the directives and judgements issuing from external authority are offered but not imposed, so that universities and their scholars have a large measure of freedom in the choice of their objectives, and of the means taken thereto. In other words, academic freedom and university autonomy, as already stated above, are rather simply the essential conditions by which the universities and scholars may properly perform their specific and important functions in society. But this must be earned by performance. A university that is preoccupied with its right to be free and unconcerned with anything else deserves to lose its freedom. The same may be said of academics.

Where the university has failed to make any significant achievements in science or scholarship and/or in its contribution to the welfare of the society in which it exists, it becomes extremely difficult for the institution to justify self-esteem and public appreciation. As a consequence, the case for academic freedom and university autonomy in these circumstances is gravely weakened.

While it is recognized that the principles of academic freedom and university autonomy, like other rights in society, are not absolute, the justification for their curtailment is not easy to make. However, it is important to be concerned by those actions which have a negative impact on the cause of these principles. For example, although academic freedom and university autonomy are considered essential to the advancement, transmission, and application of knowledge, these concepts are often used to defend privileges which are not beneficial to the well-functioning of universities, either with regard to teaching or to research. In a number of their actions against their own governments and/or university authorities, students and members of staff in many African universities claim that they are doing so in defence of academic freedom and university autonomy. But strictly speaking, the issues at the centre of the controversy or conflict have no relevance to the two concepts. University autonomy can indeed also be the cover for corporatist attitudes and for various abuses of privilege. These postures and circumstances weaken the case for academic freedom and university autonomy.

The African university remains without any doubt an institution central to the production and reproduction of ideas, knowledge, and action necessary for the social transformation of the African continent; for liberation from ignorance, disease, and poverty; for scientific, technological, and economic progress; and for the expansion and deepening of the spiritual and cultural contents of the lives of the African peoples.

But a terrorized, cowed and silenced academia is not one that can fulfil such a historic and strategic role. A terrorized, intimidated and timid academia cannot provide part of the necessary intellectual and moral leadership that Africa needs today as it prepares to enter the 21st century: an era in which collective survival and viability will be dependent on contributions and activities of what has been called the "knowledge industry".

A nation which deprives its universities of their privileges soon shows symptoms of a slow intellectual and cultural decay; and a university which is content to let its privileges slip away betrays not only itself but its country as well. Academic freedom and university autonomy are, therefore, principles which African universities should jealously guard and vigorously defend, principles which African governments and communities should, in their own interests, respect, for they go to the very root of the university enterprise. But the defence and promotion of these principles are not a one-off activity; they are a continuous, never-ending process. These are principles which all true universities must cherish and fight for.

## The Call and the Challenge

The call for proper, deeper, and a more widely spread understanding of the twin concepts of academic freedom and university autonomy is made so as to help to eliminate their abuse, misinterpretations and distortions in the fight of other causes; and thereby strengthen their defence and real value to the university enterprise in Africa. But it is useless to invoke these concepts only when universities and their academics are under attack, if nothing or little will have been done to educate and enlighten the public and the 'enemies', actual and potential, of freedom and autonomy before this happens. Perhaps such attacks, infringements, or hostile postures might have been avoided had pre-emptive steps been taken to bring enlightenment to society and the university community itself on the essentials and limitations of academic freedom and university autonomy.

It is useless to imagine that universities can be forever free from national pressures, political and social. It is also useless, indeed dangerous, to imagine that university autonomy is something capable of definition in eternally comprehensive terms. It is further useless to imagine that the elements of reciprocal influence and authority between university systems and others can ever be regarded as fixed. However, the University and its members should use their understanding of academic freedom and university autonomy to educate the general public and the influential in society, and to defend these concepts when they come under attack whether from the outside or when betrayed from inside. It is the duty of those in the University to do more than warn: it is for them to inspire. Herein lies the challenge.

This Handbook is intended to assist all concerned persons, individually or collectively, to take up the task and challenge of carrying high the torch of academic freedom and university autonomy on the African continent.

## Selected Bibliography

Alexander, J. (1986). "The University and Morality: a Revised Approach to University Autonomy and its Limits" in *The Journal of Higher Education, pp. 463-477.*

Ashby, Eric, [in association with Anderson, Mary] (1966). *Universities: British, Indian, African.* Weidenfeld and Nicolson.

Birley, Sir Robert (1972). *The Real Meaning of Academic Freedom.* World University Service.

Diouf, Mamadou and Mamdani, Mahmoud (eds) (1994): *Academic Freedom in Africa* (CODESRIA Book Series, Dakar)

Federici, Silvia (1993). "Academic Freedom in Africa". *Quest: Philosophical Discussions,* Vol. VII (2).

Hanson, J.W. (1964). "Academic Freedom and Responsibility" - in *Nigerian Education,* edited by Okechukwu Ikejiani (1964). Longmans.

Hare, Kenneth (1968). *On University Freedom in the Canadian context.* University of Toronto Press.

International Association of Universities (1965). *University Autonomy: Its Meaning Today.* Papers-7, IAU, Paris.

Millett, John D. (1984. *Conflict in Higher Education: State Government Coordination Versus Institutional Independence.* Jossey-Bass Publishers.

Odumosu, Peter T. (1973). *Government and University in a Developing Society.* University of Ife.

Shils, Edward (1958). "Self-esteem and the status of the academic intellectual". *Science and Freedom,* No. 11, June, 1958.

UNESCO-CEPES (1993). *Academic Freedom and University Autonomy.* UNESCO-CEPES, Bucharest.

York University (1966). *Governments and the University: The Frank Gerstein Lectures.* The Macmillan Company of Canada Ltd.

# APPENDIX II

## CODE OF CONDUCT FOR ACADEMICS

The integrity and reputation of a university are not achieved automatically. One cannot simply wish them and have them; or proclaim them and make them come true. They are not given, but must be fought for and won. And once earned, they have to be sustained. Among the major factors which are extremely crucial to the standing of a university, both in the achievement of the institution's integrity and reputation and in sustaining them, is the integrity of its academics. The image of the academic profession and that of the university may be protected and strengthened or damaged by the conduct and performance of the academics, individually and/or collectively. It is, therefore, essential that the academic should ensure that his/her conduct, activities and performance at all times are such as will not injure the esteem in which he/she is held by colleagues, students and society at large.

The academic profession in Africa, as perhaps elsewhere, has done very little in a systematic way to promulgate a set of guiding principles which should regulate its custodianship of knowledge in teaching and research, its role in the internal conduct of universities, and its participation in the public sphere. Thus, universities generally operate without a written code of conduct, analogous to the codes in other professions - for example, as the doctor has to his/her patient, the lawyer to his/her client, the banker to his/her customer. It is often argued that the discipline of scholarship carries its own ethical values, such as reverence for truth, with the recognition, which generates humility, that all truth may be contaminated by error. Arrogance, insincerity, prejudice, intolerance, and failure to ascertain the facts are incompatible with the academic ethic. It is, thus, taken for granted that any member of the academic profession should in the very process of learning, come to know the obligations that constitute a code of behaviour which should regulate the diverse activities of the academic. Because of this reliance on moral authority, many universities avoid dogmatic written codes and prefer merely to lay down guidelines specifying the pragmatic conditions under which scholarship can best be pursued. However, when academics are only guided by an unwritten code of behaviour, there is a danger that some of them may be unaware of the full implications of some of their actions, and go astray as, indeed, many have gone astray.

There is, therefore, a case for an unambiguous written code of behaviour for academics which should formally be drawn to their attention by their universities. Such a code, or set of guiding principles, should be broad enough to cover the main fields of activities in which academics participate, - their scientific and scholarly research and teaching, and general conduct within academic institutions; their publicist and political activities, and their performance of advisory and consultancy services for government, private businesses and civic associations outside of their campuses.

It is imperative that any such code of behaviour for academics must respect the academic freedom of the university teacher. Its aim should be to arouse reflection and fortify the values inherent in the learning process which are already at work in most academics. Thus, the code should try to encourage academics in most things, and to caution them in others. After all, it is on the natural instincts, reflectiveness, reasonableness, and moral self-consciousness of the academics that the well-being of universities ultimately depends. A possible code of behaviour as outlined below cannot cover every kind of situation in which the moral attitudes of academics in their diverse activities can make a difference for good or ill. Therefore, no attempt will be made here to be exhaustive, but to cover the essential elements and meet the general needs of the university.

## Code of Conduct

**Research** is one of the principal missions of the university. But it is recognised that the motive to do research is not always an irrepressible desire to discover new facts or ideas; nor the need to improve the quality of one's teaching. Sometimes, the motive is rather the need to publish papers in order to secure recognition, promotion and academic advancement. The urge to publish has grown with the increased prestige of research in the academic world, and with the attention given to lists of publications as a criterion in the appointment and promotion of academic staff. However, the integrity of the scholar is compromised, indeed impaired, by questionable authenticity, plagiarism, or other forms of dishonesty in his/her publications, or any false claims or declaration of scholarship made to support the case for appointment, promotion, or other academic advancement. Therefore, academics engaged in research must publish only such results of their investigations as are of unquestionable authenticity. They should note, in particular, that:

(i) Publications of scientific and scholarly works must be accompanied by truthful attribution of their authorship.

(ii)  Since careers in the academic profession are oriented towards the recog-gnition and reward of individual achievement, plagiarism, or in any way claiming credit for the work of others, infringes the obligation to acknowledge the achievements of colleagues.

(iii)  The presentation of reports of observations made by others,- regardless of whether or not they have been published, - as if they were observations made by oneself, is an infringement of this obligation.

(iv)  Claiming the exclusive authorship of a work done in collaboration, or claiming primary authorship of a work to which one's contribution was marginal, is a grave impropriety.

Therefore, while the urge to publish in order to contribute to the growth of knowledge, to gain respect for one's achievements, and to advance in one's career is expected of academics, they must avoid the pitfalls of unethical conduct in pursuing these laudable objectives. The best scholarship is honourable, passionate, and without pretence.

**Academic fraud** - the falsification, fabrication, or wilful adulteration of the product of scholarly research, or gross negligence in data collection or analysis - is not a new problem, and the world's institutions of scholarship have for centuries fought to purge their communities of fraud and plagiarism. The academic person works within an environment of competition that has been fostered to encourage single-mindedness in the pursuit of truth through scientific and scholarly research. The system, thus, exerts considerable pressure on all academics, be they young investigators or established figures in the field. If the pressure proves too great, it can lead to undue haste, rashness, lack of rigor and, occasionally, even to academic fraud.

Academic fraud is thus more than an error. It is hardly possible to exaggerate the damage that can result from such a breach of the academic commitment to truth. Academic fraud, if discovered, as it often is, shatters individual careers, bismirches the entire cause of objectivity in research, undermines the credibility of scholarship, and rends the fragile tissues of confidence between scholar and scholar, teacher and student, the university and the public. In collaborative research, the iniquity of academic fraud is compounded. The perpetrator beclouds not only his/her own academic future, but inevitably that of his/her research colleague(s), thus depriving them of the benefit of their own work, and staining their reputation in the view of outsiders who are unable to distinguish between those collaborators who are guilty and those who are in fact victims.

The seriousness of the offence of academic fraud in a collaborative work is not viewed any differently from the seriousness of the offence in an individual work. Indeed, joint authorship requires a heightened awareness of responsibility. When research is published under multiple authorship, each author sharing credit for the entire work must also share any discredit attached to it.

Any form of intellectual dishonesty or academic fraud must be condemned in the strongest possible terms. In principle, any faculty member who personally engages in academic fraud, whether or not in collaborative research, or who accedes to the publication of work, any part of which he or she knows to have been falsified or adulterated, should, in the absence of extenuating circumstances, be dismissed from the university.

**Teaching** is another of the major missions of the university. It can be said that it is not only the character of the instruction but also the character of the instructor that counts; and if the student has reason to believe that the instructor is not true to himself/herself, the virtue of the instruction as an educative force is incalculably diminished.

All men and women are fallible and the history of higher education necessarily includes examples of the unintentional teaching of misinformation - as proved by subsequent generations of scholars - but any teacher who fails to make adequate effort to keep abreast of his/her field fails to meet the only grounds for claiming the right to academic freedom - the grounds of being committed to seek for and present the truth to the best of one's ability. It is conceded that the facilities to enable one to keep abreast may sometimes be scarce to the point of frustrating the effort, in which case the effort made can still be evaluated. Academic freedom demands even more than keeping abreast so as to avoid misleading one's students: it requires also that the teacher present the material with a disciplined analysis of the issues and problems involved. The classroom is no place for unprincipled demagogy or unreflective thought. The academic freedom of the professor in the classroom is limited by the requirement that he/she present the truth as it is known on the basis of sound study, and to engage in a disciplined and rigorous exploration of the relevant issues.

The university teacher is regarded as an authority in his/her field. The acceptance of this authority is essential to effective communication between teacher and student. It is important, therefore, that the teacher should not abuse that authority by presenting controversial views - for example, concerning the nature of society - dressed up with greater veracity than the best scientific and scholarly evidence can justify. It is not that the teacher must necessarily suppress his/her own political or moral beliefs in the classroom, but he/she must avoid presenting them as scientific fact or settled knowledge.

Students must not only be taught, they must also be assessed scrupulously and fairly by their examiners. Assessment is important because it affects the students' chances in their subsequent studies and in admission to their professional careers. Assessment also affects the students' attitude towards their studies and towards themselves. Just assessment is as necessary for society as it is for the individual student. Unfair or arbitrary assessment may result from carelessness of the examiner. It may also be the product of bias due to interpersonal relations or political differences.

It is certainly desirable that teachers should be friendly with their students and it is also inevitable that they will be more friendly with some than with others. However, the teacher must guard against the intrusion of bias or favouritism into teaching or the evaluation of the work of students.

It is important too that teachers should not take advantage of their status and their power over their students. There have been numerous allegations of disgraceful subjectivity in the evaluation, grading, and examination of students dictated by immoral, especially sexual, relationships in universities between teacher and student. The marks awarded to particular students may depend on the demand for, offer, acceptance, or rejection of sexual favours. The occurrence of sexual relationships between teacher and student must be scrupulously avoided. This is not only because it can result in discriminatory assessment of the student's academic achievement. Such activities damage not only the integrity and the moral and intellectual authority of the academic concerned, and of the academic profession, but also the credibility and integrity of the university. The university teacher stands in *loco parentis* to the student, and must avoid at all times conduct incompatible with that position.

It is the duty of each member of the academic staff to carry out such teaching, examining, research, and administrative duties as are required by either the Dean of the Faculty or the Head of the Academic Department or the Director of the Institute, as the case may be. Every academic should perform his/her duties conscientiously, attending meetings and participating on committees to which he/she is assigned.

**Outside commitments** relate to the involvement of the academic in commercial, political or civic organisations, whether for renumeration or not, which are capable of diverting the attention of the academic person from total commitment to his/her duties. It is therefore necessary to stress that all members of staff of the university are deemed to be employed on a full-time basis except as otherwise specifically provided by the statutes or by the terms of a particular appointment. Outside commitments are, therefore,subject to university regulations.

**Political activities**: The university recognizes and accepts the right of academics to take an interest and participate in the political life of their country. However, this must not be to the detriment of their official duties. Normally, this should preclude office in the executive of a political party, or membership of parliament and other full-time positions. Members of staff who wish to participate in party political activities should seek leave of absence from the university.

No staff members should in any way intimidate other members of the university community as a result of the differing political affiliations. No staff member should in any way involve the university, as a corporate body or an institution, in partisan political activities. It is most improper for an academic to exploit party political affiliations to seek to advance a case for his/her appointment, promotion, or other preferment in the university.

Many academics seek publicity for themselves and for their work. In some cases, individuals who are in dispute with their colleagues or institutions break the confidentiality of the proceedings of governing and appointive bodies of the university by "leaking" to the press. The press is, thus, drawn into academic disagreements and aggravates them. This can and does cause considerable damage to the image of the individuals concerned and of their institution and should, therefore, be avoided.

An equally worrying issue is that of academic staff trade unionism. Difficult as this might be, it is expected that academics will give priority to their academic obligations - teaching, examining, and research - when faced with disruptive trade union activism.

**Consultancies**: The growing interest in university-productive sector linkages, and similar professional consultancies in which academics may be involved with government and other public or private bodies, impose certain obligations.

(i) The proportion of his/her time which a university teacher devotes to consultancy for private business firms or to the conduct of a private business firm or private professional practices of his own must be limited. A reasonable rule would stipulate that not more than one day each week be used for external activities regardless of whether or not they are for political, commercial or social causes, and whether for renumeration or not.

(ii) As a general rule, outside activities to be favoured should have some feedback to the research interests of the academic concerned and to the students who are dependent on him/her. Private practice must not mean taking up time owed to the students.

(iii) It is improper to use university resources - medical, engineering, computer, etc. - for private gain without returning to the university the commercial value of the use of such facilities.

(iv) Academics who accept elective or appointive office in government, should be required to take leave-of-absence for the  specified duration of the appointment.

**Loyalty and Pride**: The obligations that an academic owes to the university in which he/she holds an appointment go beyond a composite of obligations due to students and colleagues. There is an obligation also to be loyal to and sustain the particular university as a centre of learning and valuable national resource.  Pride in an institution is not just the gratification drawn from its fame, and the esteem in which its accomplishments are held in the society. Individual academics are proud of their university when they see it as embodying the virtues espoused in their code of behaviour or the  academic ethic.  As one distinguished scholar has said:

> A university does not have to be the greatest university in the world in order for its members to be proud of it.  Pride is, of course, sustained by achievement but not all achievement consists in the publication of ground-breaking scientific and scholarly papers and monographs or educating students who become Nobel Prize-laureates or professors in leading universities.  Pride in a university is a function of affectionate attachment to it and of its respect for the obligations of the academic ethic.

### Selected Bibliography

Ashby, Sir Eric (1969). *The Academic Profession.* The Fourth Annual Lecture under the 'Thank-Offering to Britain Fund'. The British Academy, Oxford University Press.

Hanson, J.W. (1964). "Academic Freedom and Responsibility" - in *Nigerian Education* edited by Okechukwu Ikejiani (1964). Longmans.

Shils, Edward (1982). 'The Obligations of University Teachers: The Academic Ethic'. *Minerva*, Vol. XX Nos. 1-2.

## SELECTED BIBLIOGRAPHY AND REFERENCES

AAU (1991): *Study on Cost Effectiveness and Efficiency in African Universities*. AAU, Accra.

Addis Ababa University (1980): *Three Decades of University Education 1950-1980 on the occasion of the 30th Anniversary* (Artistic Printing Press, Addis. Ababa)

Agbodeka, Francis (1977): Achimota in the National Setting: *A Unique Educational Experiment in West Africa* (Accra, Afram Publications).

Ajayi, J.F. Ade. (1963): "The Development of Secondary Grammar School Education in Nigeria" in *Journal of the Historical Society of Nigeria* vol.2, no.4.

Ajayi, J.F.A. (1973): "Towards an African Academic Community". in Yesufu (1973).

Ajayi, J.F. Ade (1979): "The Role of the University in Shaping Policy for Development" - in *Papers* No.16, International Association of Universities, Paris.

Ajayi, J.F. Ade. (1988): *The American Factor in the Development of Higher Education in Africa* (African Studies Centre, UCLA, James Smoot Coleman Memorial Papers Series No.1).

Ajayi, J.F.Ade. (1994): The Cultural Factor in Technological Development. Convocation Lecture, Federal University of Technology, Akure)

Alliot, Michel. (1961): *Enseignement supérieur de Madagascar*, 1959-1961. Université d'Antananarive.

Ambrose, D.P. & Setsabi, A.M., (1993): Historical Sketch of National University of Lesotho, unpublished Paper prepared for Association of African Universities (AAU).

Anderson, C. Arnold (1969): "University Planning in an Underdeveloped Country: A Commentary on the University of East Africa Plan, 1967-70". Minerva, Vol. VII (1-2).

Andren, C.-G. and Johansson-Dahre, U. (1993): "Academic Freedom and University Autonomy". - in *Academic Freedom and University Autonomy, Papers on Higher Education*. CEPES, UNESCO.

Ashby, Eric et als (1960): Investment in Education: the Report of the Commission on Post-School Certificate and Higher Education (Govt. Printer, Lagos).

Ashby, Eric (1966): *Universities: British, Indian, African*: A Study in the Ecology of Higher Education. Weidenfeld and Nicolson, London.

Ashby, Eric (1974): Adapting Universities to a Technological Society (San Francisco, Jossey-Bass Publishers).

Assie-Lumumba, N'Dri T. (1993): "Higher Education in Francophone Africa: Assessment of the potential of the traditional universities and alternatives for development". AFTHR Technical Note No. 5, The World Bank.

Association of African Universities (1988): Directory of African Universities (5th Edition. Accra).

Austin, Denis (1980): "Universities and the Academic Gold Standard in Nigeria". Minerva, Vol. XVIII (2).

Ayandele, E.A. (1970): *Holy Johnson, Pioneer of African Nationalism*, 1836-1917 (New York, Humanities Press).

Balsvik, Randi R. (1985): *Haile Sellassie's Students: The Intellectual and Social Background to Revolution, 1952-1977* (African Studies Center, MSU, East Lansing, and Norwegian Council of Science and the Humanities.

Bathily, Abdoulaye. (1992): *Mai 1968 à Dakar ou la révolte universitaire et la démocratie*. Editions Chaka. Paris.

Baxter, J.P. (1968): "Problems in the Administration of Modern Universities". *The Australian University*, Vol. 6(2).

Bayen, Maurice. (1973): *Histoire des Universités*. Paris. Presses Universitaires de France.

Becher, R.A. (1971): "The Effectiveness of Higher Education". in *Innovation in Higher Education*. Occasional Publication 8. Society for Research into Higher Education.

Beinart, B. et als (1974): *The Open Universities in South Africa and Academic Freedom, 1957-74* (Juta & Co. Ltd., Cape Town).

Berg, Robert J. (1989): - in World Development Forum, Vol. 7(2).

Berger, Peter L. (1974): *Pyramids of Sacrifice*. Basic Books.

Biobaku, S.O. (1969): Report from the Scholarship Committee Universities on the Inter-African Universities Scholarship Programme, Kinshasa, 21st November 1969.

Birley, Sir Robert (1972): *The Real Meaning of Academic Freedom*. World University Service.

Blair, R.D.D. (1990): "Cost Effectiveness and Efficiency in Universities: An African (in particular, Zimbabwean) Perspective". - in British Council Report of a Workshop on Cost Reduction and Recovery and Alternative Funding, Lusaka.

Blair, Robert D.D. (1992): Financial Diversification and Income Generation at African Universities. AFTED Technical Note No. 2, The World Bank.

Blair, Robert D.D. (1993): "Study of University Staff Retention". - in *Notes of Meeting of Donors to African Education Working Group on Higher Education*, Dar es Salaam, September 1993. AFTHR, The World Bank.

Blyden, E.W. (1872): The West African University (Freetown).

Blyden, E.W. (1896): The Lagos Training College and Industrial Institute (Lagos).Bray, Mark., Clarke, Peter B., Stephens, David, (1986): Education and Society in *Tropical Africa* (Edward Arnold, London).

Brown, Godfrey N. (1964): "British Educational Policy in West and Central Africa" in *The Journal of Modern African Studies*, vol.2, no.3 (pp.365-77).

Brown, Godfrey N. and Hiskett, Mervyn (eds) (1975): Conflict and Harmony in Education in *Tropical Africa* (George Allen & Unwin, London). esp. Parts I: Indigenous African Education and II Islamic Education in Tropical Africa.

Brunat, Eric and Reverdy, Bernard (1989): "Linking university and industrial research in France". Science and Public Policy, Vol. 16 (5).

Cabal, Alfonso B. (1993): *The University as an Institution Today: Topics for Reflection* (IDRC/ UNESCO, Ottawa/Paris).

Casely-Hayford, J.E. (1911): *Ethiopia Unbound* (Third Edition by Frank Cass, 1969, London).

Chideya, N.T., Choikomba, C.E.M., Pogweni, A.J.C. and Tsikirayi, L.C. (eds.) (1982): *The Role of the University and Its Future in Zimbabwe International Conference Papers* (Harare Publishing House).

Chizea, Chinelo Amaka (ed) (1983): 20 Years of University Education in Nigeria (National Universities Commission, Lagos).

Cissoko, S.M., (1984): "The Songhay from the 12th to the 16th Century" in *Africa from the Twelfth to the Sixteenth Century*, Unesco GHA, vol IV, (ed.) D.T. Niane (Heinemann Educational

Books, London).

CODESRIA (1993: "Academic Freedom Revisited: Three Years After the Kampala Declaration" *Codesria Bulletin*, No. 3.

Commission for Higher Education (1978): Higher Education in Ethiopia: Facts and Figures (Addis Ababa)

Constitution of the AAU, 1969.

Coombe, Trevor (1991): *A Consultation on Higher Education in Africa: A Report to the Ford Foundation and the Rockefeller Foundation.* (Institute of Education, University of London).

Court, David (1974): "Higher Education for Development Special Study, the Experience of Higher Education in East Africa: Prospects for a Developmental Role" International Council for Educational Development, New York.

Court, David (1974): "The Experience of Higher Education in East Africa". Special Study. International Council for Educational Development, New York.

Court, David (1993) "Lessons from Overseas Training Experiences". - in *Notes of Meeting of Donors to African Education Working Group on Higher Education*, Dar es Salaam, September 1993.

Crowder, M. 1968: *West Africa Under Colonial Rule*, London, Hutchinson & Co. (Publishers) Ltd.

Dafaala, E.N. (1969): Report of the Executive Vice-President at the Second Conference of the Association of African Universities, Kinshasa, 19th-21st November, 1969.

de Kiewiet, C.W. (1971): *The Emergent African University: An Interpretation.* Overseas Liaison Committee, American Council of Education, Washington, D.C.

de Moor, R.A. (1993): "Academic Freedom and University Autonomy: Essentials and Limitations". - in *Academic Freedom and University Autonomy*. Papers on Higher Education. CEPES, UNESCO.

Diouf, Mamadou and Mamdani, Mahmoud (eds) (1994): *Academic Freedom in Africa*, Codesria Book Series, Dakar.

Donadoni, S., (1981): "Egypt under Roman Domination in Ancient Civilizations of Africa", Unesco GHA, vol. II, (ed.) G. Mokhtar, Heinemann Educational Books, London).

ECA (1989). "Higher Education and the Future of Africa in the 21st Century: The Role of the Institutions of Higher Learning in Responding to Africa's Development Needs and Priorities". *Discovery and Innovation*, Vol. 1(2).

Education and World Affairs (1970): *Modernization and the Migration of Talent.* Education and World Affairs.

Eholie, Rose. (1993): La femme ivoirienne. Formation et intégration dans le processus du développement économique de la Côte d'Ivoire. Université d'Abidjan.

El-Abbad, Mostafa (1990): *Life and Fate of the ancient Library of Alexandria* (UNESCO/UNDP, Paris)

ESAURP (1987): *University Capacity in Eastern and Southern African Countries.* James Currey and Heinemann.

Evans-Anfom, (1976): "Technology at the Service of Rural and Industrial Development the case of the University of Science and Technology, Kumasi". in *Higher Education for Development in Africa*

Fafunwa, A.B.(1971): *A History of Nigerian Higher Education* Macmillan (Nigeria), Lagos

Federici, Silvia (1993): "Academic Fredom in Africa". *Quest: Philosophical Discussions*, Vol. VII (2).

Fletcher, B. A. (1962): *The Building of a University in Central Africa, an Inaugural Lecture* (Leeds University Press)

Forojalla, S.B. (1992): "Recent Government Policy Pronouncements on Sudanese Higher Education in the Sudan" in *Higher Education Policy, Journal of the International Association of Universities*, vol 5, 4 December 1992.

Gaidzanwa, R. Barbra (1994): "Governance Issues in African Universities: Improving Management and Governance to make African Universities Viable in the Nineties and Beyond". Donors to African Education WGHE, Dakar Seminar.

Garcin, J. C., (1984): "Egypt and the Muslim World" in Africa from the Twelfth to the Sixteenth Century, Unesco GHA vol. IV (ed.) D. T. Niane (Heinemann Educational Books, London.

Gardiner, R. K. A. (1970): *The Role of Educated Persons in Ghana Society* (J.B. Danquah Memorial Lectures, Third Series, February 1970. Ghana Academy of Arts and Sciences, Accra.)

Godeau, Rémi. (1993): Université cherche raison d'être. Paris. Jeune Afrique n° 1693.

Goldsworthy, David (1982): *Tom Mboya: the Man Kenya Wanted to Forget* (Heinemann, Nairobi).

Goma, L.K.H. (1984): *The African University: Issues and Perspectives.* Speeches selected and edited by L.P. Tembo. Zambian Papers, No.14, University of Zambia, Institute for African Studies.

Goma, L.K.H. (1987a): "The University of Zambia and the Quest for Excellence and Relevance" *Zambia Educational Review*, Vol. 7(1 and 2).

Goma, L.K.H. (1987b): Foreword. *Quest: Philosophical Discussions*, Vol. I(1).

Goma, L.K.H. (1989): "The Crisis in Higher Education in Africa". *Discovery and Innovation*, Vol. 1(2).

Goma, Lameck K.H. (1990): "The African Brain Drain: Investment in and Utilization of Human Capital". - in *Capacity Building and Human Resource Development in Africa*, edited by Alexander A. Kwapong and Barry Lesser. The Lester Pearson Institute for International Development, Dalhousie University, Halifax, Nova Scotia.

Goma, L.K.H. (1991): *The Hard Road to the Transformation of Africa*. Aggrey-Fraser-Guggisberg Lectures 1991. University of Ghana, Legon.

Grimal, Pierre (1974): *Histoire mondiale de la Femme*, Nouvelle Librairie de France, Paris, 4 vols.

Groves, C.P. (1955): *The Planting of Christianity in Africa*, 4 vols. (Lutherworth Press, London).

Habte, Aklilu (1976): "The Public Service Role of the University: the Ethiopian University Service, a Service/Study experiment" in *Higher Education for Development in Africa*

Hare, Kenneth (1968): *On University Freedom in the Canadian context.* University of Toronto Press.

Hargreaves, J.D. (1973): "The Idea of a Colonial University" in *African Affairs*, vol 72, No.286.

Harlow Vincent et al (ed.), 1965: *A History of East Africa* Vol. II, Oxford University Press.

Hart, Cherie (1991): "Looking South for Answers: The developing world is offering solutions to many global problems". *World Development*, Vol. 4(5). UNDP.

Hassan, M.H.A. (1993): "Science and Technology for the Socio-Economic Development of Africa". Resource Paper for the RANDFORUM Presidential Forum, 31st October and 1st November, 1993, Gaborone, Botswana.

Hassan, Yusuf Fadh (1991): "Some Aspects of the Development of the University System in the Sudan, with special reference to the University of Khartoum" in *Second International Sudan Studies Conference Papers, vol 2, Sudan: Environment and People*, held at the

University of Durham, 8-11 April, 1991.

Hassanali, A. (1993). Editorial. *Whydah*, Vol. 3(5).

Hayman, John. (1992): *Research on the Status of Informatics in African Higher Education.* International Association of Universities. Paris

IAU (1977): Points of View. *Bulletin*, Vol. XXV(4).

ICIPE (1988): *Scientific Institution Building in Africa.* ICIPE Science Press, Nairobi.

ICIPE (1989): *Task Force Appointed to Make Recommendations on the Future Development of Graduate Training at the ICIPE: Final Report.* ICIPE, Nairobi.

ICIPE (1991). *Insect Science Education in Africa: The ICIPE Graduate School Model.* - *Proceedings of the International Conference on the Innovative Approaches for Sustainable Capacity Building for Insect Science Leadership in Africa, Bellagio, Italy, 24-28 June, 1991.* The ICIPE Science Press, Nairobi.

IDRC (1991): *University-Productive Sector Linkages: Review of the State-of-the- Art in Africa.* IDRC.

Inter-Agency Commission (UNDP, UNESCO, UNICEF, WORLD BANK) (1990): *World Declaration on Education for All and Framework for Action to Meet Basic Learning Needs.* World Conference on Education for All, 1990, UNICEF House, New York.

International Association of Universities (1965): *University Autonomy: Its Meaning Today.* Papers IAU, Paris

International Council for Educational Development (Higher Education for Development Project (1976): *Higher Education for Development in Africa, African Regional Report*

Irung, Mulang Tshitambal'a (1988): "Pour quoi cette Fidelite Excessive de la Philosophie Negro-Africaine Contemporaine a la Philosophie Occidentale?" *Quest: Philosophical Discussions*, Vol. II(1).

Jaycox Edward V.K. (1990): "Capacity Building in Africa: Challenge of the Decade". -in *Capacity Building and Human Resource Development in Africa*, edited by Alexander A. Kwapong and Barry Lesser. The Lester Pearson Institute for International Development, Dalhousie University, Halifax, Nova Scotia.

Jaycox, Edward V.K. (1990): "Capacity Building in Africa: Challenge of the Decade". - in Capacity Building and Human Resource Development in Africa, edited by Alexander A Kwapong and Barry Lesser. The Lester Pearson Institute for International Development, Dalhousie University, Halifax, Nova Scotia.

Johnson, A. G. (1992): *Reflexions sur le developpement de l'ensignment superieur en Afrique Franco-phone an sud du Sahara: Analyses* (Lome, P.O. Box 7098, Togo).

Kamba, Walter (1993): "University Autonomy". - in *Academic Freedom and University Autonomy.* Papers on Higher Education. CEPES, UNESCO.

Kaye, Elaine (1972): *A History of Queen's College, London, 1848-1972.* (Chatto & Windus, London)

Keita, Lansana (1989): "Research Disciplines in the African Context: A Revised Paradigm". *Quest: Philosophical Discussions*, Vol. III(1).

Kerr, Alexander (1968): *Fort Hare 1915-48: The Evolution of an African College* (C. Hurst & Co., London).

Kimble, David (1963); *A Political History of Ghana: the Rise of Gold Coast Nationalism, 1850-1928* (Clarendon Press, Oxford).

Kwapong, Alexander A. (1992): "The Context of Capacity Building in Africa: An Overview". - in *Meeting the Challenge: The African Capacity Building Initiative*, edited by Alexander A. Kwapong and Barry Lesser. The Lester Institute for International Development, Dalhousie University, Halifax, Nova Scotia.

Langley, J. Ayo (1979): *Ideologies of Liberation in Black Africa, 1856-1970: Documents on Modern African Political Thought from Colonial Times to the Present* (Rex Collings, London).

Lennox-Short, Alan., & Welsh, David (1979): *UCT at 150: Reflections* (David Philip, Cape Town).

Leys, Colin (1971): "The Role of the University in an Underdeveloped Country". *Journal of Eastern African Research and Development*, Vol. 1(1).

Lopes, Carlos (1989): *Education, Science, Culture et Communication en Angola, Cap-Vert, Guinee-Bissau, Mozambique et Sao Tome et Principe* (UNESCO, Réflexion sur les problèmes mondiaux et etudes prospectives).

Lovanium University: *Calendar 1961-1962*: Leopoldville.

Luhanga, M.L. (1993): - in *Notes of Meeting of Donors to African Education Working Group on Higher Education*. AFTHR, World Bank.

Lule, Y.K. (1983): *Report of the Secretary-General to the Third General Conference, Ibadan, 9-14 April, 1973*.

Makany, Levy (1983): *Fifteen Years of Inter-University Cooperation in Africa, 1969-1982*, Accra.

Makerere University: *Calendar 1970-71*, Kampala, Makerere University Printery.

Mandela, Nelson (1994): *Long Walk to Freedom: The Autobiography of Nelson Mandela* (Little Brown & Co., Boston)

Martorana, S.V. and Kuhns, Eileen (1975): *Managing Academic Change*. Jossey-Bass Publishers.

Mayor, Federico (1991): Address at the Opening of the UNESCO/UNDP/AAU Seminar on Planning, Management and Governance of Higher Education in Africa, University of Ghana, Legon, 25-30 November, 1991.

Mayor, Federico (1993): "Academic Freedom and University Autonomy". - in *Academic Freedom and University Autonomy. Papers on Higher Education*. CEPES, UNESCO.

Mazrui, Ali (1978): *Political Values and the Educated Class in Africa* (Heinemann, London)

Mbajiorgu, M.S.N. (1991): *Innovative Responses to the Problem of Underfunding of Universities*. AAU, Mimeograph.

Mboya, Tom (1963): *Freedom and After* (Andre Deutsch).

Mboya, Tom (1970): *The Challenge of Nationhood* (Andre Deutsch)

McNamara, Robert, S. (1990): *Africa's Development Crisis: Agricultural Stagnation, Population Explosion, and Environmental Degradation*. Address to the Africa Leadership Forum, Otta, Nigeria, June 21, 1990.

McPherson, Margaret (1964): *They built for the Future: a Chronicle of Makerere University College, 1920-1962* (Cambridge).

Mellanby, K., 1958: *The Birth of Nigeria's University*, London, Methuen and Co. Ltd.

Metzger, Walter P. (1975): "The American Academic Profession in 'Hard Times'".*Daedalus*, Winter 1975.

Meyerson, Martin and Graubard, Stephen R. (1975): "The Assembly on University Goals and Governance". *American Higher Education Toward an Uncertain Future*, Vol. II. Daedalus.

Millett, John D. (1984): *Conflict in Higher Education: State Government Coordination Versus*

*Institutional Independence.* Jossey-Bass Publishers.

Minogue, Kenneth R. (1973) *The Concept of a University.* Weidenfeld and Nicolson.

Mmari, G. (1976): "The University's Response to Manpower Needs: the case of the University of Dar-es-Salaam" in *Higher Education for Development in Africa* (International Council for Educational Development: Higher Education for Development Project).

Morris, Alfred and Sizer, John (ed.) (1982): *Resources and Higher Education.* Society for Research into Higher Education, Monograph 8.

Moumouni, Abdou (1964) *L'éducation en Afrique.* François Maspero, Paris.

Moumouni, Abdou (1985); "Patterns of African Education" (History of Education) in *Encyclopaedia Brittanica* vol.18 (15th Edition).

Mudenge, I.S.G. (1993): "The Role and Function of the African University in a Rapidly Changing World". Keynote Address to the 8th General Conference and 25th Anniversary Celebration of the Association of African Universities AAU), University of Ghana, Legon.

Mudimbe, V.Y. (1991): *Parables and Fables: Exegesis, Textuality and Politics in Central Africa* (Wisconsin University Press, Madison), esp. Chapter 2 "Philosophy and Theology as Political Practices".

Mwiria, Kilemi (1992): *University Governance: Problems and Prospects in Anglophone Africa.* AFTED Technical Note No. 3. The World Bank.

Namie, Yoshiko (1989): *The Role of the University of London Colonial Examinations between 1900-1939, with special reference to Mauritius, the Gold Coast and Ceylon* (Ph.D. thesis, Institute of Education, University of London).

Ngobassu, A., 1972: "The National University of Zaire, (UNAZA)", in: T.M. Yesufu (ed.) *Creating the African University: Emerging issues of the 1970s*, London, Oxford University Press.

Ngobaasu, Akwesi (1974): "The National University of Zaire: Birth, Organizational Structure and Development." in *Bulletin of the Association of African Universities*, vol.1 No.1.

Nicol, Davidson (1967): "The Role of the Intellectual in Modern Africa". - in *The Inaugural Lectures of the University of Zambia.* Zambian Papers, No.2, University of Zambia, Institute for Social Research.

Odhiambo, Thomas R. (1993): Introductory Remarks. *Science-Led Development in Africa: Proceedings of the First Roundtable of Science Advisors for Science-Led Development in Africa.* RANDFORUM Press, Nairobi.

Odumosu, Peter T. (1973): *Government and University in a Developing Society.* University of Ife.

Ojo, J. D. (forthcoming): *Students Unrest in Nigerian Universities* (Ibadan).

Omolewa, Michael (1993): "British Universities' Response to Colonial Rule in Africa: the Nigerian Example" ISCHE XV, Conference in Lisbon, Portugal, April 1994.

Osthuizen, G.C., Clifford-Vaughan, A.A., Behr, A.L., and Rauche, G.A. (1981) *Challenge to a South African University: The University of Durban-Westville* (Oxford University Press, Cape Town).

Oruka, H. Odera (ed) (1991): *Sage Philosophy: Indigenous Thinkers and Modern Debate on African Philosophy* (African Centre for Technology Studies, ACTS Press, Nairobi).

Parent, Alphonse-Marie (1966): "Patterns of Collaboration". - in *Governments and the University: The Frank Gerstein Lectures*, York University 1966. Macmillan of Canada.

Peil, Margaret (1986): "Leadership of Anglophone Tropical African Universities, 1948-1986" *Int. J. Educational Development*, Vol. 6(4).

Polanyi, Michael et als (1958): *Apartheid and The World's Universities: Report on a Meeting held in London, November 1957* (Committee on Science and Freedom, Congress for Cultural Freedom, Manchester).

Randall, Vicky (1992): "Third World: rejected or rediscovered?" *Third World Quarterly*, Vol. 13(4).

*Republic of Zambia, Ministry of Higher Education, Science and Technology (1989): New Policy Measures for the Financing of Higher Education.* GRZ, Lusaka.

Riad, H., (1981): "Egypt in the Helenistic Era" in *Ancient Civilizations of Africa*, Unesco General History of Africa, v.II (ed.) G. Mokhtar, (Heinemann Educational Books, London).

Rice, A.K. (1970): *The Modern University*. Tavistock Publications.

Rumble, Greville (1992): *The Management of Distance Learning Systems* (UNESCO, International Institute for Educational Planning, Paris).

Saad, Elias N. (1983). *Social History of Timbuktu: the role of Muslim Scholars and Notables, 1400-1900* (Cambridge University Press).

Saint, William S. (1992): *Universities in Africa: Strategies for Stabilization and Revitalization.* The Work Bank.

Salmi, Jamil (1991): "The Higher Education Crisis in Developing Countries" *PHREE Background Paper Series*, Document No. PHREE/91/37. The World Bank.

Sawyerr, Akilagpa (1991): "Leadership and Organisation of African Universities". Paper prepared for the UNESCO/AAU Higher Education Governance and Management Seminar, University of Ghana, Accra-Legon, 25-30 November, 1991.

Sawyerr, Akilagpa (1992): "Relations Between Government and Universities in Ghana: A Case Study", in *Government and Higher Education Relations Across Three Continents: The Winds of Change*, ed. Guy Neave and F.A. van Vught (Pergamon, Oxford, 1994) pp.22-53.

Senteza-Kajubi, W. (1992): "Financing of higher education in Uganda". *Higher Education*, Vol. 23, pp. 433-441.

Seyon, P.L.N,, 1972: "The University of Liberia" in T.M. Yesufu (ed.) *Creating the African University: Emerging issues of the 1970s*, London, Oxford University Press PP.208-217.

Shepherd, Robert H.W. (1941): *Lovedale, South Africa: The Story of a Century, 1841-1941* (The Lovedale Press, S.A.)

Shils, Edward (1958): "Self-esteem and the status of the academic intellectual". *Science and Freedom*, No., 11, June, 1958.

Shils, Edward (1962): "A further step towards a West African Intellectual Community". *The West African Intellectual Community: Papers and Discussions of an Internal Seminar on Inter-University Co-operation in West Africa*, held in Freetown, Sierra Leone, 11-16 December 1961. Ibadan University Press.

Shivji, Issa G. (1976): *Class Struggles in Tanzania* (Heinemann, London).

Sizer, John (1982): "Better the Dirigiste Devils We Know". - in *Resources and Higher Education*. Society for Research into Higher Education Monograph No. 8.

Smith, Anita C., 1993: The African Experience with Higher Education: Swaziland, an unpublished Paper.

Smith, Mansfield Irving (1966): *The East African Airlifts of 1959, 60, 61.* (Dr of Social Science thesis, University of Syracuse)

Smock, David R. and Bentsi-Enchill (1976): *The Search for National Integration*. Free Press.

South African Native College (1940): *Calendar for 1940, Twenty-fifth Year* (Lovedale Press, Alice).

Southall, Roger, 1974: Federalism and Higher Education in East Africa (East African Publishing House, Nairobi.)

Springer, Hugh W. (1988): *The Commonwealth of Universities*. Hobbs the Printers of Southampton.

Sutherland-Addy, Esi (1993): *Revival and Renewal: Reflections on the Creation of a System of Tertiary Education in Ghana*. AFTHR Technical Note No. 10. The World Bank.

Talbi, M., (1988): "The Independence of the Maghrib" in *Africa from the Seventh to the Eleventh Century*, Unesco GHA, vol.III (ed.) M. El Fasi and I. Hrbek (Heinemann Educational Books, London).

Tamrat, Tadesee (1984): "The Solomonids in Ethiopia and the States of the Horn of Africa" in *Africa from the Twelfth to the Sixteenth Century*, Unesco GHA, vol.VI (ed.), D.T. Niane.

Thiam, Iba Der (1991): "The Missions of the African University on the Threshold of the Twenty-first Century". A Paper prepared for the UNESCO/AAU Seminar on Planning, Management and Governance of Higher Education in Africa, University of Ghana, Legon, 25-30 November, 1991.

Thompson, Kenneth W., and Fogel, Barbara R. (1976): *Higher Education and Social Change, vol 1: Reports Published in cooperation with the International Council for Educational Development* (Praeger Publishers, New York).

Thompson, T.J., (1930): *The Jubilee and Centenary Volume of Fourah Bay College* (Freetown).

Tsuma, Orren G.K. (1993): "Science and Technology in the 1990s". Resource Paper for the RANDFORUM Presidential Forum, 31st October and 1st November, 1993, Gaborone, Botswana.

UNESCO (1963): *The Development of Higher Education in Africa: Report of the Conference on the Development of Higher Education in Africa*, Tananarive, 3-12 September 1962. UNESCO, Paris.

UNESCO (1974): Enquête sur les possibilités d'éducation, de formation et d'emploi offertes aux femmes en Côte d'Ivoire. ED-74/WS/13, pp.1-129.

UNESCO (1976): *Buts et méthodologie des recherches de l'IIPE sur le financement des systèmes éducatifs*, pp. 1-250. Imprimerie du Journal de Genève.

UNESCO (1978): "The Brain Drain: A Hidden Subsidy from Poor to Rich". *The Unesco Courier*, November 1978.

UNESCO, 1986: EDUCAFRICA: *Etudes de cas sur l'Enseignement Superieur en Afrique / Case Studies on Higher Education in Africa* (Breda, Dakar)

UNESCO-BREDA (1992): *Future Directions for Higher Education in Africa*. Draft (June 1992). UNESCO-BREDA, Dakar

UNESCO (1992): *The African University 1961-1991: Potential, Process, Performance and Prospects.* Working Paper for the UNESCO/AAU Seminar on Restructuring the African University, Dakar, 19-24 November, 1992.

UNESCO (1993): "Strategies for Change and Development in Higher Education". Policy Paper on Higher Education prepared by the Division of Higher Education. UNESCO, Paris.

UNESCO-CEPES (1993): *Academic Freedom and University Autonomy* UNESCO-CEPES, Bucharest.

Université Officielle du Congo,(1968): *Rapport Annuel 1965-1966*, Lubumbashi.

Universite Nationale du Zaire (1979: *25 eme Anniversaire de l'Enseignement Universitaire du*

*Zaire (1954-1974)*. *Problemes généraux de l'Enseignement universitaire* T1. Presses universitaire du Zaire. Rectorat, Kinshasa, BP 13, 399, 1979.

Universite de Dakar, (1981): *Informations Statistique*, Dakar.

Université Nationale du Rwanda (1988): *Colloque sous-régional sur l'enseignement supérieur en Afrique centrale et orientale*. Kigali du 4 au 8 Nov. 1988. (25e anniversaire de l'Universite)

Université des Sciences et Techniques de Masuku. (1993): *Premier séminaire sur l'intégration des universités de la sous-région Afrique centrale*. *Mobilité des enseignants et des étudiants et régionalisation des 2e et 3e cycles*. Masuku. Du 17 au 20 mars 1993.

University of Ghana, (1974): *Annual Report 1973-74*, Accra-Tema, Ghana Publishing Corporation.

University of Zambia (1966): *Addresses at the Installation of his Excellency the President as First Chancellor of the University of Zambia* (Zambia Information Services, Lusaka).

Unterhalter, Elaine; Wolpe, Harold, and Botha, Thozamile, eds. (1991): *Education in a Future South Africa: Policy Issues for Transformation* (Heinemann, Oxford)

Uwechue, Ralph (ed), (1981): *Know Africa; Africa Today* (Africa Books, London).

Van Hook, Jay M. (1993): "African Philosophy: Its Quest for Identity". *Quest: Philosophical Discussions*, Vol. VII(1).

Wandira, Asavia (1977): *The African University in Development*. Ravan Press, Johannesburg.

Wodajo, M., (1972): "Haile Sellassie I University: A Brief Profile" in T.M. Yesufu (ed) *Creating the African University: Emerging Issues of The 1970s*, London, Oxford University Press.

Wodajo, Mulugetta (1976a): "Prospects for Regional Universities in Africa: the Case of the University of Botswana, Lesotho and Swaziland (UBLS) in *Higher Education for Development in Africa*.

Wodajo, Mulugetta (1976b): "Developing a University in a small country: the case of the University of Mauritius" in Higher Education for Development in Africa.

World Bank (1988): *Education in Sub-Saharan Africa: Policies for Adjustment, Revitalization, and Expansion*. The World Bank.

World Bank (1989): *Sub-Saharan Africa: From Crisis to Sustainable Growth*. The World Bank.

Yesufu, T.M. (edit.) (1973): *Creating the African University: Emerging Issues of the 1970s*. Ibadan: Oxford University Press.

York University (1966): *Governments and the University: The Frank Gerstein Lectures*. The Macmillan Company of Canada Ltd.

Young, Crawford and Turner, Thomas (1985): *The Rise and Decline of the Zairean State* (Wisconsin University Press, Madison, Wisc.).

Zemsky, R., Barblan, A., and Green, M. (1993): "Leadership, Coherence, and Autonomy: Perspectives for a Transatlantic Dialogue". - in *Academic Freedom and University Autonomy. Papers in Higher Education*. CEPES, UNESCO.

# INDEX